THE
McGRAW-HILL
36-Hour Course

ONLINE
MARKETING

Other books in The McGraw-Hill 36-Hour Course series:

THE

McGRAW-HILL
36-Hour Course

ONLINE
MARKETING

Lorrie Thomas

New York Chicago San Francisco Lisbon London Madrid Mexico City
Milan New Delhi San Juan Seoul Singapore Sydney Toronto

The McGraw·Hill Companies

6 7 8 9 10 11 12 13 14 15 16 17 18   QFR/QFR   1 9 8 7 6 5 4

ISBN 978-0-07-174386-0
MHID   0-07-174386-3

e-ISBN 978-0-07-174386-0
e-MHID   0-07-174386-3

Library of Congress Cataloging-in-Publication Data

Thomas, Lorrie.
    The McGraw-Hill 36-hour course : online marketing / by Lorrie Thomas.
        p.   cm.
    Includes index.
    ISBN 978-0-07-174386-0 (alk. paper)
    1. Internet marketing.   I. Title.   II. Title: McGraw-Hill thirty-six
hour course.   III. Title: Online marketing.

    HF5415.1265.T52 2011
        658.8'72—dc22   2010038169

McGraw-Hill books are available at special quantity discounts to use as premiums and sales promotions or for use in corporate training programs. To contact a representative, please e-mail us at bulksales@mcgraw-hill.com.

This book is printed on acid-free paper.

*This book is dedicated to passionate
professionals and lifelong learners
committed to understanding the wild
world of strategic online marketing.*

CONTENTS

PREFACE

The *McGraw-Hill 36-Hour Course: Online Marketing* is a book that will teach you about online marketing tools and how to apply them to support marketing credibility, visibility, and sellability. This book is written for students, entrepreneurs, marketers, and professionals—in short, anyone who wants to understand the art and science of online marketing. No matter what your academic or professional level, this book will teach you how to think critically about applying web marketing to support your goals. This book is designed to help organizations both large and small, for-profit and nonprofit, established and start-up. It can be studied individually or collectively.

Online marketing has strong distinctions over other forms of marketing, and trends and tools continue to evolve. However, one constant of web marketing will always stay intact—it is a way to make meaningful exchanges that create, maintain, and cultivate relationships.

As you read this book, remember that the true meaning of marketing is maximizing relationships. Tools like websites, e-mail, social media, web analytics, search engines, and online advertising are merely marketing support systems that help build and maintain relationships and subsequently make sales. How these tools are used to make meaningful relationships is where the key to success lies.

ACKNOWLEDGMENTS

This book would not have been possible without my support team (*team* as in Together Everyone Achieves More). Don Lipper and Elizabeth Sagehorn, thank you for helping me get more than a decade of expertise organized and in print. Although we have never met in person, the wonders of the web have allowed us to work, communicate, and connect seamlessly. To the Wild Web Women (and men!) of Web Marketing Therapy, thank you for your commitment to smart web marketing application and for making our vocation seem more like a vacation—I love you and love working with you. To my students (who asked for years, "When will your book be out?"), thank you for the "nudge." To all my social networking friends and colleagues from Facebook, Twitter, and LinkedIn, thank you for the supportive check-ins—you fueled me the entire way and solidified my belief in the power of social networking. To Michael Rozbruch, Ann Levine, and Jeffrey Sweeney, thank you for being such ideal clients, incredible professional partners, lifelong friends, and remarkable marketing role models. You all inspire me more than I can ever say. To Darrell Ross, thank you for your love, support, and encouragement. Now that I am done writing, we can spend more time hiking. I promise. There is no I in *TEAM*; this book's creation was a reminder that it is through connecting and collaborating that we can truly accelerate personally and professionally.

INTRODUCTION

I am living proof that one does not need specific degrees, high-level certifications, or vast web marketing experience to become a successful online marketer. When I received my first job offer to join the dot-com world in early 1999, I did not own a personal computer and was by no means web savvy. In fact, I initially declined the job offer, assuming that my lack of technological sophistication equaled an inability to make meaningful contributions to the web marketing world.

Fortunately, the online advertising sales director who had her eye on me did not take no for an answer. I vividly remember the follow-up phone call where she said, "Drop out of college and quit your job—there are great career opportunities working in online marketing." I decided my biggest risk was *not* taking the risk, and I accepted the opportunity to be on the founding team of ValueClick, a leading online advertising network. At the time, I had no degree, no certifications, no Internet savvy, few computer skills, and no professional experience in online marketing.

Despite my lack of experience at the time, I succeeded in the wild world of web marketing using the skills I did have, mainly the art of relationship building. Learning the "geek speak" associated with online marketing came second. Relationship development skills like listening, understanding needs, clearly communicating, educating, connecting, offering great customer service, sharing valuable information, diagnosing problems, and prescribing solutions were the little arts that, layered on top of the science of web marketing, made a big difference.

It took years of reflecting on my professional journey (and I did end up going back to school—education is everything!) to understand how I ended up as an online marketing expert, educator, and professional speaker. I credit a lack of fear of taking professional risks; a desire to learn and understand what I don't know; an acceptance that I don't have all the answers (but can find them); a willingness to test, try, and apply; and a love for serving people as the "success sauce" that allows me to work marketing wonders.

Online marketing tools do not sell products and services; *relationships* sell products and services. It is with great pleasure that I share my experience of web marketing tool options and online marketing strategy to help guide you into a practical use of online marketing. Web marketing success is not just about a familiarity with web marketing's technology or tools. Successful web marketing comes from understanding *how* you put the intricate pieces of the web marketing puzzle together to make your unique marketing goals click. Education sets a brilliant foundation for success; however, it is through applying what you learn that you truly expedite strategic web marketing success.

Enjoy this fast, fun, and strategic guide to online marketing. Learn, apply, optimize, share, grow, and love what the web can do for you. I look forward to facilitating your educational journey.

1

BUILDING AN ONLINE
MARKETING FOUNDATION

O nline marketing is like the Wild, Wild West: it has few rules, endless opportunities, and a vast open space. The innumerable possibilities can be exciting, but the geek-speak and limitless choices can sometimes seem overwhelming. Fortunately, online (or web) marketing is also very logical. Online marketing pioneers simply need to take that first step on the wagon train to get started. Journeys go more smoothly with a map and directions. And you have just picked those up.

There is a place for everyone on the web. Online marketing strategy helps define and refine what those roles are. The evolution is fast and ongoing. The rules of web marketing change every day. Smart professionals become continual learners to harness the power of the World Wide Web to brand, build relationships, and boost results. Moving slowly in the wild online marketing world is the equivalent of being at a hard stop.

The good news is that online marketing, compared to other marketing media, is still relatively new. It has little to no barrier to entry, allowing anyone to participate and strike gold at any time. Whether you have some experience with online marketing or none at all, this book will help guide and empower you on all the wild and wonderful ways web marketing can support artistic, technological, and strategic goals.

So, congratulations! You've taken the first, most important step of braving the unknown and forging ahead. Whether you're new to online marketing, need to refine areas of marketing expertise, have been recently assigned the role of online marketer at work, or are in search of a reference to support other goals, this book is your guide.

The McGraw-Hill 36-Hour Course: Online Marketing is going to lay it all out in easy-to-understand terms and actionable steps. The Chinese philosopher Laozi famously wrote, "A journey of a thousand miles begins with a single step." You have made the important first step by investing in this book. You will discover the wealth of web marketing possibilities, and learn how to apply them to support specific goals.

HOW THIS BOOK WILL HELP

Making smart strategic online marketing choices happens by understanding the breadth and depth of puzzle pieces you can work with. You make better decisions when you know your options. The art and science of online marketing "clicks" with a strategic (aka a game plan) bridge. *The McGraw-Hill 36-Hour Course: Online Marketing* will teach you about the various pieces of the online marketing puzzle so you can think critically about how to use online marketing now and in the future. Although every online marketing puzzle will vary, there are three constant online marketing rules that will hold true through continuing evolutions (and revolutions!) of this wild web marketing world.

Online Marketing Rule 1: Online marketing is not something one *spends* time or money on. It is something that (when done well) becomes an *investment*.

Online Marketing Rule 2: Online marketing success is not about what you know, it is about what you are open to learning and what you are committed to managing.

Online Marketing Rule 3: Optimal online marketing cannot occur without help. You have conquered all three rules by picking up this book. Don't let it go!

Teaching how to get the biggest web marketing bang for your buck in the shortest amount of time is what *The McGraw-Hill 36-Hour Course: Online Marketing* is all about. People do not plan to fail, they fail to plan, so the process of learning how to embrace online marketing has been divided into 12 bite-size chapters that can be digested in about three hours each. Add it up and there are 36 action-packed hours that will lead you to web greatness.

Don't think that 36 hours is enough time? Web phenomenon Facebook started with only a few hours of very simple programming (honestly), and now has a valuation in the billions of dollars. Yahoo!, Google, eBay, and IMDb all have similar simple origins. If they can do it, so can you. Approach online marketing with a "start small and snowball" mentality. Compared to Facebook, Yahoo!, Google, eBay, or IMDb, you have an even easier job. They had to invent a business. All you have to do is web-market one. There's no better time than now to get armed and dangerous to tap into the many ways that this is possible.

This chapter, "Building an Online Marketing Foundation," will define what online marketing is and show how the most important computer to use for web success is the three-pound information processor in your skull. After answering the questions in this chapter, you will have a greater edge on how to create and execute an online marketing strategy than someone with a decade of experience or a degree in marketing.

Chapter 2, "Planning the Website," covers how to plan for the most important piece of web marketing an organization can create: their website. Once again, the hard part is the thinking, but this chapter will show you how to break it down.

You continue this important process in Chapter 3, "Building the Website." Here you discover the process to create a marketing website that incorporates best practices to target an audience and prompt action. The most valuable marketing real estate is on the web—use it or lose it. Working sites are now deemed web solutions. Learn the secrets to making a website that serves, supports, and sells. This chapter will show you how to execute the website from the initial concept down to the final details like a privacy policy.

Chapter 4, "Content Marketing," addresses how to capture eyeballs with content. Often, content does not have to be created from scratch, it can simply be repurposed to create the desired results. A website is today's publishing platform, so you are what you publish. There are sensible content marketing techniques that attract and retain customers without requiring a full encyclopedia of text.

Chapter 5, "Blogging," brings the former world of online journaling into its current purpose and focus. Today, leading authorities (note the word *author* in the word *authority*) in every field have blogs. Blogging is one of the easiest ways to start building credibility and increase visibility. This chapter will disclose why blogs work, teach the types of entries that will enhance sales, and share the six steps for blogging success.

Chapter 6, "Social Media Marketing," embraces the social web. Social media may seem overhyped, but it's not a fad. It is effective, and it's here to stay. Learn the valuable impact that social media marketing has, and why it is necessary for business.

Chapter 7, "Web Analytics," dives into how vital web analytics are, and how leveraging the art and science of analytics can boost business. Creating a website without web analytics is like being a stand-up comedian who doesn't know if he's getting any laughs. Learn how to use web analytics data to optimize a site, make informed decisions, and reach goals.

Chapter 8, "Search Engine Optimization," delves into SEO. To many, SEO sounds technical and scary, but there are some very simple strategies that anyone can learn, apply, and integrate to create a big impact on the bottom line. You will also learn how social media (Facebook, Twitter, LinkedIn, etc.) can boost SEO for total web domination.

Chapter 9, "Online Advertising/Search Engine Marketing," teaches quick ways to rocket web marketing into the stratosphere and avoid blasting a crater in your advertising budget. It isn't rocket science, but you need to know the basics to be savvy about online advertising.

Chapter 10, "E-Mail Marketing," covers opt-in e-mail, one of the most effective web marketing tools. Learn best practices and how to create an enticing e-mail that will be opened, read, and generate results. E-mail marketing technologies, how to maintain spam compliance, and ways to streamline e-mail execution for high return on investment are addressed.

Chapter 11, "Online Public Relations," will show how PR can be done in your pajamas. Anyone can engage in online PR to gain media awareness, maximize selling power, and reap search optimization benefits. Online press releases are different from the old paper ones that are now ignored by newspapers. This chapter teaches a dazzling dozen tips for making online PR the secret to success.

Chapter 12, "Managing Multitasking Web Marketing," brings it all together, making all of the pieces of web marketing click with an actionable set of steps and procedures to keep online marketing on track. Online marketing's breadth and depth of options can work together and scale up, boosting a portfolio and multiplying value. Learn how to apply your education and claim your newfound web wisdom (or shall we say "webdom"?).

ONLINE MARKETING DEFINED

Online marketing is simply defined as using the World Wide Web to market products or services. Online marketing is also described as e-marketing, web marketing, and Internet marketing. The term *web marketing* is technically the most correct description and will be used primarily in this book along with *online* marketing. The *Internet* is a system of interconnected computer networks, and *online* describes a system that is connected (often electronically) to a larger network. The *web*, an abbreviation for World Wide Web, is a system of interrelated documents contained on the Internet. Online marketing means many things to many people, but at heart, it is about making, keeping, cultivating, and rekindling relationships.

There are five key components to effective marketing:

1. **Awareness.** Marketing builds awareness. You can have the best service or product in the world, but if nobody knows, what's the point? Awareness can come from many sources including advertising, search optimization, referrals, online marketing, traditional marketing, word-of-mouth marketing, and, in these online days, "word-of-mouse" marketing.

2. **Communication/information distribution.** Marketing communicates, educates, and informs. Getting a message in front of current and prospective customers is the key to success. Communication can serve as information distribution (pricing, value, competitive value, distinction, product/service information, sharing, directions, videos, testimonials, photos, how to find you, etc.). Communication can also serve as a way to help educate current or prospective customers so they understand the full value that you provide and why they want to do business with you. Communication is a critical component of marketing.

3. **Connection.** Meaningful marketing makes, builds, and sustains relationships, and all relationships are ignited with a meaningful connection. Successful marketing helps build "know, like, and trust" factors. Buyers of a product or service need to know, like, and trust you, the product(s), service(s), and organization. On the web, connections are shared by positioning expertise, evoking passion, distributing content, using the "show me, don't tell me" power of video, voicing values, and much more. Connections count for most of marketing success.

4. **Service.** Marketing is about serving before selling. Service is the most commonly overlooked form of online marketing, and can be the most powerful. Customer service helps close new sales and cultivate repeat sales. The best customers are current customers—service support reminds customers why they want to work with your

organization. Being a service superstar on the web can yield mega results and leave the competition scratching their heads. Marketing strategy needs to include web use (website, e-mail, social media, and more) for the best customer service.

5. **Sales.** There is a saying that everyone is in sales. Marketing supports sales whether you're trying to sell yourself for that new job, sell products/services for an organization, or inspire donations or volunteers to support a nonprofit. Think of web marketing as a trusty sidekick that will help build relationships and close sales. To achieve this, all the previous points (awareness, communication, connection, and service) must be part of the marketing puzzle.

The old rules of marketing involved a "one to many" approach. One message was distributed in a scattershot fashion to appeal to as many potential customers as possible. The "sell to the masses and live with the classes" approach still works. However, today online marketing allows for a much more targeted one-to-one relationship. Online marketing is not about the tools themselves (like websites, e-mail technology, blogs, social media, TV, magazine ads, and public relations). It is about how they are used to build relationships. Whether you are in B2B (business-to-business) marketing or B2C (business-to-consumer) marketing, you need to embrace the new rules of P2P (people-to-people) relationship-centric marketing. That is where the money is.

We are living in a time-crunched society that is addicted to immediate gratification. Online marketing serves this "I want it now" mind-set. Everyone under 50, and a lot of people over 50 (who are growing younger while living longer), realizes that the web is the key to immediate information and wish fulfillment. No matter what age your target market is, they are online, so your marketing needs to follow them.

The number of people who use the Internet is staggering!

- More than 75 percent of the U.S. population are online, and this number grows every day. (Sites like InternetWorldStats.com have updated statistics.)
- Ninety percent of Internet users use search engines to find products, services, or information, according to iProspect.com.
- Social media use is on the rise. In 2010, Facebook reported that every 24 hours 175 million active Facebook users (out of over 500 million total users) share about 500 million pieces of content (web links, news stories, blog posts, etc.).

The growth of the World Wide Web has changed the way we approach marketing. The power of online marketing can be accessed by anyone anywhere, as long as they have a device (computer, phone, TV, car console, tablet, etc.) with an Internet connection. There is no elitism on the web. (Most of the developing world accesses the Internet via their phones.) Relationship tools that were once available only to big businesses with big budgets can now be accessed by anyone at the touch of a button. Benefits of web marketing include:

- Twenty-four/seven availability to information and sales and product support
- Worldwide visibility
- Direct sales (no need for a storefront)
- Targeted market, or "riches in the niches" (finding and serving people who want specific products and services with a click of their fingertips)
- Competitive advantage (to open new markets, save on operating costs, take calculated risks, get found faster, connect better, and serve/sell harder, leaving competition in the dust)
- Customer acquisition and retention (using all five marketing musts mentioned above to gain and keep customers). Our best customers are our current customers.
- Savings in costs and human resources (automating processes, using the web to answer customers' questions, streamlining order processing)
- Immediate tracking to measure, optimize, and spend money where it counts

It's time to put on your online marketing thinking cap. Remember, a little can-do attitude makes a big difference. Setting goals, having an open mind, keeping your eyes on the prize, and maintaining a positive outlook works. Online marketing is a dynamic, fluid, ongoing piece of the marketing puzzle that will always have imperfections and need improvement.

What you will find is that web marketing is a lot of fun. And more to the point, it can be extremely lucrative. Making good money, connecting with people who count, and investing time and energy into something scalable is rewarding all around.

HOW ONLINE MARKETING WORKS

The key goal of online marketing is to maximize relationships, starting with increasing awareness. Online marketing, compared to other marketing media, has the lowest cost and boasts the highest potential to brand, build, and boost business. There is no right way to approach web marketing. Application varies based on target market, goals, management resources, strategy, previous history, competition, and organizational distinctions.

Online marketing methods can include online advertising, online PR, paid search, search engine optimization (SEO), e-mail marketing, social media, and affiliate marketing. A mix of methods frequently creates the maximum impact. Search engine optimization takes time, but the earlier you start, the sooner you'll see results. SEO is a mix of site architecture, use of content, linking, frequency of content, and popularity. If you are with a local organization, improve your search results by adding a local listing to Bing, Yahoo!, Google, and some online address directories to achieve great exposure for no cost.

Blogs are a huge driver for search engine optimization. The way blogs are coded (their architecture), the frequency of content added to blogs, as well as the linking built into blog content management systems (CMS), make them search engine magnets. Consider including a blog in the overall online marketing strategy to boost awareness, communicate, connect, serve customers, and support sales. A blog can serve as a source of information and become a valuable piece of marketing collateral to help build marketing alliances. Content can include company news, "insider" information about products and events, and core values, all liberally sprinkled with key phrases that best describe the products and services to help boost search visibility.

The power of social media is undeniable. Social media allows millions of people to discuss, review, recommend, and give feedback about an organization. Twitter, Facebook, and LinkedIn are not merely propaganda tools. These are two-way conversations that support P2P marketing, allowing organizations to listen, understand, educate, and share valuable information about products or services. Social media marketing executed intelligently will save time and money, boosting visibility in search engines and on multiple web channels. For instance, every time a new blog post is created, there are tools that create automatic updates with a link to the new blog post, allowing people to post to the blog and feed it instantly to Facebook, LinkedIn, and Twitter accounts. Voilà! One blog post gets immeasurable exposure. (See Chapter 6 for details on how to make social media work for you.)

E-mail marketing is a critical web marketing tool. It is also the heart and soul of spam. Don't confuse the two. Use a third-party e-mail management tool. It's more professional and legally compliant. Third-party e-mail management tools help manage contacts, maintain a current database, send e-mail blasts to appropriate groups, design professional-looking messages, stay off of ISP (Internet service provider) blacklists, and use online marketing best practices.

Your work e-mail might be flagged as spam if it's used directly to contact large numbers of recipients. While you might feel you get better results from direct e-mails, sending large quantities from a personal account can cause problems. Building an e-mail marketing program with a third-party management tool will allow you to sell, serve, and stay in touch.

No matter which online marketing tool you choose, the only constant with web marketing is change. Online marketing works to brand, build, and boost business. It can help support awareness, get a message out, serve and connect with current and prospective customers, and generate sales. No one builds a house without a blueprint. The same is true of web marketing. Building an online marketing plan on a strong foundation is the healthiest approach to ensuring that web marketing works well!

AVOIDING PITFALLS

Markets boom and bust, but smart professionals always operate as if the hounds of financial ruin were hot on their trails. Let online marketing be the proverbial canary in the coal mine. A shift in the number of website visitors or completed sales could be a warning of an imminent change. Fortunately, online marketing boasts nimble tools that can be tapped with little or no lead time. There is no need to wait for the printers to produce new brochures. At the touch of a button, it is easy to stay ahead of the curve and make the changes needed to serve, support, and sell to established and potential customers.

- **Remember that marketing means maximizing relationships (connections, leads, reselling) to grow revenues and profit.** Think about marketing not as spending but investing, and make the investments count. Online marketing collateral is a brilliant place to invest (it's low or no cost) and lives forever (unlike print ads, online ads, direct mail, or TV/ radio ads that die when you stop paying for them). Consumers today are more conscious and empowered, and they vote with their wallets. They need to know, like, and trust before they buy. Does the online marketing evoke trust? What is being said about your organization on the web? Invest in marketing that supports attracting, developing, and retaining relationships, and it will be an investment that carries an organization for years.
- **Tap free online marketing tools.** All organizations can take advantage of free online marketing tools. If a company is based in a particular geographic location, then it can get listed for free in local search directories that rank high in search engine results pages. Comprehensive web

data from Google Analytics is free to most websites. Buzz can also be built brilliantly with social media: blogs, LinkedIn, Facebook, Yelp, and Squidoo are all free to implement. You just need time to develop content and create community.

- **Be an educator.** Any industry insider can share expertise to build trust and credibility. Experts can offer value and boost marketing impact by simply sharing educational materials, content, and tips. Being an educator via online content can make leaders into authorities, and *that* is where buzz kicks in. Education and information sharing build credibility, visibility, and sellability.

- **Be authentic to differentiate your company.** Tap the power of personality to position your organization as leaders, innovators, and experts. Pack some serious pow into web marketing efforts by incorporating value, values, and voice via web channels. Whether the organization's personality is serious, funny, informative, controversial, activist, playful, or powerful, it can be a life-pump to create wild web results.

- **Repurpose marketing assets and collateral online.** Recycling is not just good for the planet, it's good for online marketing. Content like videos, photos, articles, e-mail messages, and press can be repurposed on websites and shared on e-zine sites, newsletters, blogs, sites like eHow .com, and more. If you or your organization makes the news, populate your website's press page with this information. Write your own press releases that share company news, awards, events, or new services and push them out to free PR wires. It is easy to tap existing assets to build buzz, boost credibility, and create new content that will result in higher search results.

- **Stop selling and start serving.** Build a community. Customer service via well-managed websites, educational content, helpful tips, easy-to-find contacts, FAQ (Frequently Asked Questions) pages, blogs, e-mail newsletters, and other valuable items will rise above the clutter and allow you to do what marketing is really all about: building relationships.

As organizations evolve, so will web marketing. No two entities approach online marketing the same way, and that's okay because with all the shapes and sizes of target markets, products, and services, there is opportunity for everyone and everything. Critically evaluate who you are, what you do, and whom you serve (the audiences who you want to offer your products and/or services to), then look at the website and web marketing strategy and ask if the people you are trying to reach and serve are truly being served well.

Sometimes one site does not fit all, and it's wise to create multiple sites and online marketing strategies for different audiences, or make the home page a North Star that guides all types of folks who come for various products and services. Remember, it's the wild, wild web. There are no rules.

FIRST STEPS TO SUCCESS

Your online marketing success mantra is "Strategy first, execution second." A little introspection now will save a world of heartache and bankruptcy paperwork later. Get ready to answer some pertinent questions. There are no right or wrong answers, but your responses are an assessment that will help sketch out required optimizations or smart first steps.

The answers to online marketing success are within organizational leaders. It is important to look within before planning outward marketing execution. The questions below will help facilitate the organization's value and distinction, and identify assets that can be used to support web marketing and goals. Clearly defined goals become the guide to online marketing execution. Remember, it is not the web marketing tools but rather how the online marketing is used to support goals that breeds successful results.

The first six questions help form a big picture to gauge your readiness to enter the world of web marketing. The latter questions clarify who you and/or your organization are, what you do, and whom you serve—all points that will lead to online marketing optimizations, strategy, and eventual online marketing execution. These questions can be answered singly or in a brainstorming session with a team. So grab a legal pad or open a blank Word document, sit down with a warm or cold beverage of your choice, and mull over these queries.

ONLINE MARKETING QUESTIONNAIRE

1. How will your product or service change or help your customer?

All stories or marketing messages have to do with change: A cosmetics company provides change from plain to beautiful, from self-doubt to self-confidence. A vitamin supplier provides change from poor health to good health, from feeling sluggish to feeling vibrant. A self-help program provides change from defeat to victory, from depression to well-being.

Some of the best marketing stories highlight the changes that an audience wants to make in their business or personal lives. All successful campaigns are about change for the better. People who are satisfied aren't motivated to be customers. You want to target people who are motivated: people who want to be better, stronger, smarter, prettier, healthier, and richer; people who want more out of work; people who want to make a difference and get more out of life. If the audience isn't motivated to change, and if the product or service can't deliver change, then you're wasting time and money.

2. Is what you have to say different?

If you're saying the same thing, and in the same way, as the competition, you're in trouble. You must differentiate yourself. Find that unique something that makes you different and says you are not a follower but a leader. If the product or service is substantially the same as the competitors', you should market it differently or concentrate on the "high concept" need it delivers, rather than the standard "same old same old" that everyone else is touting.

Which one of psychologist Abraham Maslow's hierarchy of needs does your product or service fulfill: physical, safety, social, self-esteem, cognitive, aesthetic, or self-actualization? Chances are, the competition has completely ignored the psychological and emotional marketing angle, and is focusing on specifications and features that have little to do with why people really choose one product over another. Spending decisions are emotional, even for the most seemingly rational products. Why? Because humans are making the choices. Doing a little web marketing therapy on the messaging can work wonders on your results.

3. Do you know how to tell your story?

Beyond having a story to tell or a message to deliver, you must know how to tell it. This is called *story-selling* in the marketing world. Strong marketing creates a recognizable corporate image that establishes a unique identity in the mind of an audience. If the audience sees no difference between you and the competition, then you become interchangeable. Apple didn't capture the lion's share of the MP3 market just because its product is better than everyone else's. It did so because iPods are more than just MP3 players—they are a lifestyle choice, as clearly demonstrated in Apple's marketing messaging.

4. Can you say your message boldly?

The meek may inherit the earth, but if they're in business they'll probably go broke. If you've got something to say, say it loudly and clearly! There are just too many organizations, too many websites, too many advertisements, too much clutter to hope people will pay any attention if you are afraid to stand up and be noticed. Go boldly, or don't go at all. With online marketing, the biggest fear is fear itself.

5. Who is your target audience?

Decide whom to target and what motivates them, then design your website, videos, and advertising campaigns to trigger every hot-button, motivating message you can. Develop a message so it speaks directly to that audience. It must have purpose, be focused and concise, and deliver a clear impression of identity. This means that you can't be all things to all people. By focusing on a clear audience with a precise message, you have a better chance of capturing nontargeted audiences as well. The fact that Apple iPod commercials are aimed at a hip young audience has not stopped them from capturing MP3 market share across all demographic profiles.

6. Can you take the heat?

Last, but not least—do you have what it takes to tell your story in a way that people will remember? Are you prepared to deliver the message in the most memorable manner possible? Are you ready to give up on nonproductive audiences and concentrate on those motivated to say yes? Are you able to ignore the odd complaint or nasty e-mail objecting to a cutting-edge approach? Are you ready for the web-video revolution? Do you agree that success comes in cans and failure comes in can'ts?

If you have made it to this part of the questioning, good work! Now it's time to delve down to a more micro level. Please answer the questions that follow with great detail, thought, and expansion. Focus and be mindful to answer the questions thoroughly. This is a critical web marketing mapping step. These questions are designed to pull out necessary online marketing musts and optimizations. Your answers will help bring clarity that you will use to move your web marketing efforts in the most effective direction.

Marketing Goals

- Where are you and where do you want to go? What do you want to accomplish? (Think big.)

Product/Service Description

(Answer these quickly, like you were giving a casual explanation during conversation.)
- Describe your product or service in great detail.
- What are the benefits of your product or service?
- What do customers get and experience when they buy, use, or engage your product or service?

Market/Competition/Niche

- Who is the competition? (Describe them in great detail. Include their websites.)
- What marketing tactics/media are the competitors using?
- What makes your product and/or service different from the competition's?
- What is the main advantage of doing business with you or your organization rather than the competition?

Target Market and Customer Description

- Describe the ideal customer/client. This could include age, income, profession, marital status, hobbies, interests, and gender. Focus on the target market and describe who they are.
- What are your customers' needs, fears, frustrations, and desires?
- What problems does the ideal target market/customer possess that your product or service can resolve? (These are called hot buttons.)
- What end result are customers looking for from your product or service?
- How do customers want to feel when experiencing your product or service?

- Under what circumstances does the target market/customer start thinking about buying what you have to sell? What would cause someone to want or need to buy what you sell in the first place? (These are called trigger points.)
- What things are important to the ideal customer when buying what you sell?
- What are the important and relevant issues customers need to be aware of before they buy what you sell?
- What objections might customers bring up when contemplating buying what you sell?
- How can you help customers overcome those objections?

Web Marketing Asset Inventory

- What do you already have to work with for your online marketing? (Assets include anything from a charismatic CEO who is a wealth of wisdom to great photos to a low-cost web-wiz intern. Identify what you have, not what you don't have!)
  - Website
  - E-mail list(s)
  - Team members (writers, web people, a strong organization leader with valuable expertise that can be shared)
  - Blog
  - Press coverage
  - Photos
  - Business alliances
  - Content (old articles, previously written content, helpful information)
  - Data from past web history or marketing campaigns to guide future decisions
  - Success stories
  - Videos

Revenue Channels

- How is your organization currently making money? What fuels the organization? How is this revenue generated? What marketing supports this?

- What are the main lead, sale, and relationship drivers? What is the average customer lifetime value (CLV)?
- What revenue-making opportunities can be explored?

Relevant Website Questions

- What do you want people to do when they visit your website or web pages?
- What is the primary purpose of your website?
- List key phrases that best describe what you offer. Approach it from the customers' perspective. If you are a "lending" company, customers "borrow money."
- Do you have testimonials or success stories?
- Does your website offer anything to prompt people to take action?
- What is the primary action you want visitors to take when they come to the site?
- Is there a secondary or tertiary action you want customers to take when they visit the website?

Okay, now go take a brain break and play for a half hour. You're in the home stretch, but there is still some serious thinking to do when you come back!

Armed with some ideas and clarity about who you are, what you do, whom you serve, where revenue comes from, goals, assets, and what the content of the site should include, it's time to nail down a tagline, value proposition, or unique selling proposition. Since web users tend to scan instead of read, one of the best online marketing resources an organization can have is a pithy and powerful central marketing message.

A unique selling proposition (USP) is used to *differentiate* a product or service from competitors, as well as *communicate unique value*. Value is not just about price. If it was, we'd all be wearing the cheapest shoes and driving the cheapest cars. Not every organization has a USP, but if you can create one, it will work wonders for your web marketing. A good USP should be:

- Only one sentence (The 140-character length of a Twitter tweet is a good limit; half that is even better.)
- Clearly written so that everyone can understand it
- Composed of benefits that are *unique* to your company or product

In order to find your central marketing message, figure out what distinguishes your product or service from the competition. This unique selling point will become the central message in the marketing copy, sales pitches, press releases, web marketing "about" description, and website. An online marketing consulting company that wants to rise above the competition might have a value message like "Making Small Businesses BIG with the Web!" to communicate their unique value and show the distinction of their approach. This one-liner serves as a marketing investment that can be used as the central tenet of all marketing.

NEXT STEPS

Remember that the heart of marketing is about relationships. Let this be your focus as you embark on an online marketing journey. Be sure to answer all the questions in the Online Marketing Questionnaire no matter what your level of experience is in business or marketing. Get clear on what the goals are, and understand revenue drivers. Critically evaluate who you and/or your organization are, what you do, and whom you serve. Then look at your website(s) and other online marketing assets, and assess the overall web marketing strategy. Ask if the people you are trying to reach and serve are truly getting what they want and need. Look at your answers to the questionnaire and see if your online marketing truly communicates distinction and value and connects with the market.

You may be surprised how many disconnects exist between an organization's marketing questionnaire answers and how well the web marketing messaging communicates them. Maybe the marketing messaging is lacking and a value proposition would help. Maybe testimonials could be collected and added. Getting the CEO's expertise into online articles or a blog to position the organization's thought leadership could be an opportunity.

Building on your answers to the previous Online Marketing Questionnaire, use these follow-up questions to help define immediate optimizations or items that need to be part of the website and web marketing messaging plan:

- Is your distinction clear on your website? What is your value proposition?
- Based on the "Who are you? What do you do? Whom do you serve?" questions, are these points clear on the site?
- Are the key descriptive words used on the website? This will help communication and search optimization.

- Are you doing the best possible job of promoting the benefits of your product or service? Like champion boxer Muhammad Ali said, "It ain't bragging if it's true!"
- Are testimonials, case studies, or success stories easily found? Try using them throughout the website.
- Does the site appeal to your ideal client? Is it designed well? Is the message clear?
- Is the website showing visitors that their needs can be met and problems solved?
- Do all of your marketing materials cater to your ideal client?
- Are current customers being served via the web?
- Are you leading them through the sales cycle as effectively as possible?

As you read the other 11 chapters in *The McGraw-Hill 36-Hour Course: Online Marketing*, more ideas for using the power of online marketing, and/or optimizing what currently exists, will emerge. Save the above questions as a launchpad for building a healthy web marketing foundation, and reread this chapter whenever an online marketing checkup is needed to bring the focus back to the ways web marketing works.

Chapter Quiz

1. There is B2B and B2C marketing. What is the new way to look at business? (Hint: It's an acronym.)
2. What are the five key components of effective online marketing?
3. What is the only constant with online marketing?
4. What are six ways to avoid online marketing pitfalls?
5. What are some free online marketing tools that can be tapped?
6. Marketing is about _____ before selling.
7. What is the online marketing success mantra?
8. Online marketing work must be done to support _____.

2

PLANNING THE WEBSITE

A fter laying out a strong web marketing foundation, it is time to start thinking about the single most important piece of web marketing...drum roll, please...the website. In this chapter we will discuss how the art (design), science (programming/ development), and marketing focus (strategy) must work in unison for a website to truly support online marketing efforts.

THE PURPOSE OF A WEBSITE

A strategic website's core purpose is to serve, support, and sell. Specific marketing goals will vary by organization. They may include sharing information, selling a product, completing a lead generation form, downloading technology, making a donation, picking up the phone, complementing advertising campaigns, building credibility, branding, and more. To accomplish these goals, effective websites come in all shapes, sizes, designs, and technologies.

By the time you read this sentence, there may be 500 million (or more!) websites on the World Wide Web. This is enough to make marketers wonder, among all that noise, how will their websites make their mark in cyberspace? The answer is to have clear marketing goals and a sound website plan.

The only constant with web marketing and website management is change. Website work is never finished. While that might seem like a weakness, in fact, the fluid nature of websites is their greatest strength. They are a scalable solution (when done right) that can expand and grow to support an organization's expansion. Websites serve an organization's goals when they serve the people using them *first*.

Whether you are building a website from the ground up or optimizing an existing website, this chapter sheds light on best practices. You wouldn't build a house without a blueprint. The same philosophy needs to be applied to building a successful website.

FIRST THINGS FIRST: DOMAIN NAMES

Before a website goes into design and development, there is one important housekeeping item that needs to be addressed. Domain names (also known as URLs, or uniform resource locators) will need to be purchased. It is strongly recommended that organizations own their domain names and website hosting for ease of management. Having a third party control these elements gives them (not you) power and can incur extra charges or headaches if transitions occur.

Selecting a Domain Name

When considering a domain name, think of factors like URL length, misspellings, and company synergy. Will it be remembered easily and work on business cards? Does the name need to sound the way it is spelled for branding? Is the domain only being used for search engine optimization (by having priority key phrases in the URL)? (There is more about this technique in Chapter 8, "Search Engine Optimization.")

When contemplating domain name selection, there are some expanded points to ponder so you can build a website using an address that will live on for the life of your organization.

- **Size may matter.** A short name could be important for several reasons. Does the website address need to be easy to remember and fit into logos and on business cards, support branding, and be easily recognizable? Does it need to be easy to spell? Some organizations have long domain names. Repeating them over a radio ad, at a cocktail party, on marketing materials, in e-mail addresses, and other venues may be difficult. If the domain is being used in marketing materials, consider the fact that long domain names don't always fit well in forms, on billboards, or in online advertising.
- **A memorable domain name may make for memorable results.** Generic names, such as Art.com and Garden.com, are easy to remember, but so

are more unusual names such as Amazon.com, Google.com, and Fog-dog.com. Say each prospective domain name out loud. Listen to how it sounds. Is it a tongue twister? When spoken quickly does it sound like something else? Whatever domain name you choose, if it sticks in the mind like glue, it may make your web marketing more meaningful.

- **Consider domain name confusion.** Trademark laws are designed to prevent consumer confusion. However, as more and more domains are being purchased, and *.com* is now neck and neck with *.net*, *.org*, *.edu*, *.biz*, and more, it is worth doing competitive research on the names you are considering. Also, if the holder of a similar domain name has trademarks secured, it could threaten your use and the ability to exercise it as a brand. Be sure to check the U.S. Patent and Trademark Office's database (www.uspto.gov/main/trademarks.htm) or the trademark database for your country. Search domain name records and the web to see if other organizations are using names you are considering.

- **Don't mistake the power of misspelling.** If people can misspell something, they will. The longer or more complex the domain name, the harder it is for customers to type it in correctly. Given the low price of domain names, it may be worthwhile to purchase the most common misspellings of your domain name, simply so your competition can't. Poachers (aka cyber-squatters) can be driven off by the threat of lawsuits, but no one wants that hassle. Securing misspelled domains is a preventative measure. Simply holding the rights to the domains (not necessarily building websites around them or redirecting) can be a safe, smart strategy.

- **Consider a domain name that relates to your organization name or core values.** Ideally, customers will be able to guess a domain name from the firm's name. If this isn't possible, then find a functional name; a unique name (Yahoo!); or one that expresses an emotion or attitude associated with the brand, person, or mission. For example, Seraphein Beyn Advertising is a name that can easily be misspelled, so their main domain is HardHittingAds.com. It may be worthwhile to purchase several domains that relate to your organization's name (and secure the *.com*, *.net*, *.biz*, etc.) so your competition cannot. It will also give you other URLs that can be used for future web marketing efforts like online advertising, affiliate marketing, and search engine marketing.

- **A domain suffix should sound solid to your target audience.** If possible, get a *.com* domain, or the domain that has the most respect in your country or region. Today, *.net* has similar clout to *.com*. However, some web surfers will assume that an organization has the *.com* and may type that into a browser's address bar first. Nonprofits are able to secure *.org* and educational institutions are able to secure *.edu*, which are also solid to their respective target audiences. It is okay to be a "domainiac." Many organizations buy all versions of their domain like *.biz*, *.info*, *.cc*, *.co*, *.ws*, *.tv*, and *.to*, just so their competitors can't. They're inexpensive. If you become successful, you'll wish you'd kept them from poachers.

To get the domain selection creative process going, write down desired domains and visit domain purchasing sites like GoDaddy.com and Register .com to see what is available. Registration sites will often show you alternatives to names already taken. Doing Google, Yahoo!, and Bing searches will reveal competitive domains that already exist so you don't buy a name that is too similar or already used by another company.

At this stage in the planning process, the most important step is to secure the names you want to build your brand around. Once you have a more detailed idea about the scope of the website you want to build, then you can comparison shop hosting providers. (Hosting providers house the computer servers where your website will reside.)

THE FIVE COMPONENTS OF A SUCCESSFUL SITE

Before getting into the nuts and bolts of making a website that serves, supports, and sells, there are five web marketing steps that should be considered in the following order so that time and money are spent where they count: credibility, usability, sellability, scalability, and visibility.

Credibility

As in life, you never get a second chance to make a great first impression online. Credibility is an absolute must, and website design is a large credibility component of web marketing. Website design includes information architecture (organization of content, color selection, and use of graphics and fonts). These elements set the tone for the user's experience. If a picture says a thousand words, then a website speaks volumes. Design is the first element to make a website credible. With competition only a click or two away, every website building block must count.

Stanford's Persuasive Technology Lab conducted a web Credibility Project to identify the top 10 points that made a web visitor trust a website (to read all the points, visit http://credibility.stanford.edu/guidelines/index.html). According to Stanford's research, "We find that people quickly evaluate a site by visual design alone. When designing your site, pay attention to layout, typography, images, consistency issues, and more. Of course, not all sites gain credibility by looking like IBM.com. The visual design should match the site's purpose."

Image is everything online. Good design evokes trust, makes navigation clear, establishes branding, appeals to target customers, and makes them feel good about doing business with the website they are on. Design does not have to be expensive for it to work. It does, however, need to represent an organization and appeal to a visitor. Professional design is not something organizations spend money on; it is something they invest in to support trust, positioning, and long-term marketing.

Usability

Web usability is best explained as "the ease with which visitors are able to use a website" (Source: www.marketingterms.com). A pleasant and easy user experience is imperative to the success of a website. Usability makes site viewers stick and click.

Usability is an important part of the design, architecture, and development of a website. Is the purpose clear? Is the site easy to navigate? Do clickable items look clickable? Are there clear calls to action ("Buy Now," "Learn More," "Watch the Video," "Sign Up Today," etc.)? Strong usability helps visitors do what marketers want them to do. Web surfers scan before they read. Usability tells visitors visually and textually what to do, where to do it, and how to do it. Remember that people who can't use your website, won't. It is that simple.

The Online Marketing Questionnaire in Chapter 1 addressed questions that need to be answered before a site's plan can be crafted. Marketing preplanning ensures that purpose and selling power points are built into the design (credibility) and user experience (usability) so a web solution serves, supports, and sells.

Sellability

The next success step is making sure the site supports sales. Showcasing case studies, testimonials, and whatever makes your organization different from or better than the competition is imperative for sellability success. Make sure contact information is easy to find. Some wavering potential customers still like to pick up the phone to consult with a real person before they make a purchase commitment.

Communicating value and distinction, sharing strong selling points, addressing frequently asked questions, helping overcome objections, and sharing success stories/testimonials are all ideas to help make a website a productive selling solution. Today's consumers are empowered—they need to know, like, and trust an organization before they contact, fill out a lead form, or buy. Make sure your site does more than look pretty. Websites become web solutions when they support sales.

Scalability

A healthy, scalable website must be architected and developed in a way that can accommodate ease of expansion (adding pages, video, content, etc.), and be built on a reputable, manageable platform so it can grow over time. Amazon.com didn't always have so many categories, products, and services. Their website was built to scale and has successfully grown over time. Usability and technological platform have strong connections to scalability.

Google Analytics (www.google.com/analytics) is website tracking technology that allows site owners and marketers to see things like traffic, sources of traffic, time spent online, actions taken, top pages visited, and more. Smart websites can scale more seamlessly when they have website statistics built in from the beginning. The data from statistics allows marketers to see patterns, track user behavior, and optimize sites over time.

The type of technological platform a website is built on needs to be considered before any coding happens to make sure that the platform is going to be supported in the future. Some organizations launch websites in phases, making scalability critical. For example, some organizations will post a "Coming Soon" page as a site is being built, and/or launch a testing site (often called a beta site) while the full site is being built out. If this is the case, the scalability phases need to be integrated into the website plan. Tools like making website wireframes before a website launches, or having site specification documents, can help manage the site build, rebuild, or optimization process. (More of this information will be addressed in the next chapter.)

Visibility

Building or redesigning a website does not guarantee that people will flock to it. You need a plan to drive traffic to the site. Web marketing has many tools (beyond the website itself, such as e-mail marketing and online advertising) that can be tapped to increase awareness. Search engine optimization best practices (to increase search engine visibility) can also be built into the site as part of the design and development process. You don't want to wait until a website goes live, wasting time and money retrofitting the site to make it search-ready.

It is important to have a clear understanding of visibility options, which will drive awareness, traffic, and actions to a website, before the website goes into design and development. There is a common misunderstanding that online marketing begins after a website is built. This is grossly incorrect. Knowing how the organization will use web marketing must be addressed before the build, so that it is incorporated artistically, technically, and strategically into the site.

If building volunteer awareness and communication is needed, then a page just for volunteers may be built into the website map and navigation. A designer may even add a box that says "Volunteers Click Here" or give a specific volunteer news feed. If increasing the e-mail list is a goal, then having an e-mail sign-up box is something that must be designed into the wireframe and programmed into the website development. If affiliate marketing is part of the program (discussed in Chapter 9, "Online Advertising/Search Engine Marketing"), then a page to promote the affiliate program will need to be added to the website map and sales copy.

Search engine visibility is one of the primary ways to drive traffic to a website. Search engine optimization, or SEO (covered in Chapter 8), is built into the website development. Website page headlines and copy can have search-friendly key phrases woven in as well as keyword-rich links in them pointing to other pages on the site. Even the URLs of inner pages can be programmed to have search phrases in them to boost natural search visibility. (As an example, the "About" page of an Atlanta-based real estate website can be simply www .websitename.com/about or it can be www.websitename.com/atlanta-real-estate for higher SEO power.)

If search engine advertising is going to be part of the postlaunch visibility plan, then it may be necessary to have pages that match the ads to help close sales or "squeeze" an action faster than driving clicks to a large corporate website. A squeeze page asks for a single action to occur, like signing up for an e-mail list or a free trial. Squeeze pages generally don't have exit links. A landing page, by contrast, may be narrowly tied to an ad campaign or demographic ("what coaches need to know about our Little League training") with several calls to action and links to the main site. Squeeze pages are very focused. For an example, do a search for "GoToMyPC." You will see that the ad clicks through to a different page than the natural search spot. This squeeze page was designed to help boost visibility and sellability.

Upcoming chapters will cover search engine optimization, social media and online advertising in greater detail.

STEPS TO MANAGING WEBSITE DEVELOPMENT

In true wild, wild web style, managing website design and development has endless possibilities. Websites can be built using do-it-yourself tools, freelance graphic artists and developers, or top-dollar agencies. There is no wrong or right way to build, design, or develop a website. However, there are steps to effectively managing website development that bridge the art and science to help ensure that the "measure twice, cut once" philosophy is intact so the site is sound, scalable, and requires minimal backtracking.

Spare yourself, your organization, your web designer, and/or your programmer any do-over work. Take responsibility for your website's development process. Nobody cares more about your organization's marketing and business success than the leaders and marketers within the organization. A website is a marketing tool first. The following will give you tips on how to best ensure your website works.

Do It Yourself or Hire a Professional?

Many times the cheapest path is the only path. Organizations with small budgets have to start somewhere, right? For most, having any web presence is better than none at all. Do-it-yourself free or low-cost templates can be customized with copy. Many hosting providers have drag-and-drop website templates that are easy to use.

The downside of these low-cost templates is that they can look generic, which may have a negative impact on your site's credibility. Sometimes a little more investment can make a big professional payoff. Many DIY templates are difficult to modify or add features to like web analytics or other more sophisticated options. Also, when websites are built on templates, the biggest risk is that any design work will have to be relaunched if the organization moves to another web designer or platform. But even with templates' downsides, a quick template-based website with great content can provide invaluable information to serve and support your web marketing objectives.

Some web template companies and even some web hosting companies (like GoDaddy.com and Register.com) offer their own web designers who will customize websites for an organization. Do note that if a designer is not experienced, all the planning in the world is not going to cut it. Sometimes marketers get what they pay for (or what they don't pay for). Ask for samples of work before moving forward with any web designer, and choose wisely.

MANAGING THE CREATIVE PROCESS

No matter who is designing the website (you, a freelancer, or a web design firm), the creative brief (see the following section) will help clarify your wants, needs, goals, and marketing message. If you can't draw a straight line, don't worry. Even the most unartistic person can sketch out the basics of a website or landing page that will serve marketing goals.

Web designers are hired to bring their creativity to the table, but their first priority shouldn't be earning a design award. The first priority is to build the most effective marketing-centric website for the target audience. Jim Sterne, author and eMetrics guru says in his book *World Wide Web Marketing* that a great website is "fast, interesting and useful." Remember this. Look at the home pages of Google, eBay, or any of the top online retailers. Function triumphs over form most times.

The Web Marketing Creative Brief

Even if you're creating this website on your own, don't skip the creative brief. Like a good business plan, it will help inform you about marketing distinctions and critical communication points, and keep you on track. The insights you'll glean from completing the competitive analysis alone are priceless and well worth your time.

If you're managing a team of web designers or serving as the marketing liaison to gather wants and needs for a larger marketing team, the creative brief is essential. Graphic artists and web designers do not always know what is in the heads of the marketing professionals they work for. Taking some "quality time" to draft a creative brief will help facilitate the hiring process and/or design management of logos, banners, marketing collateral, and so on.

Being a proactive communicator and having a common communication point (via a creative brief) will spare the need for art therapy, unnecessary drama, upset, confusion, and financial anxiety. We do not plan to fail, we fail to plan. So plan. Whether you are a web designer who needs to better manage the marketing professionals you work for, or a professional trying to manage the website development process, this brief will keep miscommunications, well, brief.

If organizational leaders hire someone to design or create marketing materials, they must still be a partner in the process. Some of the biggest problems in the website design and development process stem from leaders who do not know what they want to communicate, do not have clear/aligned online marketing goals, and have not done enough preplanning to help designers and developers execute their wants.

This creative brief can be completed and shared with in-house web designers; shared with graphic vendors; given to designer candidates; or used to get accurate costs for work like websites, banner ads, and landing page design. The brief is also a great tool to consolidate internal marketing manager opinions so the artist gets one set of directions! Key points to incorporate into a web marketing creative brief follow. Be brief—stick to the facts.

ONLINE MARKETING COLLATERAL CREATIVE BRIEF

- **Introduction.** Describe your organization—give a business overview, your marketing history, a description of your product/service, and the reason for the creative brief.
- **Project details.** Explain the scope of the project—what it's for, when it needs to be complete, and how it may or may not tie into other marketing efforts (television, advertising, new product launch, rebranding, company launch, etc.).
- **Goals and objectives.** Explain goals and creative objectives (leads, sales, branding, etc.).
- **Audience.** Describe primary and secondary audiences, demographics, target personas, and geographic location, if applicable.
- **Competitive landscape.** Describe your competition and list their websites or other competitive web marketing references. The competitive analyses of rival websites could be one of the most instructive and important sections of your creative brief.

    Learn what the competition is doing right, doing wrong, or not doing at all. Rather than wasting time reinventing the wheel, it is better to reverse engineer what the competition has done. Don't copy them or spend time critiquing why your site will be better than theirs; just learn how they attacked similar web marketing problems and goals.

To get the widest horizons possible, take a look at a minimum of five competitors: the three best sites and two of the worst. While it may seem counterintuitive, the folks who do it badly are often the most instructive teachers.

There is an old saying that a translator is like a person who looks at a beautiful tapestry and then turns it over to examine the stitching. Well, prepare to really examine this stitching. Create a simple spreadsheet to keep track of each item of the competition's tapestry:

- What is the visual impact?
- How many faces are there?
- Do they use sketches, cartoons, or photography? Are the images stock photography or original images?
- How is the navigation on the website? What are the first navigational items that people notice?
- Is there a clear call to action? Are there several? How are they highlighted? Do they use call-to-action text or a button? If so, how big and what color?
- What is the color scheme?
- What is the good, the bad, and the ugly? List what you like and what you don't like.
- What is the overall tone: fun, arty, or businesslike?
- What are the top menu items?
- How is the latest news highlighted?
- How does the website highlight the best deals?
- Where do they place their e-mail list opt-in?
- Are there social media (Facebook, Twitter, LinkedIn, etc.) links? If so, where?
- Does the website segment the home page to appeal to the desired target market(s)?
- Does the content look fresh or stale?
- Is there is an e-commerce component to this website? If so, count how many clicks it takes to buy an item.
- Is the website messaging clear? Is value clearly communicated? Does marketing messaging convey value clearly?

- **Value/Value Proposition.** What does a prospective customer need to know about the value your organization offers in order to want to work with your organization, act, or buy? Highlight the benefits and value of the product. Sometimes a USP (unique selling proposition/point) or tagline says it all. A designer needs to know the value marketing messaging as well to weave into the design. The more content given to website designers, the better they can plan and design value messaging into prominent areas of the website.

- **Critical communication points.** These are the necessary pieces that must be included in the marketing copy/messaging. Critical communication points could include features and benefits, unique selling points (how your company differs from the competition, testimonials, and so on. Address your customers' wants, needs, and fears and if possible, why your product and service can help them overcome their frustrations and achieve their desires.
- **Communication media.** Explain the ways you want to communicate via online marketing (web, print, e-mail, PR, etc.) and if any multichannel media apply (using multiple channels to complement one another). If the website design/development project is going to be coordinated with a particular event, promotion, or marketing strategy, it would help to communicate that in advance.
- **Design preferences.** Communicate any style guidelines (font, format, photographic/illustration techniques, logos, colors, etc.). Describe the look and feel you want. Examples of other websites they liked can be a great conversation starter between marketers and artists.

  Any examples of work or details that might help illustrate your wants and ideas will assist the artists. Communicate what you do and don't like about each example. For example, if there is a website where you like the photos or a font, then be specific about that. Be clear in communicating your likes and dislikes, and why.
- **Budget outline.** Call out the budget requirements, if applicable.
- **References.** Ask for examples of work and a list of past clients to contact to get to know your potential design partner/programmer.
- **Approval process/considerations.** Communicate how your organization will make their hiring decision (cost, creativity, scope of services, etc.).
- **Contact information.** Who are the primary and secondary contacts if there are questions, updates, or clarifications?

CREDIBILITY MUSTS FOR WEBSITES

As you start to sketch out your website, here are some basics to consider to ensure that your website is also a web solution. The goal of developing a website is not to simply have a site that sits on the web, but that the effort also has marketing value, serving customers, supporting sales, sharing information, educating visitors, and creating connections.

- **Home page.** The home page must clearly communicate visually and textually who you are, what you do, whom you serve, and why they should care about working with your organization.
- **"About" page.** A website needs to have a robust "About" page. Believe it or not, one of the top visited pages on a website is the page(s) about the organization. People want to know who is behind an organization; learn about its history, experience, credentials; and see photos and biographies of company leaders. Do not discount the credibility power of an "About" page.
- **Professional design.** Sometimes a well-designed logo living on a template-created site is all that is needed to show professionalism. Good website copy with clear navigation and a nice layout can be all an organization needs to succeed in supporting sales.
- **Easy-to-find contact information.** This credibility must is reinforced by the Stanford Web Credibility study. Sites that are more trusted have visible contact information, making a statement that an organization is available, ethical, and ready to work with the website visitor.
- **Clear calls to action.** Most website visitors scan and don't read text. Tell visitors where to go, whether that is calling an 800 number, filling out a form, or hitting a "Learn More" button (a great way to lure people into the site past the home page).

Employing credibility musts is critical when creating a site that will make visitors feel secure about doing business with you.

Web Credibility Best Practices

There is no commandment requiring everyone to slavishly follow website best practices. You may have an innovative design idea that shatters all previous conventions. Good! By all means test this design. But like Picasso said, it's important to understand the rules before breaking them. Here are some tried-and-true web design tips to consider.

- **Success breeds success.** Own your online marketing success (and don't be shy about touting your successes, awards, and affiliations). Credibility supports sellability!

- **Be consistent for credibility.** It is imperative that all marketing collateral (business cards, website design, e-mail design, blog) is consistent. Consistency applies to design, marketing messaging, and calls to action. Be sure calls to action are similar across all web marketing materials, including e-mail newsletters, blogs, messaging, and advertising banners. Have a consistent design tone. For example, if the brand's pitch is as a low-price retailer, the site design should be simple and uncomplicated. If you're selling upscale homes, you'll want your site to have a more rich, sophisticated look. The feel of the site needs to match the expectations of your audience. If you sell children's clothing, think bright, primary colors. If you're marketing meditation seminars, choose the soothing tones of a pastel palette. The niche you occupy informs the site's look.

- **Show, don't tell.** Pictures are worth a thousand words. Studies have shown that websites that are illustrated, specifically with faces, are more trusted and more profitable than sites that aren't. If you have a product or service that is difficult to understand, hire a graphic artist or photographer or buy great stock art to paint the picture for your audience. Don't forget video as a way to show and tell. Used correctly, videos can be very persuasive. Google and Apple have turned the explanatory video into a true art form. If you can't afford to hire a photographer or an artist to design art, here are some sources for free, safe stock photos that are "I didn't steal them"–proof:
  - Stock.xchang—http://www.sxc.hu/signup (requires an account)
  - FreeFoto—http://www.freefoto.com/index.jsp
  - OpenPhoto—http://www.openphoto.net
  - Photocase—http://www.photocase.de/en
  - Stockvault—http://www.stockvault.net
  - Flickr—www.flickr.com/search/advanced (read their Creative Commons page before using).

Note: Stock photo sites such as www.gettyimages.com sell stock art that has superior aesthetics that may be worth investing in.

Tackling search engine optimization will come in a later chapter, but for now, decide on the keywords and phrases that best describe what you do and use those in web messaging to attract visitors. Be sure that your subject headings and offerings also include them. If you know keywords that prospective customers may search to find you, include them in copy that goes in the design phase. If you don't know these phrases, guess. You can always edit website copy later.

Don't design a layout with large paragraph blocks. Especially on the home page, design the text to be short and sweet. Remember that you want to get people *to* the site, then *through* the site. Use teaser text ("Learn More," "Click Here") to invite users to click on links for more detailed information. This practice will clean up your home page with more white space and have the added benefit of highlighting what your users are interested in by tracking their clicks. Here are three tips to writing web-friendly, credible copy.

- Use a maximum of five lines per paragraph.
- Use a combination of upper- and lowercase letters in URLs if you are mentioning website links in website text to help readability (www.Web MarketingTherapy.com vs. www.webmarketingtherapy.com).
- Keep lines of text to 21 words maximum to boost readability.

Establishing a solid website foundation makes spending time and money on a website a smart marketing investment that will support online marketing efforts. As more layers of online marketing are uncovered, the more you will see how they end up pointing to a website and how the marketing questioning work from Chapter 1 is reinforced through all steps. Now that you understand the points needed to consider before building a website, it's time to put the pieces to work and actually build the website.

Chapter Quiz

1. What are the five components of a successful site?
2. What critical step needs to be taken for website planning, before design and development?
3. What are important points to ponder when selecting a domain name (or URL)?
4. What are the five credibility musts for web development success?

5. Name three tips to writing web-friendly copy.
6. List the key points that need to be included in a creative brief.
7. Are there free stock photo sites, or do all images have to be purchased before using them on a website?
8. What is the biggest risk of having a website on a template-based web foundation?

3

BUILDING THE WEBSITE

Great ideas are only great if they are executed excellently. This chapter helps move your strategic art and science website planning into smart website building. Let's learn the tools to make your website idea a reality.

MAKING IT HAPPEN

By this time you've gone through the hardest part of building a website, the thinking. Now comes the easy part, the technology (believe it or not!). Once the goals are clear, it is simply a matter of choosing the right tools for the right job.

Selecting a Host

Now that you have an idea of the scope of the website, you can compare hosting providers. A website needs to reside on a hosting computer somewhere (unless your organization hosts the website on its own servers). The hosting provider business is competitive with vendors constantly vying to top each other with new features, services, and pricing plans. Your best bet is to read the latest reviews. Do a simple Google search for "hosting reviews" using the name of the company you want to investigate. You can also ask fellow organizations of roughly the same size about their hosting experiences.

Size Does Matter

But in this case, it's traffic size. Hosting plans are generally priced based on levels of site traffic (also called bandwidth) and server space. If you go over your allotted bandwidth, some hosting companies will hit you with a penalty or, worse, your site may simply crash, making it impossible for anyone to view. Most hosting companies offer the option to upgrade your bandwidth on the fly. If you know you are about to make a huge marketing push, it is wise to choose a hosting provider that can instantly upgrade your bandwidth to handle the traffic spike. Also, if your site houses its own videos (not embedded from other video-sharing sites like YouTube) or large files for users to download, you may need to increase your bandwidth package. When Oprah declared the Amazon Kindle as her "most favorite thing in the world," her loyal fans briefly crashed Amazon's servers. (You should have such problems.)

Uptime Reliability

How much reliability do you really need? While 99 percent uptime reliability sounds great, realize that it means up to 87.6 hours of downtime a year. Here's a quick breakdown of what the "Nines of Reliability" mean:

Nines of Reliability

Two 9s (99 percent)	=	up to 87.6 hours or 5,256 minutes or 315,360 seconds of downtime per year
Three 9s (99.9 percent)	=	up to 8.76 hours or 525.6 minutes or 31,536 seconds of downtime per year
Four 9s (99.99 percent)	=	up to 0.876 hours or 52.56 minutes or 3,153.6 seconds of downtime per year
Five 9s (99.999 percent)	=	up to 0.0876 hours or 5.256 minutes or 315.36 seconds of downtime per year
Six 9s (99.9999 percent)	=	up to 0.00876 hours or 0.5256 minutes or 31.536 seconds of downtime per year
Seven 9s (99.99999 percent)	=	up to 0.000876 hours or 0.05256 minutes or 3.1536 seconds of downtime per year

If you have a high traffic site that you want to be up 99.99999 percent of the time, expect to pay almost as many digits for only three seconds of downtime a year. Hosting companies guarantee uptime service by making virtual copies of your website on a variety of servers all over the planet so that if one crashes, another somewhere else takes over instantly. For most organizations, seven "nines of reliability" is overpriced overkill.

Other Hosting Features

If you are going to have an e-commerce element on your website, you will need to do your homework to select the right solution. Many hosting providers have off-the-shelf shopping carts, credit card processing, and more, which are robust enough for most clients. If you plan to blog (which could be a good marketing idea), some hosting providers also include blogging software. (We will explore more on this topic in Chapter 5, "Blogging.") If you're going to accept and store customer information on your website, then you'll want to ask about the levels of security they offer. One of the most trusted things an online shopper can see when buying online is the *s* in *https://*. The *s* means it is a secure site.

Dedicated vs. Shared Hosting

Less expensive hosting packages are "shared," with a number of websites hosted on a shared server. Having a dedicated, exclusive server hosting your website costs more. However, for some organizations, peace of mind is paramount. If one of the other sites on that server sees a huge spike in traffic, that could affect the speed of your website. A dedicated server means you "own" that server and no other website's traffic will affect your speed. For most small to medium-sized organizations, web hosting via a shared server is sufficient.

The Prelaunch Website

Some people think they have to wait until all of the design plans are fleshed out before they can launch a website. Here's a web marketing tip—start small, then snowball. Consider building a professional and informative holding page for visitors who stumble onto your website to boost credibility while creating contacts and connection. A well-designed holding page (also called a prelaunch website or "Coming Soon" page) with essential information like contact information, logo, tagline, and address attracts visitors to stay longer to learn more about the organization. It bolsters credibility and increases the chances of these viewers returning to the website once it has launched.

You can even ask users what's most important to them and benefit from the free market research. Let them help you design your web marketing. Give them what they want by asking them for it!

An online marketing best practice for a prelaunch website includes having clear contact information and inviting people to sign up for your e-mail list to be notified when the full website launches. Being able to e-mail a list of opt-in recipients to promote the full site is a solid way to begin online marketing.

USABILITY MUSTS FOR WEBSITE DEVELOPMENT

A website's ease of use can make or break an online experience. Having strong website usability is directly correlated to the success of the site. The more solid the website foundation, the better it can be scaled, too. Usability ease must be planned first, using tools like a website map, an asset inventory list, and wireframes. These tools will help dictate healthy website development or optimization. Think of usability as putting all the pieces of the website puzzle together to make online marketing (and visitors) click.

Mapping Out a Website Map

A website map is a list of pages that will be accessible to website visitors. It also visualizes a hierarchy that will help a designer manage all the criteria that will be part of the website.

Some website maps are as simple as a list of typed pages and subpages in a Word document, whereas other website maps are more visual with boxes (Figure 3.1). Either way, a map simply maps out the important pages to ensure that website development includes all of the important pages, in the right order. Sometimes pages are broken out by top navigation (the pages seen in the navigation bar at all times), sub-navigation (pages that live under top navigation pages), utilities (like login links that are normally in the top right corner of a website), and footer links (like a privacy policy at the bottom of the page that is not important to show prominently, but must live on the website). People on a website need to easily know where to go, how get back to previously visited pages, and browse the site. A good user experience means that when people visit your website, they know what to do, where to go, and how to navigate back to other pages they previously visited. Following is a simple website map:

Website Map Example: Simple List of Top Navigation and Sub-Navigation for a Small Site
- Home
- Blog
- About
- Services

- Search engine marketing
- Copywriting
- Marketing strategy
- Training/education
- Press/news
- Hot off the press
- Press releases
- Testimonials
- Shop
- Contact
- Member login (in the top right corner)
- Privacy policy (in footer)
- Site map (text with links of all pages in website footer)

Figure 3.1   This website map example demonstrates the site map previously listed in the text, but in a visual format to further convey hierarchy and organization.

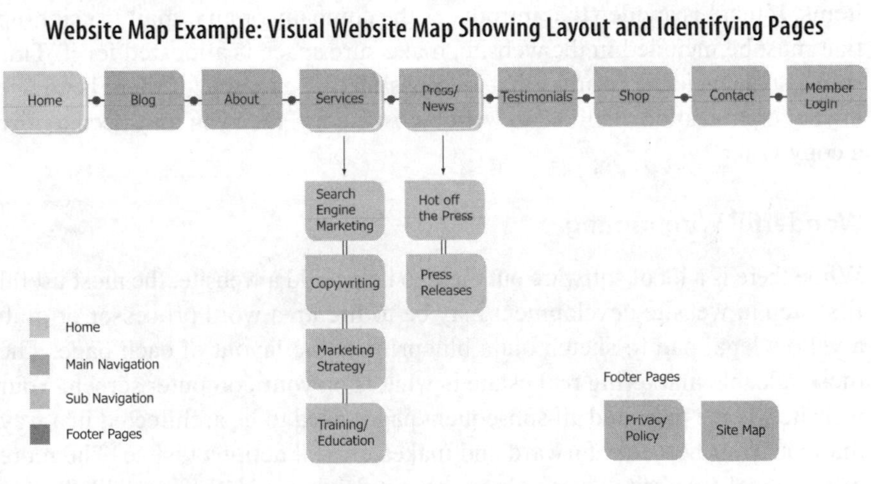

Website Map Example: Visual Website Map Showing Layout and Identifying Pages

Listing all the pages of a website helps a developer know what they are building and gives an artist a clear idea of what must be included in the navigation, which they design into the mockups of the web pages. Website mapping helps build a consensus if there are multiple decision makers in the design process, ensures all pages that must be included are part of the design/development, and helps organize how all the pages will fit together (with top navigation and sub-navigation).

The website map is where the architecture of a website begins. Next comes identifying what the pages will have in them (content, technologies, calls to action). Then comes wireframing. Once the blueprint of a website is set, the pieces start to come together.

Usability tip: There is an unspoken usability rule that the logo on a website always clicks through to the home page. Many web users expect that clicking on the logo will guide them back to home, so make sure this functionality exists.

Asset Inventory List

Once important website pages are listed and their order is determined, the next step is making sure all the important assets are included where they'll count. Assets can include anything from previous media coverage, descriptive sales copy, taglines, e-mail sign-up, and demonstration videos. It is very important to know what assets will be part of the website so they are designed into the wireframe (see below) and eventually included in the website.

Making a list of assets creates clarity of all the tools that can be used on the website, ensuring nothing important is left out, especially sales-worthy items. If there is a video that introduces the company or an e-mail list sign-up that must be included in the website, make sure space is allocated for it. This step also helps identify areas that are missing. For example, if there is no one at your organization qualified to write website copy, then you may need to hire a copywriter.

Wonderful Wireframing

While there is a lot of software out there to help build a website, the most useful first step in website development may be to fire up a word processor or grab a yellow legal pad to sketch out a blueprint of the layout of each page. The most valuable marketing real estate is what is on your computer screen. Your website's home page and all subsequent pages need to be architected in a way that puts your best foot forward and makes critical actions visible. The more professional a website design/development company is, the more likely it is that they will use wireframes before they begin the coding of a website.

If you really want to make your web designer's job easy and have already listed the features you want, along with layout and design elements, you can try to create a preliminary wireframe to visually show what you want and where.

Just as the name implies, a wireframe shows the basic architecture, or "bones," of a site, minus the skin (see Figure 3.2). There is plenty of free software to help you wireframe (do a Google search for "wireframe tools").

Things to note to support the wireframing process include:

- Create a menu of navigation items from your website map. Will that navigation be horizontal across the page or vertical down the right or left side?

Figure 3.2   An example of a wireframe shows that no color is used; the purpose of this execution is to plan page layout, important components, and navigation.

- Show calls to action ("Learn More," "Buy Now," "Call 866-IRS-PROBLEMS").
- Include an e-mail list opt-in. E-mail management companies provide code that webmasters can embed into the site to capture e-mail sign-ups and feed the names right into your database. If this is an asset that you want included, make sure it is in the wireframe.
- Make a decision about social media widgets. Do you want to have icons for Facebook, Twitter, LinkedIn, and other social media networks on the site?
- If there is an e-commerce component to your website, have this designed into the wireframe.

Note: The wireframe will not normally look pretty. Think of it as a digital napkin sketch, with just enough detail to get the placement ideas across. Color is not included in a wireframe. The reason for this is to keep the focus on architecture and components, not get into a conversation over how light or dark the blue in an image should be. A wireframe is a conversation starter to make sure that before design and coding begin, all of the important pieces of a web puzzle are included. You or your web designer and programmer are virtually guaranteed to change it. A wireframe helps focus structure, organization, and placement.

Decide which features must be present at launch. If some items need to be put into a Phase Two or Three, note this. Don't be afraid to think big! It's better to design a website with room to grow, rather than having to redesign it every time a new function is added—this is what scalability is all about. For example, even if starting a blog isn't in today's game plan, it might be a good idea to leave space in the layout to include it later.

For strong usability, think about the things you want this website to accomplish. Here are some sample questions:

- What do I want my first-time visitors to do first?
- What do I want my repeat visitors to do first?
- How do I inspire them to keep coming back?
- What is my primary marketing goal (leads signups, branding, positioning, etc.)?

Usability Constraints for Optimal Creativity and Results

To help the creative process as you work to create ease in which visitors use your website, imagine your site appearing on a mobile device to determine your top three usability musts. To employ usability best practices, ask yourself what the website would look like on an iPhone. What has to be seen? Constraints, whether they involve a haiku, a screenplay, or the challenge of cramming a full website onto a tiny screen, force people to be creative. Given the limitations of a 3.5-inch screen, what are the most important information points, features, or functionality that must be included? Whatever these features turn out to be, they must be very visible on the website.

Place Calls to Action Above the Fold

All opening information must be visible on the page with no scrolling needed. The top right corner of a site frequently emerges in tests as the best place for a call to action. Amazon uses the rotating box in the top center of their site to showcase products, which also works well as an attention-getter. By enhancing your website with obvious calls to action and intuitive navigation, you will improve user experience. Calls to action can include:

- Making a phone call
- Encouraging visitors to join an e-mail list
- Promoting a discount deal (the fewer clicks needed to purchase, the better)
- Filling out a contact form

Don't Get Cute

It is not helpful to devise new lingo for standard web sections (for instance, instead of "Contact Us," you label the link "Smoke Signals" or "Hailing Frequencies"). Such moves will make site navigation difficult and alienate most users. Speak to them in an easy-to-comprehend way. Tools like the HubSpot Website Grader (see page 44) will scan your website for free, and part of the grade is the educational level in which you write. They advise that simpler is better with messaging (unless you are a company catering to academics).

Keep Usability Strong: Plan for Testing

Before a web design concept moves into full coding, it might be wise to test any proposed website basics on a small subset of clients or prospective customers first. Tracked web results will validate or nullify some of the initial creative designs. There can be a huge difference between what people say and what they do, so make sure data is from live user web tracking, not from a chatty, opinionated focus group. While the boss might love the color scheme that mimics her alma mater's jersey colors, if the target market does not, it's back to the swatches.

Whether your website is launching from the ground up or making simple optimizations, plan to include postlaunch usability testing. There are a number of free tools to help ensure the best user experience. Below are three resources.

- HubSpot's Website Grader (http://websitegrader.com/) will produce a free website grade report that gives an overall score based on items like how easy your website language is, the use of images on your website, and whether or not you have a blog on the site. Website Grader even allows you to factor in competitive sites to see how well your site ranks against theirs. This report can help give you user experience optimization ideas.
- SiteTuners (http://www.sitetuners.com/) is a multivariate testing website optimization company. You may want to budget in their services a few months after the launch to help ensure your website is as user-friendly as possible.
- Google Analytics (http://www.google.com/analytics/) is a free website statistics service that can be built into the website from day one to track traffic, where people click, how they are funneled through the sales process, and more. Google Analytics also has a Site Overlay tool that "overlays" the percentage of clicks per page of the site to see the top places people click. With the Site Overlay tool, you can easily find ways to improve user experience, simply by making top-clicked areas higher or more visible to increase actions.

Software tools will give you ideas on how to make continual improvements on user-focused design. You can use these tools before a redesign to help map out optimizations or after web work to track and continually improve the site.

Remember that the best designers of a website are the users. Sometimes the best usability measurement comes in showing your website to someone who has not used it before but is in your target market. Ask this person to take a series of steps (buy a product, navigate your site, etc.), and then sit back and watch. You can learn a lot by silently observing people use your site.

Whether you use technology or live usability studies, listen to what you are told so you can do better. A customer who calls to ask for information that's on your site has just handed you a nugget of information gold for free. Whatever they need isn't easily found, and needs to be more prominent.

Other Usability Notes
- Remember KISS: Keep It Simple, Silly—no welcome letters or music.
- Be conventional, because conventions work. Consistency is key.
- Cut the clutter. Busy overwhelms visitors.
- Design the website to move vertically, not horizontally.
- Create a visual hierarchy. This is like having a North Star that continually serves as a high-level guide to get visitors to where they want to go.
- Design your site so that every page is self-evident (where am I and why am I here?).
- Make navigation easy. If something is hard to use, visitors won't use it.
- Make clickable items obviously clickable. Designers can include buttons that look raised to create this feel.
- Try breadcrumbs. This is a usability design/development technique that leaves "crumbs" at the top of the page that allow visitors to easily find their way back. Example: Home > Snowboard > Snowboards > Beginner-Intermediate > Women's
- Use color. Green means "go," which is the best color for your sign-up or buy button. Red can also be a good attention-getter if used sparingly (it can also be seen as a warning color).
- Check out a great book on usability called *Don't Make Me Think* by Steve Krug. It has great visuals and a smart commonsense approach to web usability.

SELLABILITY MUSTS FOR WEBSITE DEVELOPMENT

There is a common saying that if you don't toot your own horn, nobody else will. When communicating the value of what your organization does, it is critical to help website visitors understand why they should work with you. Some of the strongest selling points on a website are testimonials, value propositions, clear calls to action, self-generated news releases, and sharing your story or credentials.

Tackle Those Testimonials

If you don't want to toot you own horn, let your customers do it for you. The best sales tools are testimonials from satisfied customers. They are more credible, applicable, and real. Once you have them, you'll want to design space in your layout to sprinkle them liberally throughout the website. The trick is getting them.

- If you do great work and people sing your praises, ask for testimonials. If your product/service is not something people want to confess they use (like "getting the IRS off your back"), then offer to use their first name and last initial. When people like you and compliment you, the likelihood that they will help with a testimonial is huge. Just ask politely, and make it easy for them.
- Ask top clients to give short, sweet testimonials and let them know that you "want to brag that they are a client." Build the testimonial list and add to it as the organization grows.
- To make collection seamless, you can offer to transcribe the testimonial and send it to them for their approval. One of the biggest barriers in getting a testimonial is that the requestee thinks you want a formal recommendation letter. They can get overwhelmed and not act simply because they don't totally understand that you want something short and sweet. Offering to write it takes the pressure off and omits inconvenience.
- Pepper testimonials throughout your website. Most folks are not compelled to go to a testimonials page. Keep a page on your website with a list of testimonials, as it's great to be able to e-mail a link to a compiled list of accolades, but sprinkle them throughout your site as well to keep the sales power strong. Often the best structure is to make a claim and then have a testimonial (sometimes in a box) that speaks to that claim.

Clearly Communicate Value

Online marketing must clearly communicate value so that website visitors understand why they should work/shop/buy/donate. Many organizations make the first words or headline of their website their unique selling proposition. Sometimes showing versus telling works wonders. Video can be a very compelling way to show value in an easy and enjoyable way.

Calls to Action Need to Be Called Out

In Selling 101 courses, the largest lesson taught is to "ask for the sale." This same lesson applies to website development. If you want website visitors to buy, sign up, download, contact you, or refer a friend, you have to ask them to do so. Calls to action can be woven into website copy, can be designed into the wireframe and built into the website development (e-mail sign-up boxes, contact submission forms), and can even be at the end of videos that live on your website.

Become Your Own News Department

One of the biggest misconceptions organizations have is that they cannot have a press or news page if they haven't been covered by mainstream media. Wrong. It is the job of marketers to become their own media department, creating properly formatted press releases that live on their websites. Creating self-generated news is a sellability strength that communicates the value of what is happening at your organization, shares sales-worthy updates (new products, services, pricing, etc.), and keeps a strong P2P (people-to-people) conversation going. Becoming your own news department also helps boost credibility. Seeing all the great happenings, awards, and more on your website can help visitors feel secure about doing business with you.

Story-Selling

Stories sell. Online marketers must accept that they are in the story-selling business. An easy way to start sales-rich content creation is to communicate the company's history, the professional backgrounds of its leaders, and so on. Website visitors need to know, like, and trust an organization before they open their wallets, and a surefire way to start the story-selling process is to share credentials. Be interesting so you can get prospective buyers interested in working with your organization.

Online Privacy Policy

A credibility must is an online privacy policy. Believe it or not, online privacy policies can be sellability boosters. Even if no one ever reads it, you still need one. Privacy policies address the use of personally identifiable information (e-mail addresses, contact information, website activity, and credit card information). The second a website asks for a prospect's e-mail, the law requires a privacy policy. "You need to update or add a privacy policy" is one of the last things marketers want to hear. They'd rather be talking sexy online marketing ideas like social media and web design. Cool or not, an accurate privacy policy is a must for all organizations (small, large, for profit, or nonprofit).

Knowing how to construct a good privacy policy is essential to an online presence. A good privacy policy should address how your firm uses personally identifiable information (PII); collects e-mails; or uses cookies on the site (if you use any form of web analytics, you have cookies on your site); if you sell or rent PII to third parties or sell online ads on your site; and more. It is

critical to have a current, accurate policy on most websites (usually housed
in the footer).

The good news is, you are not alone. There is privacy policy support out
there for nearly everyone. TRUSTe (www.truste.com), provider of the leading
online privacy seal and an Internet trust authority, has a success-backed Privacy
Policy Generator. They provide custom privacy policies for a wide range of
websites, from retailers to publishers, backed by the TRUSTe certification and
seal, boosting credibility and sellability. TRUSTe's privacy policy service asks
all the critical questions to help you produce a compliant policy and also scans
the site to ensure its legitimacy and to verify the presence of certain security
and privacy elements, such as cookies and other tracking technologies. Having
the TRUSTe seal on a website, due to its reputation and quality assurance, has
been proven to boost sales.

SCALABILITY AND MAINTENANCE

Building a website to serve both immediate and future needs means the incre-
mental costs of building a website (time, money, and energy) are a scalable
investment. You don't have to pay for every feature up front, but planning
ahead for it means you won't have to pay a premium to include it down the
line. Ensuring a site can be scaled by adding pages and new functionality and
features is the final online marketing imperative to have your website serve
as a web solution.

In order to have a website that is scaleable, there are tools that need to be
automatically built into every page. While this might seem like overkill for a
five-page site, five pages can quickly balloon to 500 pages before you know it.
Including the following best practices and tools will help you scale up without
headaches:

- Google Webmaster Tools is a free service powered by Google that allows
  webmasters to verify they are the owners of their website. The technology
  shows website errors and page problems, and also allows you to submit
  a XML site map that helps Google read and index your site better to
  support search engine optimization.
- Keep an ongoing asset inventory list so you can scale your website with
  any new press releases, articles, photos, audio and video files, and more.
  Use what you have on your site. Keep a running tab of tools and technologies you can build into your website postlaunch.

- Keep a website map in the footer of your site and be sure to update it frequently as it evolves with new pages.
- Update the copyright in the footer as your site matures. Use a date range (© or Copyright [company name] 20xx–20xx) with the year of the site's oldest material as your first date and the current year as your ending date. This longevity enhances your credibility.
- Make sure you have metadata (title, description, and keyword tag) on every page of your website to help classify pages within the search engines. (There is more on this in Chapter 8.)
- Establish a naming convention to use descriptive file names for all photos. For example, if you sell Apple products to elementary schools, instead of labeling a photo "image56.jpg," use something key phrase–rich like "ElementaryStudentEnjoyingHerNewiPad.jpg."
- Place photo descriptions via the alt tags, HTML code that can be set by a webmaster to label the image to help describe that image in the code for organization of images. When you label photos with strong key phrases, this also supports search engine optimization.
- Make a list of existing advertising campaigns that may need dedicated landing pages so online ads click through to specific content to maximize sales power.

Website Maintenance

One of the reasons that many websites fail is a lack of follow-through. Here are a few things to think about to ensure healthy scalability:

- How will you update the site? (There are some firms where only the IT department can change a comma. A web marketer will want to update the site himself or herself or have a very reliable and speedy webmaster or web team able to make updates.)
- How long will content approvals take? (Technically website changes can happen instantly, but if every change needs to tunnel through five layers of approval, you need to build those roadblocks into your schedule.)
- How much new content needs to be created each month? (Pencil out a schedule.)
- How long will it take to create that new content?
- Who will create the new content?
- Do new graphics or photography need to be created for your website? If so, by whom?

- Who will update the site?
- Who will answer e-mails?
- Who is in charge of quickly responding to your social media communications?
- Who will moderate any forums or message boards?
- Who will take care of regularly scheduled maintenance?
- Who will be in charge of maintaining and cleaning up e-mail lists?
- How much time will each of these elements take each day/week?

Web Marketing 101 Checklist

Online marketing requires a smart strategy. Part of that sound strategy includes smart management. Online marketing management requires attention to detail and organization. Be sure to keep your online records current and note the following information:

- All the domains you own, whom they are owned by, how long you have owned them, logins to your domain company
- Your hosting records (logins, how to submit help tickets, etc.)
- FTP (file transfer protocol) access for your websites
- Logins and access to your web analytics (If the webmaster owns this, get access, but try to own all of this on your own.)
- E-mail system logins
- Access to your logo files, templates, and designs
- Login and password to any third-party provider service
- Blog login and password
- Social media logins (Facebook, Twitter, LinkedIn, YouTube, Flickr)
- The contact phone numbers and/or e-mail addresses for all your service providers (domain, hosting, etc.)

NEXT STEPS

As you learned in this chapter, designing a website requires a lot of preplanning and an art-meets-science approach. Building a website requires a clear strategy, and reaps fantastic rewards as a scalable online web marketing solution.

Review the current state of your organization's online marketing status to see what the haves, have-nots, nice-to-haves, and need-to-haves are based on credibility, usability, sellability, scalability, and visibility. Assess the situation, optimize areas that need improvement or attention, and once the foundation is set, move to new channels. For example, if a website is poorly designed or the value proposition is not clear, then buying online advertising does not make sense...yet.

Baking the online marketing cake in the proper order will help ensure success. It will make online marketing meaningful and more effective so that it can serve, support, and sell.

Chapter Quiz

1. Describe a website map.
2. What is a wireframe?
3. List a few of the elements to possibly include in a wireframe.
4. List some of the usability tips from the chapter that are important to know when developing a website.
5. True or false? Organizations cannot have a press or news page if they have not been in the mainstream media.
6. What does an online privacy policy address?
7. List several strong selling points on a website.
8. What are examples of assets that can be used as marketing tools and included on pages when planning your website?

4

CONTENT MARKETING

The saying "Content is king" is heard repeatedly in the online marketing world. Content is king because of its power to educate, inform, connect, and boost credibility, visibility, and sellability. This sound statement is also one of the more scalable ways to put the power of web marketing to work. *Content marketing* is simply defined as publishing content on the web that educates and empowers readers. Online content marketing can also multitask by attracting search engines. When it comes to healthy web marketing, you are what you publish.

You can't get a better definition of content marketing than Joe Pulizzi's "Five Pillars of Content Marketing–The Ultimate Definition":

- *Editorial-based* (or long-form) content. It must tell a relevant, valuable story. Must be informative, educational, or entertaining.
- *Marketing-backed*. The content has underlying marketing and sales objectives that a corporation, association, or institution is trying to accomplish.
- *Behavior-driven*. Seeks out to maintain or alter the recipient's behavior.
- *Multi-platform* (print, digital, audio, video, events). It can be, does not have to be, integrated.
- *Targeted* toward a specific audience. If you can't name the audience, it's not content marketing.

(Source: http://blog.junta42.com/content_marketing_blog/2007/07/the-ultimate-co.html)

Content marketing goes by many names, but according to a survey by Vertical Leap, while only 45 percent of marketers and business owners in the U.K. were aware of the term *content marketing*, 100 percent were already engaged in the development of content for marketing purposes. Applying strategy to current engagement can boost selling power.

Too many professionals erroneously believe that content creation via a blog will solve all their content marketing problems. But blogging (discussed in more detail in Chapter 5) is like limiting an organization to only one tool in the wild web toolbox. Content marketing goes above and beyond blogging. Content can live on a website, on a blog, as online press releases (expanded on in Chapter 11), on free article marketing sites, on social media outlets, in e-mail marketing, and more. All these options will be covered in this chapter.

There are so many ways to attract eyeballs online. As you spend more time reviewing the competition, pay attention to the different ways they use website design and marketing messaging to serve current customers and attract new customers. How are they building awareness, distributing information, connecting with current and prospective customers, serving visitors, and selling products and services? After this chapter, you will have a better idea how to use the power of web content as part of an overall marketing strategy and how to apply it to support goals.

The good news about content marketing is that previously produced content can be repurposed in many ways to minimize new creation and maximize impact. The biggest fear of overworked marketers is that producing content will become one more daunting task on their already overbooked calendars. In many cases, the most brilliant content marketing comes not from an organization but from the website's users. This chapter will address what marketing professionals can create as well as what can be user-generated.

Content marketing lives both on the originator's website and on the websites of others. For example, a blog entry may have content echoed in online press releases, social media, article websites, e-mail marketing, video sites, and so on. Content marketing also exists in the "real" world with print materials, direct mail, events, and more.

One of the primary goals of online content marketing is creating as much inbound traffic as possible. Online marketing is most powerful when your content has made its way onto the wild, wild web and lures people to your main website where they can hit the information mother lode. Putting your content in some form on other sites creates more awareness, information sharing, connection creation, and traffic building.

USER-GENERATED CONTENT

The good news is that from a content marketing point of view, some of the most successful content may be easiest to create. User-generated content has a big impact on both readers and search engines. Often, user-generated content gets higher rankings than an organization's home page. This is due to the popularity of this type of content and where user-generated content is housed on the web.

User-generated content includes:

- Message boards
- Product reviews
- New uses for your product or service (sometimes called "hacks") such as using clear nail polish to treat insect bites and stings, using a dishwasher to cook a whole salmon, etc.
- Testimonials or case studies (how users solved problems)
- Social media pages
- Twitter feeds
- Video contest submissions
- Q&A interviews with users
- Online groups or communities like LinkedIn, Ning, etc.

Many organizations have a following or fan base that will happily create content if given the web space to do so. Some organizations are afraid of user-generated content for a variety of reasons. Their first concern is that the users will create something illegal or immoral. It is possible to set up a system where other users can flag content as inappropriate, or have a moderator in place to review content to maintain its quality. In many cases, user-generated content can be self-policed by the community with minimal moderation by the host organization.

The other main concern about user-generated content is that people (maybe even the competition) will write false or bad things about the organization, its products, its services, or even its personnel. While that does happen, a loyal fan base will often refute the charges with more authenticity than someone inside could. Savvy marketers include a content management plan in their online marketing strategy to monitor user-generated areas and keep them fail-safe.

Create a participation policy that includes no personal attacks, no immoral comments, no solicitations, and other basic ground rules. Few users will protest if you remove user-generated content that is objectionable or just comment spam (people promoting their products via your website's comments field). But if a debate rages in the message forum and the discussion gets heated (as at some point it could), ask people to debate the topic, and refrain from personal attacks. If inappropriate fighting persists and the moderators need to ban someone, be up front about it. Address the line(s) crossed, and include a link to the policy code that the user agreed to when he or she signed up to participate on the site. For most sites a flame-war happens once in a blue moon or, in some cases, never. Often the payoff of user-generated content is more than ample reward to compensate organizations for any possible trouble. The cost of moderation is small and knowing the risks helps organizations be proactive.

Content That Converts: Customer Reviews

If a website sells a product or service, consider the gold standard of user-generated content: customer reviews. These can have a *huge* impact on site traffic (increasing it by as much as 80 percent), overall conversions (60 percent increase), and average order value (40 percent increase). RarePlay Trends Research Analyst Bob Rattivarakorn reported in 2007:

> According to a study by Deloitte Consumer Product Group, 62% of US online shoppers read product reviews written by other customers when researching products and 99% of respondents believe that the information they get is very or somewhat credible. According to a study conducted by E-consultancy and Bazaarvoice of online retailers in the US, UK and Europe, from a retailer's perspective customer product reviews are increasing retail e-commerce conversion rates, site traffic and average order value. Other added benefits identified by online retailers in implementing product ratings and reviews are they improve customer retention/loyalty and search engine optimization.

Many e-commerce website managers are afraid that negative product reviews will hurt sales. Opening up the conversation can sometimes attract negative comments, but the negative feedback can help solidify the desire to buy if tough feedback is managed strategically. The saying "All press is good press" can be true, if managed well. Listening to the market allows leaders to improve products and services and it has been shown time and time again that users trust organizations that post both negative and positive reviews of their product *if* organizations address the feedback constructively. Acknowledging customers and owning your product's imperfections with authenticity have tremendous online selling power. Dianna Dilworth wrote in *Direct Marketing*

News about how retailer Bath & Body Works increased sales using ratings and reviews.

> In the recent e-mail campaign for the FitFlop, Bath & Body Works used customer ratings and reviews in its e-mail messaging and found a 10% higher conversion and 12% higher sales per visitor as compared to campaigns that do not include customer ratings and reviews. "We've seen an 87% growth in reviews in the past two months," said Shannon Glass, director of Internet operations for Limited Brands, parent company for Bath & Body Works. "We are seeing a higher conversion rate for products with reviews versus products without reviews," she added. "Consistent with this, item abandonment rate is decreasing. Customers are making more informed choices prior to adding the product to their shopping carts."

It isn't just having reviews but showing users how to sift through the reviews. For example, Amazon.com added one question to their customer reviews that netted an additional $2.7 billion in sales, according to Jared M. Spool's article "The Magic Behind Amazon's 2.7 Billion Dollar Question":

> Amazon makes the best of both the positive and negative reviews easy to find. . . . In our studies of Amazon shoppers, we found many start by looking at only the negative reviews, using them to try to "talk them out" of buying the product. Interestingly, Amazon now has a feature to easily see the more negative reviews together. . . . As we've watched Amazon customers make purchases on the site, we can clearly see that promoting the most helpful reviews has increased sales in these categories by 20%. (One out of every five customers decides to complete the purchase because of the strength of the reviews.) From this, we can project it has contributed to Amazon's top line by $2.7 billion.

How to Handle True Negative User Comments

If the charges against your product or service are true, then user-generated content allows you to give great customer service in full view. Look at negative customer postings as free product testing that will allow you to fix problems in real time. Even if you can't give an immediate fix to the problem, users appreciate that your organization is on top of the issue and dedicated to investigating problem resolutions.

Rubbermaid was getting a lot of negative customer reviews about a product line called Produce Saver. From the negative reviews Rubbermaid discovered that the product wasn't meeting consumers' needs because consumers weren't using it correctly. (The Produce Saver keeps produce fresh past its expiration date only if the produce is put in whole, not cut up.) According to Jim Deitzel, Manager of eMarketing and Brand Communications for Rubbermaid, in an interview with Bazaarvoice:

> We knew the usage guidelines. But why didn't these reviewers seem to know? Wasn't it printed on the packaging or inside the container? It wasn't. . . . We immediately went to work with the product manager to create instructions and recommended usage for Produce Saver. We posted the usage document on the actual product page of the website and linked to it from other areas of the site that highlighted Produce Saver. Then the product manager wrote an informative blog post describing the recommended usage of the product and why it works best that way. Finally, we took this new content and responded directly to the consumers (who submitted the reviews) via the website.

DEVELOPING A CONTENT STRATEGY

Customer reviews are addressed as part of this content marketing chapter because reviews serve as content that search engines crave to populate their results pages. When users are researching a problem, a search engine will often elevate an article, a knowledge base page, or a forum page to the top of the listings. Blog posts and sales pages may get indexed, but often reviews or forum posts get a bigger piece of the visibility puzzle. There are many third-party forum sites that get more traffic than official company websites. Remember that content marketing is all about garnering the most eyeballs. Once the eyeballs are attracted, creating a connection with constructive content is what counts.

To create a cohesive content marketing plan, start by looking at the existing reference materials your organization already has. What are the most frequently asked questions (FAQs)? What materials do users use to solve their problems faster? Engage the people who have direct contact with the user base (usually the customer service teams), then start to assemble lists of questions and procedures that help clients solve problems. If content ideas are still coming up small, ask users what their problems are. Your sales force is another great source for user questions.

For existing websites, use analytics to figure out what terms visitors are using to find your website. Make a list of the top searched phrases or the phrases that you would like your organization to be found around, then create more content around those keywords. If you don't have an existing website, do a search for the Google Keyword Tool (or use your favorite keyword research tool) to find relevant keywords and phrases in your topic area. Be sure to check out your competitors' keywords as well. If you see that one of the competition's offerings is getting a lot of traffic, then create content that compares your product to theirs. Such comparison pages usually rank very highly because users will frequently search for "Product A vs. Product B." Do a search query like "Quicken vs. Microsoft Money" and see what kind of results appear.

Content creation, as part of an effective online marketing strategy, connects to the hearts, minds, and wallets of the users, helping them research and make decisions faster. Create a repeatable process to think about ways to help educate and empower prospects. Some organizations assign a content manager to make sure that all of the content that is created is part of the overall online marketing strategy. Too many companies produce huge volumes of content without looking at strategy. Content that supports strategy converts, making the time, effort, and costs pay back.

Content That Website Owners or Marketing Professionals Can Create

To get started, first focus on content that an organization can create itself. Most organizations already have a lot of content that can be repurposed into new formats. In many cases people within the organization who don't think of themselves as "in marketing" have created useful information that could be used for content marketing.

To get the biggest bang for your content buck, figure out how much of your existing material can be reused. Make a spreadsheet with the original content item on the left and all the categories (from the list below) that it might be converted to along the top row.

Content marketing can take the following forms:

- Blogs
- Online press releases
- Articles
- Product/service descriptions
- Technical support
- User guides/technical manuals
- White papers
- Case studies
- E-books

- FAQs
- Tutorials
- Videos
- Podcasts
- Reference materials (from a simple glossary to a full encyclopedia on your topic)
- Printable items (procedure checklists, guides, recipes, flash cards, posters, etc.)
- Diagnostic questionnaire (designed to help the user solve a problem)
- Help desk or knowledge base
- Q&A advice
- Demonstrations on how your product/service works with a third-party product/service
- Company news
- Deals/coupons
- Online store
- Calendar
- Online utilities (online mortgage or retirement calculators, calorie counters, etc.)
- Software downloads
- Games
- Music
- Your commercials (Believe it or not, this can be a huge draw.)
- Twitter feeds and other social media updates
- Activism tools (tools that will allow users to promote your message)
- Industry news aggregating (an automatic feed of the latest headlines in the topic area)
- Lists of outside blogs, industries, or resources that users might find useful

Notice that almost all of the items on the list require action on the part of the website owner. While this may seem like a lot of work, the payoffs of repurposing content in multiple channels can be huge. The marketing rule of "Tell them, tell them what you told them, and tell them one more time" helps diversify the online marketing portfolio, giving more opportunities to capture awareness and create connections. Don't know how to prioritize which items to add? Ask your audience. A simple survey on the home page asking each user's preferences is a simple way to start. Also, review analytics to see what repurposing options yield the most traffic and conversions. Allocate time and effort where it will count.

Use the Magazine Model of Content Development

One way to plan content strategy is to think like an editor-in-chief of a magazine covering your topic area. What are the monthly departments? What are the features? What are the advice columns? Think about your audience in the life cycles within your topic area. Then start creating content to serve inquiring minds what they want to know. Brainstorming about each of these segments in your user base's life cycle will generate lots of areas for you to explore.

Think about creating multiple content strategies. What does a first-time visitor to your site need to know versus a returning visitor? If you have different audience segments, you might direct them via e-mail offerings or pay-per-click ads to individualized landing pages and content. Think about the decision trees each segment must go through to reach their (and hopefully your) desired goal. For example, a youth sports line might offer one type of information for the child and another type for the parent. What information do you give to the foot soldier and what information do you give to the general? In some cases you will have to arm the foot soldier with information for him or her to advocate to the general.

Don't reinvent the wheel: if there is a third party who has good content and who is a potential partner, see if you can acquire some of their content for your site. Often, content creators are thrilled to have the additional web exposure and would be happy to share as long as they are credited properly and have links back to their website.

Content creation needs to have success criteria attached to the effort. Define quantifiable goals. If the desired action (buying the product, writing the senator, filling out a content form, etc.) occurred, or at least moved the visitor further down the sales funnel, it can be measured with analytics. Build content strategy around goals and define how the content makes progress toward them. Feel free to test content. (It's a good idea to have an ad hoc focus group run through your site anyway.) Measure what types of content or call to action messaging get more eyeballs and/or convert better.

Remember that relevant, helpful, quality converted content (not spammy puffery) is what makes sales. Content needs to perform a service for the user.

DIFFERENT CONTENT STREAMS

A lot of online marketers focus on just one tool: words. Words are powerful, but they are only one part of the content stream.

Photos = Sales

A picture is worth *more* than a thousand words. The right picture could be worth a thousand sales. Who would buy a used car online without seeing photos? Even generic computer servers are sold with photos. Those photos need to be shared via social media such as Flickr (even the British royal family is on Flickr now), Facebook, and Twitter (via TwitPic). Look at these social networking sites as a much larger extensions of your organization's website.

Don't forget "fun" photos of your team in action too. This helps to put a human face on your organization. Studies show that people buy more from companies that have faces on their main website than those that don't.

Words That Sell

Many organizations put out a printed or digital newsletter. Repurposing the newsletter as blog posts, online articles, tweets, Facebook updates, and more helps make those words sell. Unlike a printed piece of paper that eventually makes its way to the recycling bin, online content compounds over time and never expires. Use and reuse online and off-line content to get the word out. The whole newsletter does not have to be published on a website or even in a digital newsletter. Using short introductions and subject links as teasers leading to more content on a website allows readers to go where they want. Remember that web surfers scan rather than read most of the time. Words that sell are scannable. Use interesting links with descriptive words in each story section of a newsletter to link to a blog post, online article, press release, or page of a website.

Putting RSS (Really Simple Syndication) feeds on online content also sells. Creating separate RSS feeds for blogs, press releases, newsletters, and content areas of a website helps marketers help readers. RSS spoon-feeds content streams to the interested parties, making content receiving and distributing a passive and automatic act. It is a great feeling when RSS lists grow and content managers know their content not only lives online, but is also automatically sent to opt-in recipients for multitasking marketing power.

Most organizations put out press releases only when news happens. Consider press release creation as a planned part of online content marketing strategy. When marketers create something on a website that is a new resource for your audience, repurpose it by creating an informative press release. Online words that sell often ride the coattails of current events. To capture interested readers, plan in your editorial calendar content (like blog posts and press releases) around current events such as holidays, media buzz (as it hits and relates to your industry), and regular government reports.

E-books and white papers are some of the best conversion materials you can use to sell. Even if content is given away for free (free often includes some registration), content managers can assign an artificial value to help illustrate perceived value. Many marketers call this type of content a "sample taste" (think of ice cream samples that are a free taste but make you want to eat more). The content generosity approach can help create a connection, launching a relationship that leads to sales.

Professionals are more time-crunched today than ever before. Sell with words by offering organized, helpful content that includes phrases that will be searched by potential customers and/or journalists. Well-written content that is searchable and ready for journalists to turn into stories can work wonders for online public relations (more on this in Chapter 11). The key is making sure content is widely distributed across multiple channels (when in doubt, refer to the article marketing directories list found later in this chapter and the online public relations distribution list in Chapter 11 to get repurposing ideas). You can even become a content aggregator. If people trust your website, blog, Twitter feed, or Facebook page as a source of helpful information, they will stop scanning the web and come to you first. Simply signing up for news feeds and posting them on your site can be a powerful place to start. If you tell prospective and current customers what's important in your topic area, even if your competition is the big news of the day, people will treat you as a trusted resource. Chances are, you already check out the headlines as part of your daily workflow. Making a small online marketing adjustment to publish helpful content (like sharing great headlines and linking to other articles) can make your online marketing strategy a serving, supporting, and selling system.

Online ads and e-mail marketing are also considered parts of a strategic online marketing content stream. Think of the content in online advertising as a cheap testing ground to try new approaches and get performance feedback. A simple text ad and a landing page's content can say what sells. Use the power of all online marketing data to cross-support the web marketing puzzle. If online ad content is successful, you can then deploy it across content on the website, in blogs, on Twitter, in articles, in online press releases, and more.

Video: Are You Ready for Your Close-Up?

Video is one of the most important content tools to convert web users into becoming customers. A picture is worth a thousand words and video is 30 pictures per second. Do the math. Video production does not need to break the bank. All that is needed is creativity, a web camera (some are built into mobile devices or laptops), off–the-shelf video software (some is free or low cost), and a willingness to roll up your sleeves to publish the content online. Many organizations have catapulted themselves into new marketing success territory by becoming a "weblebrity," using the power of online video to create connections and initiate conversations.

Simple videos can include a welcome message to introduce your organization and give it a warm human face. If your founder is part of your brand, have him or her star in the video. People want to see who is behind an organization. Pushing products or services is not the purpose of video; instead, show a bigger message like how the organization solves problems for their audience. For example, Wal-Mart's slogan is "Save Money. Live Better." and their television ads show people doing fun things like visiting their grandkids with the money they save at Wal-Mart. This same concept can be applied to video content created for the web. Steve Jobs is a master at showing how Apple products will make people's lives better. These Apple videos get repurposed as content on the web, getting viewed long after the live launch date.

How video is used needs to be specific to the target market and product and/or service. Ideas for videos may include using video to demonstrate the feature(s) of a product, or providing tutorials on how to use a product in a specific circumstance.

Media/Branding

Starting a video "magazine" can boost business. Any organization can become the *60 Minutes* of their given field. Creating consistent video content that people want to view can become a great addition to marketing. Videos shouldn't just promote a product or service. They should give viewers a handle on the big issues in your field. Chapter 5, "Blogging," shares the six steps to blogging success. These steps can be applied to a video magazine as well.

Republishing Speeches

If someone in your company is giving a presentation or speech, record it on video. Recording and republishing a presentation or speech can allow the content to work for you again and again. Also, a recording can be cut into short clips (quick "best of the best" videos often work best) and republished on video sites like YouTube and Vimeo.

Entertainment
Don't forget to have fun with video. Compelling content needs to be enjoyable to watch. Funny is not the only form of entertainment, but humor has a strong success track record. Look at videos that have gone viral, like Blendtec's famous "Will It Blend?" series (www.Blendtec.com). They demonstrate their products by blending objects like an iPhone. The videos went viral immediately, had a significant impact on sales, and have become a meme (cultural reference point). Make music videos, faux commercials, or instructional videos in the style of Shakespeare. Let your imagination go wild, and don't be afraid to have personality.

User-Generated Community Video Contests
You can create a video phenomenon without even picking up a camera. Sponsor a video contest where users can make videos extolling an organization's product or service. Giving a community any needed elements like logos, visuals, audio tracks, and so on empowers it to trumpet your brand. Set basic rules, such as no obscenity (just search "video contest rules" online to get some ideas). Once videos have gone through a moderator to gauge appropriateness, then users can vote on the one they like best.

Set the submission deadline long enough in advance to give folks enough time to create quality work. Because procrastination is a popular time management technique, you'll see submissions spiking as the deadline looms. The final benefit of having a community video contest is that proud video producers will promote their work on their own social networks and ask all their friends to vote. (**Note:** Community videos can have a downside. Chevy Tahoe had a video contest in 2006, and some ardent environmentalists created very anti-brand videos. Be aware of your market, and have a clear video management plan in place.) A video contest doesn't take that much effort, but you have to budget time and internal resources, create guidelines, conduct an analysis to consider opportunities and threats, and have prizes (make sure the prizes are worth something to your audience so people will be committed to creating quality work). Prizes can include products, services, money, trips, and more.

Audio

Video is the largest growing content-creation medium, but marketers must not forget the value of audio. Simple sound (without images) in the form of podcasts or audio clips playing on a website can create a meaningful connection, making a bottom-line impact on marketing. Podcasts are the most common form of audio, where assigned "hosts" talk as if they were on the radio, sharing expertise, tips, and advice and interviewing a topic area's expert. Interested audiences can listen to podcasts on their music players, on their phones, or on their computers while they do other work. Search for podcasts in your niche market to get inspired and learn best practices.

BlogTalkRadio.com is a great place to search for podcasts and sign up for an account to become your own podcast host. Audio tip: Many strategic marketers also offer web transcripts of podcasts to help multitask their audio effort with website text that helps boost search engine optimization. Some marketers transcribe video content into text as well to maximize impact.

EXTERNAL CONTENT MARKETING

A lot of the best content marketing does not live on an organization's website; it is out on external sites attracting eyeballs. External content marketing is a low-cost (and often no-cost) way to help build awareness, distribute information, connect with and serve customers, and boost sales.

Marketing Rule: Tell Them, Tell Them What You Told Them, and Then Tell Them One More Time

Multiple placement offers more exposure and more likelihood of a meaningful impact. A lost-opportunity content marketing case in point: a company announces a local workshop event in an e-mail, yet there is no mention of it in their blog, on their website, in an online press release on their press page, on article marketing sites, or in local event calendars online (if the organization has a local target).

Never make assumptions that content published in one place will be viewed. Online marketers have to make their message available for their current and prospective customers in many formats. People read e-mails, then delete them. If it was memorable and they want more information later, they will likely go online or to a website to follow up. If web users can't find the info again somewhere else, marketers may lose them and that's not good customer service. Own all the great tools at your fingertips to make your online marketing work!

Re-communicate and make marketing consistent. Does the website look like the blog? Do e-mails look like the website? In most cases, design consistency is important. Be mindful of branding and positioning to show professionalism, and ensure that consistency is in place to make the most of the content.

The Best External Sites to Showcase Your Content

Here are some external venues to consider as part of your coordinated content marketing strategy:

- Online press release sites (more on this in Chapter 11)
- Video sites
- White-paper sites
- Guest posts on industry blogs
- Guest blogs on a popular site for your audience
- Radio shows or podcasts
- Social media sites including, but not limited to, Facebook, Twitter, Linked-In, Squidoo, online communities, eHow.com
- Online newspaper guest columns
- Online trade magazines
- Consumer magazines in a topic area
- Third-party websites that don't compete but reach the same audience
- Affiliate marketing
- How-to sites
- Article marketing sites

Most of these opportunities are free of charge; content simply needs to adhere to the external guidelines. Posting content needs to be done where there is clear value presented. Test, track, and put energy into the areas that drive traffic and sales. Make the content count so you can count on external publishing as a way to build awareness, share information, connect, serve, and sell!

Article Marketing

By far one of the most underutilized online marketing strategies is using article marketing sites. With article marketing you can subtly promote products and services (very soft sell, never promoting the company or its services directly) via online article directories. Most directories receive a high volume of traffic and are considered authority sites by search engines, so the articles rank highly in search and generate lots of *free* traffic.

You'll need to submit your article to multiple article directories. Most search engines filter duplicate content to prevent the exact same content from reappearing in searches. You can get around this by modifying articles slightly to keep the content diverse and increase your chance of getting multiple high rankings.

Although you won't be able to promote your organization overtly on these sites, you can still build credibility and visibility for your organization (most article sites have an author biography section that can link to the main site). When content is authored and it's good, the source can start to become an authority. Note the word *author* in the word *authority*!

This is also an opportunity to put your analytics to use. You can generously sprinkle your articles with whichever keywords or phrases your website readers are using to find you. In fact, if you conceive content around the key phrases people are searching for, searchers will find your site, and your articles, and familiarity will breed awareness and hopefully conversions.

To get you started, here are some top article marketing directories to consider submitting to:

www.ideamarketers.com
http://ezinearticles.com
www.goarticles.com
www.oneminuteu.com
www.articlesbase.com
www.amazines.com
www.addme.com/article-submission.htm
http://digg.com/submit
www.selfgrowth.com/expertform.html
www.authorsden.com
www.scribd.com/upload-document#files
http://bx.businessweek.com

How to Create Your Own Wikipedia Entry

One of the top-ranked items in a search engine on any given topic is the Wikipedia entry. Wikipedia (www.wikipedia.org) is an online open encyclopedia.

This means that anyone can add or change any entry, with a few minor exceptions. Your company's Wikipedia entry should describe your organization or company and its history, mission, services, and/or products. All assertions must be provable and citations must be provided. Solid non-company-produced references include published articles in newspapers, independent magazines, academic journals, and books. These references need to be on the World Wide Web as Wikipedia editors will check references against web sources.

Anyone can post or edit an article on Wikipedia. The hard part is ensuring that the article will be allowed to stay. As an online encyclopedia, Wikipedia wants just the facts. Terms like *solutions* (unless referring to liquids), *best*, *leadership*, *state of the art*, and *cutting-edge* are too promotional and will flag a posting for deletion. In addition, an organization whose Wikipedia entry has been previously deleted will be targeted for a follow-up deletion. Any new entries must be posted according to their guidelines (http://en.wikipedia.org/wiki/Wikipedia_policies).

A tool like Google Analytics can show you exactly how much traffic is funneled from Wikipedia to your website. Because of Wikipedia's high volume, you should sign up to be alerted to any updates people make, to monitor your article for quality and truthfulness. Wikipedia's policies also help protect other people from using your entry as promotion for their own organization. If someone places a link to their company's website in your article, it will be swiftly deleted, appropriately, by an editor. Every article in Wikipedia is intended to be informational and neutral, contain no stealth advertising, and be a valid contribution to the online encyclopedia.

A content strategy can seem imposing at first. It is easy to get overwhelmed with all the possibilities. Take small steps, repurpose content, and focus on quality. Little efforts over time will make a significant impact as the content compounds. If you allow user-generated content, you'll have something better than a free-content-creation staff. You'll have a group of users who are paying you (by buying your organization's products or mission). The more you let them contribute, the more it will pay off in customer loyalty.

Even if your organization won't allow a user-generated content strategy, you should still pay attention to what your customers have to say. When you install an analytics package on your website, you get a silent partner at the content table. If you listen, they will tell you how to grab their attention, how to communicate with them, and in many cases how to sell to them. In the next chapter, we'll address one of the best ways to react and sell to them in real time: blogging.

NEXT STEPS

Think of online content creation as the glue that brings the online marketing puzzle together for credibility, usability, visibility, sellability, and scalability. Compelling content can be website text, images, video, blog posts, online press releases, social networking posts, podcasts, articles, and (ideally) a combination of several. The beauty of content creation as an online marketing tool is simple: authoring content creates authority status. Sharing ideas and bringing relevant web content to a target audience on a website, blog, or social site or via press releases or third-party article sites creates more web tentacles to help create connections.

Don't forget the power of repurposing content. You don't have to write everything from the ground up. Recycle content that was already written, engage guest writers, and "Tell them, tell them what you told them, and then tell them one more time" with content in multiple places to increase readability and visibility. Share content to serve, support, and ultimately sell your audience and embrace your inner web gemologist—start publishing and aggregating the "best of the best" content to help make a meaningful marketing impact on the web!

Chapter Quiz

1. Define *content marketing*.
2. What are Joe Pulizzi's "Five Pillars of Content Marketing"?
3. True or false? Content should only exist on an organization's website or blog.
4. What are different types of user-generated content?
5. What is needed to produce video as part of content marketing?
6. What are some of the different types of video content?
7. What is a way to get more out of audio as a content marketing medium?
8. In addition to Wikipedia and external content sites as places for off-site content placement and exposure, list some sites that articles can be posted to.

5

BLOGGING

Some marketing professionals believe blogging is too frivolous to be a real marketing tool. Does writing about a cat's reaction to breakfast produce real business leads? Probably not, unless that topic is written by a leading veterinary dietitian. Fluffy's transformative reaction to "Feline Kidney Regenerative Recipe #456" could be very important news to customers, stockholders, and even humans who are struggling with kidney disease. Suddenly that seemingly frivolous blog posting about a healed cat could get the writer or the organization media recognition, boosting their credibility, visibility, and sellability. Great awareness does produce business leads.

Web marketing is about creating a relationship. Blogging supports relationship building in that it creates a conversation. Blogging serves a number of vital web marketing purposes simultaneously:

- Blogging is a powerful search engine optimization tool to pop an organization's name to the top of search engine results pages listings.
- Blogging allows professionals to leverage their expertise, positioning themselves as authorities in their field, boosting credibility and sellability.
- Blogging paired with RSS (Really Simple Syndication) feeds allows postings to instantly fill the mailbox or feed reader of everyone who has opted in.
- Blogging allows free feedback due to its ability to allow readers to post their own comments, critiques, and questions.

BLOGGING DEFINED

What we call blogs today started in the early 1990s. Originally diarists and journalers would write about their experiences in online text-based groups like Usenet or on bulletin board systems. Blogs (short for *web logs*) gave people an outlet to publicly purge their passions.

Today blogs have evolved into multimedia communities where bloggers (and the blogging community) have grown in size, stature, and impact to eclipse all but the largest media outlets. Blog aggregator *The Huffington Post* has a larger readership than the *New York Times*.

In their truest form, blogs are a web-based log of entries (or posts) about a particular subject or subjects. The content can be educational, inspirational, political, or whatever the theme supports. While most postings are text-based, blog entries can also be drawings, photos, video, and audio. In addition to sorting blog entries by date, blog entries are categorized based on subject, keyword, author, and type of blog entry (list, quiz, video, etc.).

There are various technologies that support bloggers, including WordPress, TypePad, Squarespace, and Blogger. Blog technology also allows readers (the recipients of content) to have the ability to respond. Blog managers can moderate and respond to comments, allowing for a two-way conversation. Although blogs started as one-way conversations, by today's standards, a blog is not a blog unless comments are allowed.

It is important to understand that it is not the blog tools or technology that yields marketing success, it is *how* a blog is executed (the strategy and management) that makes all the difference.

BUILDING A BUSINESS CASE FOR BLOGGING BENEFITS

Blogging often gets a tremendous amount of push back from within organizations. Some organizational leaders fear they will lose of control of their messaging. They fear there will be negative comments or theft of content, or that blogging will become a huge time suck that exposes the organization to risk and ridicule without any tangible return on investment.

For the web marketer, the first web marketing challenge may be within the organization itself. To make the business case for blogging, address the concerns above to make sure blogging makes sense for your organization. Focus on these benefits:

Blogging Drives Traffic via the Production of New Content

Search engines are constantly sending their "spiders" out for new content to index so that their search engine results pages have relevant data. Blogs often get a higher search priority because of their frequency of content. Blog posts can drive traffic to the main website via links and informative content.

As far as content stealing is concerned, the risk is the same risk as any public website copy. Most marketers use simple tools like Google Alerts to get free feeds on key phrases that relate to their organization and to help monitor media coverage and other websites.

Blogging Gives the Organization a Human Face

Putting a human face (or many faces) on an organization builds empathy and trust. Studies have shown that consumers are more likely to buy from organizations that put a human face on their websites. A blog can do that with text, photos, and video. In short, blogging builds bonding. In the era of P2P (people–to-people) marketing, professionals need to leverage social media like blogging to create a personality.

Blogging Demonstrates Customer Service in Full View

Lack of trust is a barrier for many first-time customers. Blogging allows the organization to demonstrate its commitment to customer service by having the blogger relay stories about how the organization helped a user solve a problem. Many organizations publicly show negative comments on a blog and, by immediately responding to the comments, demonstrate their client commitment. Showing vulnerability can be a very compelling selling point.

Blogs Can Develop Niche Markets

If the organization has a niche market that isn't being fully served in the main website, blog entries that speak to that niche can have a powerful impact. You can look at the blog as a micro-site targeted to that niche. Watching your traffic or comments in that area increase can boost your confidence that you can develop that niche into a more robust business.

Blogs Help You Make "Long Tail" Sales

Internet stores like Amazon and Netflix make money from blockbusters, but it turns out that they make more money from obscure, low-demand products that are not readily available in brick-and-mortar stores. The "long tail" demand curve graphically represents top-selling products or services at the top (head) with a downward slope for its more obscure (long tail) options (Figure 5.1). Because the total volume of low-popularity items exceeds the volume of high-popularity items, the demand curve resembles a long tail.

Figure 5.1   The long-tail demand curve represents best-selling items at the top with more-obscure items at the long tail.

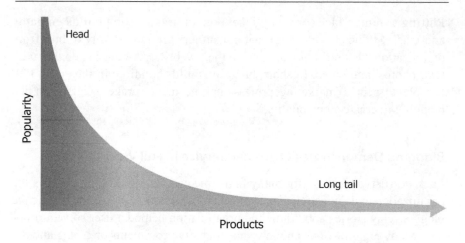

Blogging Helps Reputation Management

While many organization leaders fear that blogging will hurt their reputation, in fact it can help save it. There's an old proverb, "A lie will go round the world while truth is pulling its boots on." A blog can help organizations quickly respond to a false accusation or a true crisis. Public relations firms often manage company blogs or participate in content creation and moderation due to their viral "round the world" speedy nature.

Blogging Is a Free Way to Promote Your Press Releases

Some press release distribution services can cost a pretty penny (we'll discuss this more in Chapter 11). Blogging is a no-cost way to instantly distribute press releases to an organization's user and press base. In addition to a regular blog RSS feed (which sends blog entries to readers who opt in), creating a blog "press release only" RSS feed works well for online marketing. Look at current press release distribution costs on sites such as www.prweb.com, www.prnewssire .com, www.pressreleasepoint.com, and www.pitchengine.com to review costs and see the savings of having a blog as an free PR tool.

Blogging Can Function Like Focus Groups

Instead of hiring an expensive market research company to do focus group testing, you can ask website visitors or current blog readers questions via blog posting or a poll. The results won't be scientific because only the minority who care about an issue will chime in, but the feedback can be very authentic and compelling. Knowing what readers are passionate about will help organizations create products, services, and marketing campaigns that speak directly to their users. Web statistics like Google Analytics can be embedded into blogs to show the most popular blog posts. Widgets like Retweet tools (which allow readers to hit the Retweet icon and share that item with their Twitter followers) can show popularity via the quantity of retweets.

Blogging Saves Money on Support Calls and E-Mails

Take common questions and post the answers as a blog post. The next time that question comes in, customer service can be expedited by sending a link to the answer on the blog. Looking at the organization's customer service budget might show additional savings that can be reaped with an active blogging effort to address recurring issues. A service-centric blog can also help reduce the number of questions in the first place.

BLOGS AS WEB MARKETING POWERHOUSES

Blogging should not be treated as separate from other online marketing execution; it needs to bridge various aspects of web marketing (like e-mail, online public relations, content marketing, education, search engine optimization, and other social media marketing) for multitasking marketing power. Understanding the art (the art is the true heart of blog success) and science of blogging will take this web marketing medium and lay the foundation to put it to work to boost credibility and visibility and support sellability. Blogs are a vital part of making the web marketing conversation happen. A blog serves a number of web marketing functions simultaneously.

Blogs Build Communities

Blogs' ability to allow readers to post comments creates a true conversation. Often, the conversation is not just between the blogger and the reader but between all the readers. Organizations use their blogs to share relevant content, sometimes posting links to other blogs or websites that may be interesting to their readers. The more bloggers aggregate great content and information, the more likely readers will go directly to their blog.

Blogging Grows Your User Base

New customers may find your blog before they ever hear about your website. Blog postings are shared with people who care about your organization's mission or who thought your take on a given topic was worth sharing with the wider world. Blogging is one of web marketing's greatest stealth lead–generation techniques.

Blogs Can Build Existing Partnerships and Cultivate New Ones

Building partnerships with blogging can be as simple as exchanging links or engaging in affiliate marketing or true cross-promotional and even strategic partnerships. Organizations with similar target markets, which complement rather than compete with each other, often cross-promote blog posts to educate their readers about each other. The blogosphere is filled with stories of industry leaders who are fans of each other's blogs who decide to form a strategic partnership or even a whole new business together.

Blogs Allow Multitasking Marketing by Repurposing Old Content

The most difficult part of online marketing is creating content. There is no need to reinvent the wheel. Blogs allow previously created content to get recycled or repurposed, amplifying eyeballs and exposure. Photos, articles, videos, or even old commercials are great blog fodder. Think of your old content as free online marketing collateral that increases search engine optimization (SEO) and branding while allowing for feedback from readers.

Blogging Can Create Great Free Press Coverage

Blogging is a great way to sell how the organization faces the daily challenge of meeting its goals, serving their customers, addressing needs, and showcasing value and values. Blog content can make an organization interesting and exciting to their market. When journalists discover an organization's blog, they can get great background and a real feel for the organization. This makes it far more likely that when they do a news feature on the organization (free publicity!), it will include more of your story with the spin you want.

Blogging Is a Quick Way to Announce News

Putting news on your blog will increase web traffic. Blogs are often indexed faster than other pages, with their most current information presented at the top of search listings. That means a short blog entry on a keyword-rich news-worthy topic can get a top search ranking, while a more exhaustive article on the same topic written a year ago without the best use of strong key phrases that attract readers may not make the search engine's first pages.

Blogging Allows the Organization to Quickly Respond to Industry News

Responding to industry news via a blog has a number of benefits:

- Blogging provides instant freshness to a stale site.
- It shows the organization is on top of industry trends.
- It allows the organization to put its spin on the industry news.
- If the organization's competition is in the industry news, it allows the organization to comment about the competitor's shortcomings and how the organization's product/service is really better.
- Blogging about an industry trend can also allow the organization to promote their product or service as the answer to the news. It presents a sellable moment.
- When a topic is in the news, more people will be searching the keywords in that topic. Blogging on industry news increases the chances that people searching those keywords will find the organization's website.
- Current news is what the media is craving to write about. Being on top of current events can educate readers on subjects they are interested in and attract a journalist who needs a thought leader to give a sound bite on that subject.

Blogs Help Promote All Aspects of Social Media Marketing

Having social media links or widgets on a blog allows visitors to see and visit an organization's Facebook pages, Twitter feeds, LinkedIn profiles, and more. Blog content can be set up to automatically feed to opt-in readers via RSS feeds and link new posts to Facebook, LinkedIn, and Twitter for multilevel visibility. The social media (as others see their friends as fans of your blog) will bring new eyeballs to the blog.

HOW BLOGS WORK

As Chapter 2 clarified, blogging serves the five main web marketing components of credibility, usability, visibility, sellability, and scalability.

The architecture of blogging platform technology makes content organization simple, creating strong user experience. The coding of blogs is clean, allowing for frequent content publishing and building in a lot of links, which boosts search visibility. Overall, a well-managed blog can create connections, share information, increase visibility, and boost sales. The potential for blogs to scale up with more and more content is endless.

The number of blogs in the world is growing at a speed that is almost too fast to track in real time, although Technorati's annual "State of the Blogosphere" report is a good source (http://technorati.com/state-of-the-blogosphere). The orders of magnitude are mind-boggling. It is safe to say that worldwide blogs number in the hundreds of millions, with hundreds of thousands being started every day. With millions of posts hitting every day, blogs have become a primary news source for the vast majority of Internet users.

Customers crave a point of view. Buyers are using the World Wide Web to research and find products, services, and information. A resourceful blog becomes a force in visibility, credibility, sellability, and scalability. Blogs educate, get found easily in search engines, and allow for conversation in an asynchronous way, often working to support organizations 24 hours a day. Sharing a point of view helps people help themselves, and some organizations can't ever anticipate what it will do for business in the process.

That said, blogging is *not* worth doing unless you have:

- Something valuable to say
- The tools to blog with (These are easy to find.)
- The ability to create community (Just because you build a blog does not mean people will read it.)

- A purpose—a clear reason to blog (and a smart strategy)
- The most important piece: passion

A blogger who blogs for the sake of blogging will not be able to keep the love alive and sustain it as an online marketing solution for the long haul. Blogging isn't a sprint, it's a marathon. Commit to blogging as an online marketing investment to share information, educate, voice values, and engage in ongoing social dialogue. Bloggers blog because they care. Understanding why blogs work and how to create a sound strategy will help ensure that execution is done in a way that is clean, clear, consistent, and conducive to making a meaningful marketing impact.

FREE BLOGS VS. HOSTING YOUR OWN BLOG: PROS AND CONS

One of the first decisions an organization needs to make about its blog is seemingly small but could have big repercussions: should you host a blog on your own website under the organization's domain name, or use one of the free blog sites? There is no universal right choice. There are pros and cons to each option to consider for immediate and long-term blog success.

Pros and Cons of Free Blog Sites

You'll find many choices if you're looking for a free blog site. Some of the best known are Blogger (powered by Google), Weebly, LiveJournal, and WordPress.

Advantages of Free Blog Sites

- The most obvious benefit to having a blog on a "no charge" platform is that it is free.
- A second benefit is the speed and ease of launching a blog that is provided by free blog sites. You can launch a blog in a matter of minutes with tools like Blogger.com.
- Third, free blog sites are also easy to use. Even the least experienced webbie can launch, post, and publish content (including videos and pictures).

See Figure 5.2 for an example of a free blog built on Blogger.com that matches the look and feel of its websites.

Santa Barbara Luxury Rentals uses the free Blogger platform but designed the layout so that it expressed stronger brand and design similarity to their website.

Figure 5.2   Example of a blog built on Google's free Blogger technology that was designed to match the look and feel of a business's main site.

Disadvantages of Free Blog Sites

There are some downsides to using free blog sites. First, the URL has the name of the free site or "blog" included in the name, which can be tough to verbalize if you are trying to tell someone the blog address for them to remember. Although you can link to your blog from your main website, if the blog isn't hosted on your site, when users leave your website to visit your blog, they are on a different destination, which is a usability point to ponder. The URL of a free blog is often longer, less attractive, tougher to remember, and lives on a destination other than your website. Example: http://webmarketingtherapy .blogspot.com/ (free blog site) versus http://www.webmarketingtherapy.com/ blog (hosted on main website, all under one umbrella).

Another negative is that the free templates offered can be limiting. Marketers are usually limited to a certain structure, have to pay to get advanced templates, or have to hire a web designer who is HTML-savvy to help further customize the blog's design.

Blogs that are on free blog sites do not live on the main company website, so all the content being added and indexed is "credited" to the free blog site. This could offset results, *if* optimizing the main website is the goal. Some companies use free blog sites as a separate SEO strategy that ultimately links to the main website, but if optimizing a main company website where having all the search-friendly content under one domain is the priority, then it may be worth considering building a blog into the main site.

Another factor to consider is that a blog on a free site can be shut down if for any reason the blog site doesn't want to keep your blog live. Access can be denied if the blog site feels that you are violating any blog policies. For example, some users only use free blog sites to build key-phrase links to help boost search engine optimization for another site, which flags the account. Free blog providers can deny a blogger access if they choose. Hosting a blog on a main domain gives marketers more control over content.

Pros and Cons of Hosting a Blog on Your Own Domain

Hosting a blog on your own domain is not necessarily more expensive. In fact, you can still use software from free blogging platforms like WordPress but have the blog hosted on your main website server. It adds a level of company connection by having the blog live under one company umbrella. This tactic can create ease of user experience, streamlined website management, and enhanced brand affiliation.

Advantages of Hosting a Blog on Your Own Domain

Having a blog on your own domain creates a seamless correlation between blog and brand. If you are on a company website like www.taxresolution.com then a simple click on www.taxresolution.com/blog will bring readers to all the blog's content. The ongoing content being added to the blog is indexed by the search engines under one domain, creating more pages to index and a more visually attractive and easy-to-communicate URL.

There is also a greater level of customization. Free blog sites tend to be very template-structured for ease of management, whereas blogs hosted on a main domain can give more flexibility in structure, design, and placement.

Disadvantages of Hosting a Blog on Your Own Domain

Whether a company has a single blogger, or dozens of bloggers like The Huffington Post, when a blog lives on a main domain, the content has a direct connection to the company and brand. Although nine out of ten companies *want* this strong connection, some bloggers prefer to have their own space. Some companies may not want their writers' opinions directly connected with their brand. A strong company/blog tie-in could be seen as a disadvantage. The desire to affiliate (or un-affiliate) with content is worth building into your setup strategy.

Deciding where to host the blog is a first step. But remember, it's not the tools that make web marketing matter, it's how you use them that makes all the difference. A little blogging attitude adjustment will make a big difference. If you want to take your blogging to the next level, read on.

SIX STEPS TO BLOGGING SUCCESS

Blogging is more than an online marketing option—it is a responsibility. Blogging requires dedication, passion, discipline, commitment, respect, patience, education, generosity, humility, and understanding. There are six success steps to make blogging time and energy count. The success steps are voice, theme, content, design, search engine optimization, and outreach. Pay attention to popular blogs—they all employ these steps.

Blog Success Step 1: Voice

The first success step for blogging is having a clear voice. Once a blog lives in cyberspace, people can copy and paste points made and write whatever they want about it on their blogs or websites. Commentary happens even if comments are not allowed on a blog. An organization's voice is amplified via a blog.

Blogs are about conversations, not preapproved press materials. Blogs put a human face on an organization and help convey professional and company personality. To clarify your blog voice, it is best to think from an end-user perspective. Get over any ego issues and be willing to give your readers valuable content. When composing blog posts and creating a consistent strategic blog voice, ask yourself:

- Who is the end user?
- What is the purpose of the blog?
- How do you or your company want to connect with the reader?
- What content will be valuable to your readers and target market?
- Will emotional appeal be a factor?

Use humor (when applicable), fun topics, entertaining content, and pithy, powerful quotes. A blog voice is less serious and more conversational, friendly, and informative.

Blog Success Step 2: Theme

The best blogs are a marriage of fact and opinion. No matter what the blog theme is, readers want perspective. Some blogs are educational, some are controversial, some are customer service oriented, some are employed to give a firm a more "personal" feel. Many organizations set up blogs to get to know their users better. These types of blogs have a "lifestyle" theme where the blogger is sharing ideas and opinions about more than just the product(s) they have to offer. These blogs are appealing to many people because readers feel they are not just connecting with your product(s), but that they are also connecting with you.

In the March 2010 issue of *Inc.* (http://www.inc.com/magazine/20100301/lets-take-this-offline.html), Joel Spolsky wrote, "[A] well-known game developer and author named Kathy Sierra blew me away with an incredibly simple idea. . . . To really work, Sierra observed, a blog has to be about something bigger than his or her company and his or her product."

How does your organization's mission contribute to a larger goal for customers (making life easier, for instance), for the industry, or for the world? A blog needs to be a resource to support the bigger cause, and content needs to become a community itself so that outreach efforts drive traffic and repeat traffic.

Blog Success Step 3: Content

The saying "Content is king" is especially true with blogging. Blogs that have interesting, authentic, valuable content geared toward prospective and current customers are the most appealing and ultimately the most successful. Blogging does not need to be time consuming. Some of the best blog posts are short, sweet, and to the point. Many blog posts link to other sites that are valuable and have great content. Blogging does not require professionals to be expert writers, just enthusiastic experts in their fields who are willing to share tips, advice, and sometimes links to other web content that serves, supports, and sells readers.

Organization of content is also a point to consider for scalability. Blog technology allows for tagging or labeling posts. Tagging and labeling entries often multitasks as:

- Labels help keep track of your content.
- Labels allow readers to search more specifically for something on the blog.

Labels (in some blog technologies) can create mini-sections that cover specific topic areas, allowing both readers and search engines to find content on that topic easily. Tracking label links can reveal which hot-button keywords are connecting with readers and adjust marketing and blogging efforts accordingly.

Blog Success Step 4: Design

Just as design is a huge factor in website credibility, design and usability are also critical to blog success. Often, blogs are built into a website or have a similar theme to an organization's main website if it is not on the site itself. Having a game plan for design before the blog is built is very important. Online marketers rarely have a second chance to make a first great blog impression. Make blog design count. If you hire a blog designer, draft a creative brief (see Chapter 2) so he or she knows what you are looking for.

Putting a professional design spin on a blog can have a big impact. Look at the before-and-after images in Figure 5.3. The after version of the blog header has the following advantages: the organization's logo in the top corner that shows who is behind the organization, building trust and boosting cred-

Figure 5.3 Example of an optimized blog header. See how the addition of a logo and widgets to the "after" illustration enhances branding and integrates social media use.

Before

After

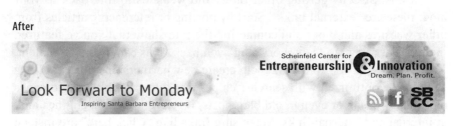

ibility; a more visible RSS feed widget; and the addition of a Facebook widget to increase interactivity.

Simple optimizations to a blog template (even just to the header) made content easier to read, adding the logo boosted credibility, and the widgets for RSS and Facebook were included.

Blog Success Step 5: Search Engine Optimization

A blog is also a great tool to help boost search engine visibility. The constant addition of fresh content and the ability to create links within blogs all work to attract searches. Use priority key phrases when writing copy, headlines, and hyperlinks (links to other blog posts or to pages in the blog or main site) to make the blog as search-ready as possible. Get into the habit of using key phrases that describe your products and services, especially in the titles of blog posts. Often, the title of the blog post becomes part of the URL, and search engines give priority when URLs and content have consistency. Remember that categories or labels can also be named with valuable key phrases to increase search engine visibility.

The bottom of a post is where the blog categories and tags appear. A category may be applied to more than one post, whereas tags are keywords or short phrases used to describe a single post. In most blog platforms, the editing area where you write your blog is where you to enter tags for that post.

Key phrases picked as tags are used for search engine ranking and allow potential subscribers to find the blog easily. When you post, tagging the article with relevant keywords assists a reader/visitor who may be searching for particular content, and helps the search engines index the site.

Search engine optimization is an ongoing process. Stay on top of SEO by tracking the keyword searches of visitors who are finding the site (using a tool like Google Analytics), noting which keywords are most commonly used, and writing and using label/category/link names to reflect those searched terms.

Boost SEO by getting other blogs and websites to link back to your blog; these are "external links." Start by posting or referencing articles from other websites and blogs and contacting them to show that you've featured them and ask them to feature or "plug" you back. This can diversify content, ignite interest in your blog, and help create new partnerships. Internal links can also be optimized with search-rich phrases that can link back to pages of a main website or even to old blog posts, if relevant. Search engines look at internal and external links. Make sure links like "Click here" are instead search-friendly with descriptions people may be searching for, like "Click to read the social media checklist article."

Think of SEO-friendly writing as a healthy marketing lifestyle. It doesn't happen overnight and takes some getting used to.

Blog Success Step 6: Outreach

Building a blog does not mean that people will magically come to read it. You must network and do web marketing outreach to build traffic and attract readers. Include an outreach plan:

- Announce your new blog via press release.
- Form blog partnerships with other bloggers.
- Offer to guest write on other blogs or websites to increase traffic back to your blog.
- Interview influential people on your blog. Interviewees will likely send their "famous moment" to their own blog readers, e-mail list, Facebook, Twitter, and more!
- Find blogs that are complementary to your blog. Endorse them on your blog and contact them to let them know that you did. The favor may be returned.
- Build readership. Equip the blog with widgets (widgets, also known as snippets, modules, and plug-ins, are chunks of code that can be embed-

ded in an HTML page) to make it easier for readers to subscribe to your blog via e-mail or RSS feed. Place widgets on the front page of your blog for easy access.

HOW TO PROMOTE YOUR BLOG

Whether the blog has been around for ages or is brand new, there are a number of ways to increase its exposure. Taking the time to go through each step will increase blog readership and provide a solid return on investment for only a few hours of work.

List Social Media Directories to Submit to for More Visibility

There are two steps involved in submitting to social media directories. The first is getting the blog listed in social media directories. The second step is getting people to vote on your content, once it is listed in the directories, so that more people see it. The more popular the blog is on social media directories, the higher it appears on their pages. First, register the blog at the following sites:

- Technorati.com
- Best of the Web Blogs Directory: Blogs.botw.org/
- Blogged.com
- BlogSearchEngine.com
- BlogCatalog.com
- Blogarama.com
- The Open Directory Project/DMOZ (for search engine optimization): Dmoz.org
- PitchEngine.com (to get press releases socially submitted)
- Article marketing sites (to repurpose your blog's content into articles for more visibility)
- Industry or subject-area directories (Conduct a web search for these.)

Note Appropriate Social Bookmarking Sites to Increase Traffic

Instead of using the bookmark tab on browser bars, now web users use social bookmarking to save, store, organize, and share links. This is an opportunity for bloggers to gain visibility and get people to vote on their blog. The top vertical search engine (with a social media emphasis) indexes more than 1.5 million blog posts in real time.

- Digg.com: Submit blog posts to be voted on or "dug" by others. If enough "diggs" are received for a post, it will be on Digg's front page for millions of viewers to read.
- Reddit.com works the same way as Digg.

Be sure to consider using some of the social media sites for content ideas and get your blog listed (when you can) on the following sites:

Twitter
Digg.com
Reddit.com
Mixx.com
Technorati.com
StumbleUpon.com
Yahoo! Buzz: http://buzz.yahoo.com
Google Buzz: http://www.google.com/buzz
TweetMeme.com
Delicious.com
Kaboodle.com
Ma.gnolia
BlinkList.com
coRank.com
Slashdot.org
Propeller.com
Folkd.com
Netvouz.com
Mister-Wong.com

Additional Ways to Increase Traffic to the Blog

The following are additional ways to drive traffic to your blog:

- Add social media widgets to the blog sidebar right above the "Categories" for Twitter, Facebook, YouTube, Flickr, and LinkedIn.
- Add RSS feed and e-mail sign-up widgets to the blog. This will capture fans and keep readership up, as RSS feeds automatically send new posts to opt-in recipients. Some blog readers do not recognize what an RSS widget does, so an e-mail sign-up box option can increase responses.
- Optimize your Twitter background. Have a brand-centric design with contact information. (See an example at http://twitter.com/treehugger.)

Optimizing the Twitter account to be more about the blog writer and less about the organization will boost followers.

- Create a Facebook page for your organization (http://www.facebook.com/pages/create.php). Get other Facebook pages to promote the blog—use your personal connections. A Facebook fan page will boost awareness and drive traffic to the blog. The blog can automatically feed into Facebook for exposure.
- Create a YouTube account (http://www.youtube.com/create_account). This account can link back to the blog and will increase search engine optimization if it is set up with search-rich phrases in the account description.
- Create a Flickr.com account to show photos that support your mission
- Create a LinkedIn company profile (http://www.linkedin.com/company/linkedin).
- Use Twitterfeed.com to feed your blog to a Twitter account.
- Use the NetworkedBlogs.com application to import the blog to your Facebook fan page.
- Add a Retweet button to the blog (http://tweetmeme.com/about/retweet_button).
- Use HootSuite.com to manage multiple social media accounts at once.
- If a team is managing one or more Twitter accounts, use CoTweet.com to provide tweet assignments, notes, and on-duty status.
- Add share buttons to each blog post using AddThis or AddToAny so readers can share the blog posts (www.addthis.com/ or www.addtoany.com/).
- Make sure that all the links on the blog and in the blog sidebar open in a new window so your blog still stays open to readers.
- Add a "tag cloud," which is a cloud of phrases that shows the most popular tags and links to blog categories for optimal blog usability. Try to give each blog post three to four tags (make sure tags relate to the blog post).
- Be strategic with category titles on the blog and links within posts (that link to old posts or other organization pages) using relevant keywords and phrases such as:
  - Your organization's name
  - Name(s) of top blogger(s)
  - Keywords related to your products or services
  - Keywords related to your larger mission
  - Keywords related to the community you serve
- Try to add three to four categories to each blog post when labeling them (make sure categories relate to the blog post).

- Every site that is listed under "Sites I Like" or "What I'm Reading" are sites that you can also ask the site owner to link back to you.
- Ask to interview other influencers in the field. Hopefully they will blog about it, tweet it, add it to LinkedIn, and more. Remember, relationships are everything on the social web.
- Have a link to your blog in e-mail signatures to increase exposure and traffic.
- Have fun! Social media helps you communicate, collaborate, and entertain. Concentrating on these three foci will ensure success. There has to be a reason for readers to come back. Make the content value-rich, helpful, educational, and enjoyable to read.

BLOG CONTENT IDEAS

A good blog theme is an umbrella that content ideas can flow from. If a blog theme is "Healthy Marketing Advice," content can be about anything marketing related, as long as it has smart marketing tips. When content ideas are tough to come by, look to the theme as the North Star—a guiding light that helps shine ideas on valuable content to share with readers.

For many people inspiration strikes only when they have a specific mood: last-minute panic. Professionals need to have a plan to produce great content without inspiration. (If inspiration strikes, that's gravy.) Here's the plan.

What to Blog

- **Write as simply as possible.** Studies have shown that online content that is shared most often is readable to most elementary school kids. This is about providing instant clarity. Most readers want a blog to comb through the relevant subject matter and show them something that is worth their attention. A blog entry can be as simple as "Hey, look at this" with a little narrative as to why blog readers should look at the link, photo, or video that is being shared. If you want to write long essays on the topic, that's great as long as your analytics numbers show that long essays are what your readers want.
- **Keep it short.** Someone once said that blog posts should be like a miniskirt—long enough to cover the subject, but short enough to keep reader interest. One of the best bloggers in the business, Seth Godin, writes very short blog entries. Check him out at http://sethgodin.typepad.com/.

- **Plan a writing schedule and keep to it.** You'd be amazed at how creative you can be when filled with last-minute panic. Until you've got your sea legs, start with a weekly entry and then grow to three to five posts a week. Some bloggers have "Weekly Wednesday" or "Monday Motivation" or "Friday Funny" themes so they have a clear focus and day of the week to prompt writing.
- **Make a list of topics to cover.** If you're stumped by what to write about, go back to the blog theme and start thinking about your target customers. Think about how the blog can best educate, enlighten, and engage them. Brand, build, and boost your business. Your expertise, ideas, perspective, tips, tricks, and stories won't help anyone if they're all stashed away in your brain.
- **Look at the calendar.** Every industry has annual, seasonal, or in some cases monthly events that are content creation–worthy. In some cases you can create a draft about a seasonal event long in advance and then plug in the latest news at the top of the posting. For example, the fashion industry has a large focus on spring and fall fashion, accountants get very busy around tax time, and professional organizers have a lot of buzz around spring cleaning.
- **Create editorial departments.** Look at pertinent trade magazines to discover which departments you can adapt to regular blog entries. Any time there is big media buzz around a certain topic that relates to the blog theme, put on that journalist hat to blog about related current events to maximize interest and exposure.
- **Stay informed.** There are a number of tools to keep you up to date on the latest industry news so that when news hits, you'll know and can write about it:
  - Create Google Alerts for topic area keywords or phrases (http://www .google.com/alerts).
  - Create an industry news dashboard in iGoogle and then customize the feeds. This will allow you to see all the industry news at a glance.
- **Look to the key phrases for inspiration.** There are key phrase clusters around every organization and industry. Use a web analytics package to look at the keywords and phrases that people are using to find your site. See if any of those keywords lend themselves to regular blog entries. Check out Google Trends for the keywords in the given topic area to see which keywords are on the rise and which are declining.
- **Take advantage of inspiration.** Sometimes the muse strikes. Don't forget it. Write it down and post it. If you want to develop the topic more fully

later, you can with the knowledge that you've created two blog postings (a short one and a long one) out of one inspiration.

- **Plan "think pieces."** "Think pieces" can sound scary and formal, but it is simply a three-pronged way to write that includes a quick analysis, background material, and personal opinions. All you need is an opening, three points, and a closer—keep it to 400 words maximum and you're done. Remember that, with blogging, done is better than perfect. The web is flexible; you can always go back and edit.

- **Slice the onion thinly.** Don't feel you need to write everything about a topic in a single entry. You can say, "Stay tuned for Part Two," and give readers a reason to come back (or sign up for the RSS feed) to get more of the story.

- **Author how-to articles.** The web is one of the main places people go to find information. How-to articles are great for customer service and to show expertise.

- **Include educational articles.** Web users are in need of authoritative articles about millions of topics. When readers are educated, they feel empowered. When an organization empowers people, a relationship is built that can launch business.

- **Share your checklists.** If you've got a procedure that works, share it. Lists are easy, organized, and very helpful to those web readers who scan rather than read, and they show expertise.

- **Try a Top 10 list.** Thanks to David Letterman, Top 10 lists have become a staple for content creators. For interesting and relevant blog posts, try a Top 10 list of things people don't know about your topic.

- **Interview people in your industry.** A blog is a great excuse to network with big names. Create an interview sheet with top questions you would like answers to. Interviews can be conducted via phone or e-mail.

- **Embed videos from YouTube or other sources.** Video is more than just eye candy. It is one of the top content creation ways to engage readers. Video links are clicked on and shared more often than any other content on the web. Regularly search for videos in the topic area of your industry, and when there is something worth sharing with readers, post it.

- **Link to podcasts.** If your organization or someone in the industry has a relevant podcast, link to it. Add some opinion to the piece being shared on the blog.

- **Outsource to experts.** Get guest bloggers to write and keep content diverse. Diversifying writers helps create fresh content and can appeal to more readers. Guest writers gain exposure and the blog owner gets content—it's a win-win.

- **Get the best blogging advice every day.** Seeking help will inspire the content development process. Get blogging advice or inspiration from people who do it professionally. Make ProBlogger (www.problogger .net) regular reading.

HOW TO WRITE A BLOG QUICKLY

The most prolific writers in the world swear by these simple steps to get writing projects completed quickly:

1. Schedule a regular time to write when everyone knows you should not be disturbed.
2. Create a writing ritual that gets your head in the game. Sharpen pencils. Freewrite. Pet your cat for two minutes. Spin around three times. Do whatever it takes.
3. Outline first. Quickly sketch out your opening, basic points, and closer, then assign a rough word count to each. You can veer off your outline if inspiration strikes, but without an outline too many bloggers get stuck.
4. Write as fast as you can without editing along the way. Creative writers teach this technique because it works. Think first, edit later.
5. If you need to drop in a fact that requires research, write in a place-holder and find the fact later. Don't stop writing for anything, but do get your facts before you publish. Here's an insider's trick: Most publishers use the letters *TK* to signify "To Come" (as in "On date TK, Joe Smith, age TK, married Sue Jones, age TK"). Writers frequently fall down the research rabbit hole, never to emerge. Write first. Find the missing facts later. Enjoy life. Repeat.
6. Use the phone. If you can speak, you can write. Most cell phones can record audio files that can be synced to a computer. If that doesn't work, just call your voice mail, leave a message for yourself, and type it out later. Some voice-mail systems like Google Voice, Vonage, and others will machine translate voice-mail messages with accuracy somewhere between the uncanny and hilariously wrong. A service like iDictate.com will allow you to dictate blog entries just like making a voice call. The return on investment on

blogging (hands free, of course) while stuck in traffic is well worth it. You could transform your commute from road-rage-inducing to the most fun and creative time of your day.

When Is the Best Day to Blog?

Remember that writing a blog entry and releasing it to the public don't have to happen in tandem. Planning and working ahead are excellent habits. The decision when to unleash a blog entry is based on a few considerations.

- **Monitor web traffic patterns.** For some professional websites, traffic tends to decrease a lot on weekends, because they serve working professionals (who put in most of their hours Monday through Friday). Professionals may consider blogging more during the week because Google Analytics web data shows that's when people are on the site. It pays to pay attention to patterns and then act accordingly.
- **Blog when you have something valuable to say.** Blogs and news are best served freshly squeezed. Don't worry about the day; just get it out there. If the content serves and supports your readers (and has value), then post it. If you feel like you want to blog only Monday through Friday, then you can always set the post to auto-launch during the week. It is easy to queue up blog posts so they launch at a later date.
- **Leverage media relevancy (buzz).** If there is industry news that is buzzing, then it is prime time to blog about it. Piggyback on what is out there in the news and blog your point of view as the trends hit.
- **Focus on your audience.** Who are you trying to serve? What content can you blog that will help them? Focus more attention on creating content that will serve your audience and less on which day of the week it appears.

As for days of the week, some recommend Monday morning while others swear by Thursday afternoon. Make note of when comments are coming in to the blog and listen to the feedback you get off your site. You can learn so much when you just open your eyes and see what feedback you are getting (comments, tweets, retweets, data, etc.). Follow the six blog success steps, focus on quality over quantity, and blog to serve (not just to sell) and you will be light-years ahead of the other bloggers in cyberspace who are scratching their heads over how to blog to boost business.

BLOGGING DANGER ZONES

Don't Get Your Hand Caught in the Copyright Cookie Jar

It is great blogging practice to comment on other people's stuff, but it is against the law to copy and paste a large portion of what they've written. Always cite and link to the original source. How much is too much to quote? Try to quote no more than 15 percent of original material. Single digits are even better. Directly quote only the barest minimum you need to make your point. If you want to write a point-by-point counterattack of something someone else has written, write a very quotation-lite rebuttal that links to the original.

Bloggers Must Disclose Payments for Endorsements—It's the Law

Most bloggers use blogging as a marketing tool to promote a product, service, mission, or expertise. The blog serves as a credibility, visibility, service, and sellability booster. But for some, the blog itself is the moneymaker. Some bloggers have blog "tip jars" for loyal readers to thank them for their great content, and some bloggers endorse other products or services in exchange for compensation (commission, sponsorship, free products, etc.). To keep blog content as authentic as possible, the Federal Trade Commission has mandated that bloggers must disclose payments for endorsements.

Most see this as a great rule, since bloggers will have to be transparent about their recommendations and readers will know what content is truly a recommendation. If the online marketing strategy includes making money from ads that live on the blog, then make sure it is crystal clear to readers that there is compensation involved for certain product or service endorsements.

THE TYPES OF BLOG ENTRIES THAT ENHANCE SALES

In addition to creating relationship ROI, blogging is a great way to generate sales. You will need to use unique links (the Google Analytics URL Builder is a fantastic tool for this) in your blog to track the blog's and specific entries' effectiveness over time. Here are some types of blog entries that have been proven generally to enhance sales.

- **Comparison blogs.** Comparison blog entries readily translate into sales because they highlight the differences between two competitors. Potential customers are looking for a reason to buy Product A over Product B.

Benchmarks and feature comparisons are good, but don't be afraid to toot your own horn. Remember that your product or service must not just have features, but be able to solve problems. For some organizations, the entire website is the blog.

- **Problems.** Sometimes people don't use a product properly and this leads to negative customer reviews on your website or on outside consumer review sites. A blog entry that addresses the problem will go a long way to making people comfortable about buying the product.
- **A better way.** Some users find a better way to solve a problem using a feature of your product. Think of this as a "cool tricks" entry. In truth, this doesn't have to be something really new, just new to the user.
- **New uses.** Sometimes people will create a new use for a product. If this happens, blog about it. Perhaps some of your users have come up with new uses—ask them. Don't be afraid to have fun and make creative, fun, or funny posts. Stephen Colbert cut vegetables with the edge of his new iPad; this video made it to many blog posts as fun, entertaining content.
- **New features, new prices, and overall news.** Product or service news is often highlighted on web pages, but such items are also worthy of a blog entry (and a press release, but more on that in Chapter 11).
- **User stories.** Web surfers are more likely to trust "people like me" versus a company, so let your users help create compelling blog content. Interview a user who is very happy with your product or service. Better yet, invite guest blogs so you don't have to do any of the writing, only editing. A real customer can also be effusive in a way that the company blogger can't.

Before You Start Your Blog, Some Final Thoughts

There are plenty of tools on the market, such as Blogger, WordPress, or Type-Pad, that can be used to launch a blog in minutes. It is easy to get lost in the technology. Bloggers need technology, but as with all aspects of online marketing, it's not so much about the tools as how you use them. Remember, be authentic and give great content.

NEXT STEPS

Read some blogs in your relevant subject area and note the good, the bad, and the ugly. Aim to copy the good. Make notes about their theme, voice/tone, content, design (look, feel, colors, widgets, RSS, etc.), SEO, and outreach.

Write your blog strategy out. The blog strategy document can become an internal training or blog optimization tool. It can lead to more service-oriented content on the blog, a better user experience, optimized design, heightened search engine visibility, and more.

Chapter Quiz

1. Define *blog*.
2. What is RSS?
3. Is a blog truly a blog if it does not allow comments?
4. What are the four main factors to focus on when deciding whether to use a free blog site or host it on the organization's main domain?
5. Make a list of blog content ideas, what to write about, and blogging best practices.
6. List two main ways to promote a blog.
7. True or false? It is okay for bloggers to get compensated for endorsements and not disclose it.
8. Note the types of blog entries that enhance sales.

6

SOCIAL MEDIA MARKETING

Social platforms are doing more than driving buzz. Social outlets like blogs, Facebook, LinkedIn, and Twitter are driving purchases; travel; and romantic, political, and other real-world decisions. As social networks grow, so does the power of word-of-mouse chatter to shape consumer conversations. Social media works like a virtual cocktail party where all attendees can discuss your products, services, experiences, and new ideas.

Now that you've got the basics of web marketing securely under your belt, it's time to get savvy about social media. By the end of this chapter you'll understand how to:

- Effectively use social media best practices as a low-cost marketing tool.
- Use these popular platforms to gain a competitive edge.
- Build a powerful voice in this "influence economy," where anyone with an opinion can effect great change.
- Use social media content to boost brands, bond with customers, and build business.
- Understand ways to quantify social media as a marketing effort.

HOW SOCIAL MEDIA SERVES AND SUPPORTS GROWTH

Social media has become extremely popular because it allows people to connect in the online world to form relationships for personal and business purposes. Social media is also called user-generated content (UGC) or consumer-generated media (CGM).

While the previous case studies and numbers prove that social media can help organizations big and small, the next big question is how to apply it specifically to your organization. Before you get started, understand that social media serves users and organizations as an online marketing media option in three main ways: communication, collaboration, and entertainment.

Communication

Marketing is all about building relationships, and relationships start with communication. Communications students learn the rule "You cannot *not* communicate." Conversations will take place about your organization whether or not your organization is an active participant in social media. New web tools, such as blogging, micro-blogging (Twitter), social networking (Facebook, LinkedIn, Ning), podcasting (BlogTalkRadio), video distribution (YouTube), event coordination tools (Meetup), wikis (Wikipedia), photo sharing (Flickr, Photobucket), and product review sites (Epinions), allow firms to communicate, educate, and share information directly with their current and prospective customers.

Social media's direct communication distinction serves and supports organizations as it brings the people you want to attract directly to you, allows them to connect with each other, and makes direct communication possible. Many marketers ask if social media is more for business-to-business (B2B) or business-to-consumer (B2C) marketing, but the answer is that social media is all about people-to-people (P2P) marketing. Social media makes communication a *conversation* so you can share, receive feedback, and connect on equal ground with the target markets.

Collaboration

When consumers are empowered with information and support, they feel powerful—they trust you, buy from you, and stay with you. Social media collaboration transforms consumers into "prosumers" (consumers who have done enough research to have gleaned some professional-grade knowledge). In an era of social media, prosumers (not companies) make, shape, or break purchase patterns. Companies do not sell things, people sell things. With social media, online collaboration sells companies' products and services to each other, often without the company initiating the collaboration.

Organizations can ignite collaboration for marketing by creating and/or joining communities. By doing so, they can listen and connect to their target customers and build a free forum to bring a community of like-minded people together. People want to connect, converse, and belong to groups. Online collaboration equals marketing acceleration. A community under your organizational brand can be a huge marketing booster.

Entertainment

The most important reason that social media works as a marketing tool is because it's fun. People want to go where they feel they belong, have a voice, are listened to, and enjoy themselves. You need to be where your target markets are, and these days the masses are on Facebook, Ning, Twitter, LinkedIn, Photobucket, YouTube, and more. Why? Because they are fun.

Remember the "Will It Blend?" campaign by Blendtec? It was a perfect example of social media marketing in brilliant action. The campaign's videos were relevant (they showed the product), were entertaining (they blended an iPhone!), and were viral. People could easily share the fun with friends due to the ease of social media sharing.

SOCIAL MEDIA STRATEGY: THE THREE Vs (VALUE, VALUES, AND VOICE)

It is easy to get overwhelmed with the multitude of social media options, but the secrets to successful social media boil down to the three Vs: value, values, and voice.

Value

Social media content has to be bigger than a single person or organization. Writing about just you or your organization may keep the search engines happy, but it will bore readers to tears. The first secret is to deliver value to readers. Think of how to improve their lives (not by simply selling a product or service, but by talking about it in a way that has an impact). Content doesn't have to be profound but should provide a reason for someone to stay and play. Create value for readers via the content posted in social media.

Values

Values means writing about principles that are important. Some organizations, because of their industry, mistakenly believe that their use of social media must be formal, noncommittal, and sterile. But compliance or regulatory issues do not dictate that social media communications must be boring. A good financial social media maven can write about basic investing principles and strategies, and share links to other articles to illustrate the need to plan wisely. A company selling rafting trips can use social media to share valuable content by sharing their values about the pristine beauty of the location, how people are cleaning it up, and what the reader can do to save the planet (and mention at the end of the post that the reader might want to book a rafting trip to see this beauty for themselves). Hit the big issues first, then talk about you or your organization second.

Voice

Have an authentic voice. The simplest way to figure out what your authentic voice is, is to write the way you talk. If an organization is in the medical industry, the authentic voice may be more professional and compassionate and geared toward making readers feel confident in their medical facility. The CEO of a company may have more of an opinionated, strong voice in social media. Just converse with the readers on issues you care about, and your voice will ring through loud and clear. Through an authentic voice, you create connections.

SMART SOCIAL MEDIA EXECUTION TO SUPPORT SALES

As with all other online marketing solutions, one social media site doesn't fit all organizations. The key thing that organizations need to remember is the need to serve and support. That is the way to sell. Social media efforts must have *value*. There has to be value to get people to engage. Social media doesn't sell things—people sell things. Engaging in social media marketing starts the relationship-building process.

The focus of many organizations is usually the bottom line. The new bottom line is that the organization is now in the relationship business. Social media is not going to magically make sales. Instead, it supports organizations in making, building, and growing relationships. Look critically at online marketing and see how it communicates who the organization is, what they do, and who they serve. Does the organization's web marketing have valuable information, attract quality visitors, share helpful information, educate, and enlighten people to build the know, like, and trust factors? When there is a connection, sales happen—and happen again.

When a web marketing strategy has a clear purpose, intention, desire to offer superlative service, and partnership, and it employs commitment to communication, then it supports sales. It is time to start thinking in terms of relationship ROI.

Is every blog post or tweet going to make sales? Probably not. But when users continue to learn, connect, become more empowered, and have a great cyber-relationship with an organization through social media connections, a professional success equation happens that yields results every time: Responsibility + Relationships = Rewards.

- **Responsibility.** Regardless of where the primary online marketer resides on the org chart hierarchy, they should own the use of web marketing and be a proactive participant in social media. Organizations really thriving with social media have all team members taking a responsibility role. When we take responsibility, we take our professional contributions personally and the outcome is always greater than not feeling a sense of ownership. Taking responsibility for social media will increase the chances of success.
- **Relationships.** Relationships are everything. Repeat—relationships are everything! To make social media work, get out of the business of selling and into the business of serving. You build relationships via social media with meaningful marketing messages, social media community networking, and content, and by being authentic.
- **Rewards.** Social media can show rewards via increased traffic (web analytics will show this) and conversion rates. Sometimes customers may tell you that it was a blog post that made them want to call. That may not compute in web traffic logs, but it is a relationship return on investment that helps build trust and differentiate an organization enough to prompt a potential customer to want to work with you.

C.O.U.P.L.E.: The Secret of Successful Marketing Relationships

Success in a marketing relationship is just like success in a romantic one. Social media has distinct strategic online marketing power that allows companies to C.O.U.P.L.E.

- Commitment: You need to show that you'll go the distance in this social media relationship. You need to invest your time-building social connections without demanding a payoff. Slow and steady wins this race.
- Outreach: Social media is a partnership across a variety of social networks. Outreach also means looking for partners that you may collaborate with to amplify your message.

- Understanding: Try understanding the relationship from the customers' (and potential customers') points of view. What do they want? What problems can you help them solve? Often, they simply want to be heard. Understanding what they want and using social media to listen will lead to a symbiotic relationship.
- **Passion:** Believe in your organization and how it can help people. Get excited about the possibilities and use your authentic voice to share your value and values and help people. Passion is contagious and engaging.
- **Love:** Yes, love. Put some heart in the art and science of social media to make it work wonders. Online marketers are used to the old ways of pushing propaganda. Love your customers instead. If you care about the other person, it will show. If you don't, this will also show.
- **Effort:** Social media needs management every day. Little things like making regular updates, responding to questions, and commenting on what is going on in your industry are little gestures that can pay off big-time.

MARKETING MULTITASKING

At its most basic, when marketing multitasks (we'll go into marketing multitasking more in the final chapter), social media is used as a platform to announce the latest blog entry, press release, deal, coupon, video, podcast, and more. Taking social media marketing to the next level means online marketers create content specifically with a social media channel in mind, such as Burger King's Whopper Sacrifice Facebook application, Twitter-only promotions, and so on.

The Right Social Media Tool for the Right Job

The social media universe is always expanding, and while there is a lot of crossover, different networks specialize in different ways of communicating. The social media universe evolves and combines in new forms every day. To get the most ROI, these social media tools are used together. In some cases this can be done automatically, such as linking a Twitter feed to a Facebook or LinkedIn profile. The important takeaway here is not the list of individual social media sites but their subcategories. Each of these subcategories is a powerful tool in the online marketing toolbox.

Communication
- Blogging: Blogger, LiveJournal, Open Diary, TypePad, WordPress, ExpressionEngine
- Micro-blogging: Twitter, Plurk, Tumblr, Jaiku

- Social networking: Bebo, Facebook, LinkedIn, MySpace, Orkut, Skyrock, hi5
- Social network aggregation: FriendFeed
- Events: Upcoming, Eventful, Meetup, Foursquare

Collaboration

- Wikis: Wikipedia, PBworks, Wetpaint
- Social bookmarking (or social tagging): Delicious, StumbleUpon, Stumpedia, Google Reader, CiteULike
- Social news: Digg, Mixx, Reddit
- Opinion sites: Epinions, Yelp, MouthShut

Multimedia

- Photo sharing: Flickr, Zooomr, Photobucket, SmugMug
- Video sharing: YouTube
- Livecasting: Ustream.tv, Justin.tv, Skype
- Music sites: The Hype Machine, Last.fm, ccMixter

Entertainment

- Virtual worlds: Second Life, Forterra Systems
- Game sharing: World of Warcraft, FarmVille

Reviews and Opinions

- Product reviews: Epinions, MouthShut
- Q&A: Yahoo! Answers, WikiAnswers
- Local business reviews: Yelp, Citysearch, Yahoo! Local

Refer to Brian Solis' Conversation Prism (http://www.briansolis .com/2008/08/introducing-conversation-prism/) to see a visual representation of the multitude of social media options (and this chart still does not cover all of them!).

A particular organization will derive substantial relationship ROI by spending more of their online marketing resources on a few industry-specific social media sites. Review sites are a great case in point. For example, for those in the dining or hospitality industry, a list of relevant review sites might look like this:

10Best.com
ChefMoz.org
Citysearch.com

Dine.com
DiningGuide.com
DinnerBroker.com
Frommers.com
Gayot.com
Giatamedia.com
Greenopia.com
HolidayCheck.com
HotelChatter.com
hotelguide.com
HotelGuide.net
InsiderPages.com
MenuPages.com
MyTravelGuide.com
Priceline.com
RestaurantRow.com
Travelocity.com
TravelPost.com
TripAdvisor.com
VirtualTourist.com
Yahoo.com (local business reviews)
Yelp.com
Zagat.com

But for a local doctor, the list of relevant review sites might look something like this:

DrScore.com
Vitals.com
CheckMD.com
RateMDs.com
Vimo.com
SuggestADoctor.com
HealthGrades.com
AngiesList.com
DoctorSecondOpinion.org
WhereToFindCare.com
Google.com (business reviews)

Why Review Sites Are So Mission Critical

No matter what the organization's mission is, there is someone reviewing it. Find those review sites and start a dialogue. Review sites are among the top-ranking listing for people searching for something generic ("excellent sushi, Rockville, Maryland") to evaluating something specific ("Dr. McDreamy, physician, Seattle, Washington"). These sites are mission critical because people searching reviews are in a transactional mind-set. These potential customers already know exactly what they want and are ready to buy now. They just need to know where. This is where a well-positioned social media placement can have a huge real-world ROI.

A stumbling block to the use of social media may be concern over possible reputation sabotage. Smart organizations prepare themselves and proactively reply to comments (when they are rational comments and deserve a reply), and trust that one or two negative comments in a sea of positive ones will be put in their proper perspective. Simply showing that your organization is actively listening can set an incredibly powerful impression. Let's face it, organizations are not perfect, and people do not expect them to be. But being a dedicated professional and showing that there is a voice in cyberspace can make a meaningful impression. Encouraging happy clients to post comments about your organization can also boost credibility and visibility for sellability.

THE TOP FOUR SOCIAL MEDIA BEHEMOTHS

There are too many social networks to give a detailed blow-by-blow account of how to maximize online marketing efforts on each, so we'll focus on the top four: Twitter, Facebook, LinkedIn, and YouTube. The lessons learned here can be applied to other social media.

Twitter

Twitter is a free online social network that allows users to write brief messages up to 140 characters in length on their profiles and view those of other users. Organizations that use Twitter are flexible, connected, have direct relationships, and can communicate with their base more rapidly. They can trumpet their brands without blowing their budgets.

Chances are, people may already be tweeting about your organization (or its mission). Twitter is the most authentic focus group ever made. Eavesdropping on what people are saying is easy. Just use the Twitter search engine (http://search.twitter.com) to read the buzz about an organization and industry.

Twitter allows an organization to deliver great customer service to an individual or a group, and because all subscribers can see the response, many people will benefit from that one example of customer service. But organizations have got to walk the walk. Setting up an account that isn't maintained isn't savvy execution. Use Twitter to engage in authentic conversations with customers, not as a self-serving propaganda tool. Lots of organizations are starting to use Twitter to answer customer service questions in a short, succinct, community-shared way.

These days, having a Twitter account is a necessary tool to stake territory in the wild, wild web. Just as organizations need to have a good website address, a Twitter account is prime real estate that needs to be claimed. A Twitter site is often one of the top listings in a Google search. Don't believe it? When the British Petroleum oil disaster hit the Gulf of Mexico in 2010, the primary Twitter account that most people (including journalists) saw was a BP parody account launched by critics.

If the organization has a blog, posts can automatically populate onto Twitter by using Twitterfeed.com. Having a blog post live on a blog and also automatically feed to Twitter helps boost visibility and increases the potential for people to see the content.

For mom-and-pop shops with little or no ad budget, Twitter can serve as their main marketing outlet. Businesses as small as mobile coffee kiosks can tweet new locations or deals. Because small business owners can tweet right from their phones, it is immediate and easy.

Even if the organization only has a small website, its Twitter page can be changed so that it is visually consistent with the website and other branding. Unfortunately, there are some major Internet entities that don't bother to do this, losing a prime opportunity for brand emphasis. Just because an organization may be small doesn't mean that it can't outshine the big guys.

Twitter Tools

Twitter seems like a lot of work, but there are hundreds of tools that can help you get the job done as efficiently as possible. Twitter tools are changing very fast. To learn about the latest and greatest tools, just Google the phrase "Twitter tools" and read the latest reviews. Here are a few that many people swear by:

- **HootSuite.** An organization's Twitter feed doesn't have to be written live in real time. Use tools like HootSuite to schedule tweets in advance. By the way, you don't even need to tweet yourself. You can hire a web marketing firm to do it or use HootSuite to manage tweets among multiple social media accounts for one easy login (www.hootsuite.com).

- **Twitter Search.** This is a great way to streamline your "Twitxperience." To see what is going on in Twitter right now (because everything with the web is right now), just go to Twitter Search, type in your search subject, and voilà! The latest, greatest Twitter scoop. You can see who is retweeting posts, review comments about an organization, and quickly check in on your favorite social media influencers and industry leaders (http://search.twitter.com).
- **Twitter badges.** To tout tweets, "pimp" your blog with Twitter badges. It marries fashion and function with fabulous flair, all via a simple widget. (Do a search for "Twitter badges" or "Twitter widgets.")
- **Twitterfeed.** If your organization has a blog, posts can automatically populate onto Twitter by setting up a free feed (http://twitterfeed.com).

Twitter: The Business Case

Technically speaking, Twitter is micro-blogging, but don't look at Twitter as a mindless collection of tweets. See it for what it really is: a very powerful real-time search engine/relationship tool. With roughly 200 million users and 65 million tweets a day (as of mid-2010), Twitter has reached a critical mass that provides an important number of business functions such as:

- **Marketing multitasking.** When your organization does anything new, from posting a blog entry to starting a video contest, announce it on Twitter. Twitter feeds can automatically update most social media outlets including Facebook, MySpace, LinkedIn, and others.
- **Displaying your brand.** Twitter is a prime location and interaction tool to help you build a brand in real time. The 140-character limit means you can't just repost your organization's slogans. You have to show folks that you are living those values.
- **Conducting research.** Using Twitter, you can find real-time keyword trends (how many people are talking about my brand right now?). You can also do research about how people are conversing about a topic. Twitter Search (http://search.twitter.com) is the easiest Twitter trend tool to get started. Type in a key phrase and you'll see a live feed of the current conversation on that trend. If you want to see a graph of how that key phrase has trended, go to Trendistic.com. (For more great business and marketing Twitter tools, search for "Twitter trend tools.")

You can be even more proactive in your research. If you've got enough Twitter followers, you can ask them a simple survey question such as, "How many of you would like X over Y? What about Z?" You can ask your Twitter followers about anything from advertising on your website to which CEO headshot is better. (Just keep in mind that the results aren't scientific and you'll be hearing mostly from a vocal minority.) If you want to conduct a more comprehensive, 20-question survey via Twitter, Facebook, or your e-mail list, you can use tools like Twtpoll (http://twtpoll.com/). Twtpoll will combine responses across all social media.

If an organization doesn't have a lot of followers, follow the Twitter feed of someone in the same topic area who has a lot of followers and pose questions there. Just be sure that the questions have conversational value and are not a sales pitch. ("Hey, Pepsi Twitter followers, want a 50 percent off coupon to try Brand X cola?" is not cool, but "Hey, Pepsi fans, what do you think makes Pepsi a better soda than the others?" or "Why is Pepsi better than Brand X cola?" or "Who has better advertising: Pepsi or Brand X cola? Why?" is okay.)

Discover New Customers and Have Them Discover You

When someone uses your organization's key phrases in their tweets, feel free to follow them and invite them to follow you. These people are already talking about the topic or brand, so it is likely that they might be interested in your Twitter stream.

The key to social media is that it is social. It is shared. That means if one of your followers retweets your organization's Twitter posting, all their friends see it and might become new customers. And their friends retweet, and so on, and so on. Not to mention all the link sharing that happens on social bookmarking and news sites like Digg, Reddit, Delicous, and Google Buzz.

Believe it or not people often search for brands on Twitter before they search for a company's main website. Twitter is the perfect no-cost way to promote introductory offers. When you think about your Twitter content stream, think about what you might offer longtime followers as well as first-time potential clients.

As you continue your "Twitorial," consider these Twitter tutorial best practice tips as you venture into the wild world of Twitterville:

- **Handle complaints before they become a big issue.** Major hotels and airlines have people who are dedicated 24/7 to monitoring the uses of their name and finding people who are complaining about their service. When someone complains, that person often gets a quick Twitter response that helps to resolve the issue. This real-time customer service helps the individual, and it also displays the organization's commitment to customer service.

- **Find business partners.** While B2B connections are what LinkedIn touts as its value proposition, in reality Twitter is also a great place to find people who can help your organization (not to mention you personally) achieve your goals.

- **Create an authentic persona.** Companies present different faces on Twitter, from the corporate entity to individuals. Choose a user name and focus on establishing a relationship with users. Users need to feel they are connecting either with a real person or with an organization that shares their values. They follow tweets because they have a passion (or at least an interest) in their topic.

    When setting up a Twitter account, you can have just one link to your main site or blog. A link to a blog may be the better choice because social media is about relationship marketing, and a blog allows readers to get to know the blogger/organization in greater detail.

    Pick a friendly photo. Most photos that work best are natural-looking ones with a smiling face, plain and simple. People want to connect with a person, not a brand. Don't think that's important? Some people will decide whether to follow a tweeter based solely on his or her profile picture. You can always test between a company logo or personal photo to see which works best.

    Twitter offers standard page designs, but more brand-conscious marketers will opt to customize a Twitter page so that it visually matches the rest of the organization's branding. For details on how to do this, check out http://support.twitter.com/entries/15357-how-to-customize -your-twitter-design.

- **Tweet responsibly.** Tell folks "what's happening." Share comments that are relevant, entertaining, and useful. Tweets are best when they are "news you can use." Once again, it is about delivering value through online marketing. Tell folks about products in development and share interesting information. Don't sell, relate.

- **Discuss, don't sell.** Social media is, well, social. Don't be the bore who only talks about him- or herself. Join other discussions and contribute. Don't sell. Discuss. Listen to what the other folks are saying and respond as a human being would, not a brochure. Just keep in mind that every reply (with the exception of direct messages) on Twitter is in public view.

- **Ask questions.** Answer questions. Ask survey questions, discussion questions, branding questions, and more. Then discuss the answers.
- **Share.** Sharing is caring. Share links to other tweeters, blog posts, quotes, interesting pictures, and so on. Most likely anything on the topic (or even off topic, if it is entertaining) will be appreciated by Twitter followers.
- **A picture is worth a thousand words.** When you've only got 140 characters, sometimes a twitpic can be the most eloquent posting ever.
- **Retweet.** If you find something interesting as you read other folks' Twitter feeds, retweet it (click on the Retweet link on the original post) to share it with your followers. This isn't just good Twitter etiquette, it is micro online marketing. Retweeting is a gift that keeps giving. When someone retweets, the original poster gets new eyeballs. The traffic works both ways. If you retweet a top tweeter, her followers will see your name and may start to follow you.
- **Tweet your blog, blog your tweets.** When every new blog entry posts, tweet a link to it. On your blog, include your Twitter feed (or at least links to it). Use URL-shortening tools like TinyURL (http://tinyurl.com/) or bit.ly (http://bit.ly/) to shorten long URLs to get the most out of your 140-character maximum space.
- **Become a top tweeter.** For most organizations, the more followers, the better. Pop singer Lady Gaga hit five million Twitter followers in July 2010. Presumably she delivers value because all five million followers are interested in Lady Gaga, her life, and her music. While even a fraction of that number would be fantastic for almost any organization, what matters most is communicating with a specific audience interested in your product or service. Think quality, not just quantity. Organizations can have a substantial ROI on Twitter with just a handful of the right followers. But usually Twitter ROI is a numbers game. The more quantity, the greater the chance for quality. So how do you become a top tweeter? Create value, of course, but as with other areas of life, in order to lead you must first follow. Follow a lot of the top tweeters to learn from the best. Follow people in the relevant topic areas. The more people you follow, the more likely others are to follow you in return.
- **Use other social media to increase your Twitter audience.** Share links to your Twitter profile everywhere. Make it your first way to connect with your audience.
- **Don't forget to use Twitter to connect to the real world.** Politician Sarah Palin has turned her Twitter followers into a mobilized grassroots

force. Her tweets often get more mainstream press ink (and airtime) than a full-page editorial would. Why? Because they are short and to the point. They offer her world view and are action based.

President Barack Obama did the same thing in the 2008 election. His Twitter profile (http://twitter.com/BarackObama) was everywhere in his print literature. Obama's casual Twitter followers became donors (most of them were small donors who collectively had a huge impact). Some of his followers became activists using Twitter to mobilize some real-world door knocking to get out the vote. The Obama team also used Facebook, MySpace, and YouTube and made sure his online marketing campaigns worked together hand-in-glove. For example, a new blog entry that included a new YouTube video was announced on Twitter, and events were posted on both Twitter and Meetup.

Twitter has a lot of pluses for marketers. It is immediate. It is short. You can add photos easily. You can update it from your phone. But as with Superman, the source of its greatest strength is also its kryptonite. Twitter's 140-character limit restricts conversations to Q&A ping-pong. To deeply interact with a customer base requires more than tweets. To take the relationship to the next level, you've got to become *friends*. By now, you know what that means.

Facebook

If Facebook were a country, it would be the third largest in the world. Facebook reached over 500 million users in just six years. According to Cecilia Kang's July 19, 2010, column in the *Washington Post*, "the population inhabiting Facebook now equals that of the United States, Japan and Germany combined."

The Top Five Ways Facebook Can Boost Business
Facebook's power goes beyond simple relationship building. It is a muscular online marketer that delivers results. Here are five ways Facebook can boost business.

1. **Facebook builds awareness.** Facebook can build connections via personal profiles, pages, and groups. It also offers affordable, targeted, cost-per-click advertising options that can be laser-targeted to the city where the organization does business, the age range desired, or the interest groups wanted. When someone sets up a personal Facebook profile, that person usually adds his

or her age, gender, interests, location, and other information. It's easy to advertise to people on Facebook based on geographics and psychographics.

2. **Facebook brilliantly distributes information.** Facebook allows marketers to leverage personal and professional contacts to share information for free. Facebook can even help revive dead venues. When a leading Santa Barbara restaurant called The Wine Cask closed and reopened a year later under new management, a simple announcement by the general manager on his personal Facebook page spurred new business and boosted awareness to old restaurant fans.

3. **Facebook creates community.** Social networking serves to bring people together. Building and branding a Facebook page or group allows local contacts to converse with each other and boost business. Let your community become your best salespeople and free focus group. Listen to the conversations and allow raving fans to share and get in on the conversation. Seth Godin, a marketing guru and author, talks about tribes. Tools like Facebook allow tribes to come together and create communities. Companies do not sell, people sell. Put the power in people's hands and go where they are—on Facebook.

4. **Facebook can offer additional low-cost customer service.** Through Facebook, organizations can answer questions, receive feedback, promote events, and provide news to their target audiences for free.

5. **Facebook can boost sales.** Let's face it, organizations have to fight harder than ever to survive in a tough economy. But your organization (for profit or nonprofit) can have a competitive edge with Facebook. When Facebook is used to serve (not push propaganda), organizations will do well.

When used with the right intention and managed regularly, Facebook can be a no-cost marketing tool to help organizations gain a competitive edge. Converse directly with customers and create a community where you can learn, share, and connect, all in a fun way.

Facebook Best Practices

For marketers, Facebook is a social networking platform that is beyond pokes, jokes, and friend-finding. It is about boosting marketing and sales. Organizations and public figures can have pages, people have profiles, and groups that want to have more regulated discussions have, well, groups.

Think about it this way. Sarah J. Smith has her personal Facebook profile page where she posts updates about her son, Luke, and her dog, K9, and their private adventures that only her friends can see. Sarah, a big fan of *Doctor Who,* reads everything she can on the official BBC Doctor Who Facebook page. Seeking like-minded fans, she creates a Facebook group for Doctor Who fans in Ealing, London. These fans meet both online and in person, sometimes going out to meet with other London-based Doctor Who fan clubs. When they meet via Facebook or in person, they discuss which Doctor Who products they plan to buy, news, favorite episodes, and more.

Facebook pages and groups like this are an online marketer's dream because they are actively mobilized around a topic. And you do not have to rely on fans to create a Facebook page. These pages can be created by marketing managers, consultants, or by organizational leaders. These brand-conscious fans define themselves by their consumption and are primed to buy even more. Organizations can create their own pages, but people can also create their own fan pages and groups. The downside is that the official brand has little or no control over what these groups do on Facebook as long as they don't violate Facebook's terms of service. Once they are started, the group's members are in charge, but if you feed them well then they will feed you.

Most online marketing will involve creating an official page for an organization (http://www.facebook.com/pages/create.php?). Some public figures still use their personal Facebook profile for their online marketing (http://www.facebook.com/Ashton), but most have opted for an official page (http://www.facebook.com/eddieizzard). If the Facebook profile gets a lot of traffic, Facebook may change a personal profile to an official page.

Facebook Page Invites

After you create a page for your organization on Facebook, you can message your friends on your personal contacts list and send them your page link, then invite them via a personal message to join. Random strangers may also stumble upon your page and opt to "like" it or request to join your group.

You can go also to the left area of your Facebook page (under the page logo on the left side) and click on "Suggest to Friends."

With people spending more and more time on Facebook, organizations cannot afford *not* to spend time there. Whether the investment is managing a personal profile, page, or group; supporting a group of fans; listening to social conversations; or paying attention to competitive Facebook use, this social platform is not going away anytime soon.

LinkedIn

With over 85 million professionals, LinkedIn is a professional's social marketing network to exchange information, ideas, and opportunities. A public LinkedIn profile acts as an individual's résumé, creating the opportunity to share expertise and credentials. Recruiters actively search LinkedIn for qualified professionals to fill job positions. Many professionals use social tools like LinkedIn for personal online marketing, making sure their profile is tagged with descriptive words and phrases that a headhunter may be searching.

Many companies want their employees to have active profiles to enhance visibility and boost connections for sales. LinkedIn offers the ability to create groups where organizations can launch discussions with like-minded professionals or participate in other groups to gain visibility, make contacts, and more.

Organizations can post a profile so people who may be researching them can see who they are, what they do, whom they serve, and who works for them. Lastly, LinkedIn multitasks, allowing links to websites, blogs, and Twitter accounts to be added to profiles. LinkedIn also has a feature under the applications setting that allows a blog to automatically feed into a profile. Many marketers do not see LinkedIn as a messaging tool like Twitter and Facebook, but the power of content with credentials can help boost an individual's career and help get an organization more eyeballs and enhance contacts. LinkedIn is one of the best "interactive Rolodex" tools out there for online marketing.

YouTube

According to comScore's rankings, YouTube is the number two search engine on the World Wide Web and tops all social media activities. Video watching is the number one activity dominating social media (we know what you are doing during work hours!). Organizations are using video sharing sites like YouTube to search for content, share tips, and make "show me to tell me" content that is very easy to take in (remember that social media content sticks due to the entertainment factor). Whether a CEO is making a personal announcement, a customer service rep is talking though tech tips, or a customer is giving a testimonial, online video supports social media by creating a visual and audio connection to make a meaningful impact.

Videos can be embedded into blogs and on websites, shared on Facebook, and tweeted to followers. In true social media form, videos can be rated and shared, and have social media widgets that make sharing very easy.

Many professionals have become "weblebrities" (web celebrities) by creating their own YouTube channels. Like blog posts or tweets, great video content can make a measurable marketing impact.

NEXT STEPS

The million-dollar question is how to measure social media success. For some, the number of clicks from these outlets to a main website will matter. For companies like Dell that could directly account for dollars spent thanks to driving traffic from Twitter messages alone, it is revenue. Whether the metrics are traffic, leads, sign-ups, or sales, organizations need to be aware of the new form of ROI that social media supports so strongly—relationship ROI.

The last measurable impact is visibility. Social media like LinkedIn profiles, YouTube videos, Wikipedia entries, blogs, and Facebook pages dominate search engine results. Do a Google search for "Darth Vadar." You will likely see images, videos, and/or Wikipedia at the top of the search results. Organizations can achieve "TWD" (total web domination) for visibility when social media is put to work.

Chapter Quiz

1. What are social media's three main marketing functionalities?
2. True or false? Conversations will take place about your organization whether or not your organization is an active participant in social media.
3. What are the three Vs of social media?
4. What does C.O.U.P.L.E. stand for as a social media marketing acronym?
5. What are the five main ways Facebook can boost business?
6. True or false? An organization has to have fans create pages for them.
7. What is LinkedIn?
8. How can social media boost search engine visibility?

7

WEB ANALYTICS

O ne of the biggest distinctions of online marketing is its immediate tracking capability. Web analytics are the lifeblood of an online marketer, offering insightful information about online advertising performance; easy monitoring of patterns; and comprehension of web marketing initiatives, conversion rates, and more. Web marketing is the most trackable marketing medium out there. However, the real value of web analytics data lies not in the science of the statistics but in their artful interpretation. This chapter will teach you how to comprehend, set up, and analyze the art and science of web analytics.

Having a website without analytics is like being a stand-up comedian who doesn't listen to hear if the audience is laughing. A comedian measures success by the kinds of laughs (polite pun groans versus aneurysm-inducing belly laughs), who laughs (men, women, kids), and what kind of material is working. That immediate feedback loop allows a comedian to improve his or her act on the fly. Web analytics allow marketers that same type of feedback to continually improve performance (minus the two-drink minimum).

While *web analytics* may sound techy and complicated, in reality it is just a single line of code you paste into your website's source code to track use and behavior on web pages. The whole operation, from getting your analytics code to pasting it into your website, can usually be completed in under five minutes (depending on the size and complexity of the website). But don't underestimate the power of this one simple change. This line of code will change your web marketing forever.

Once your super senses come alive, you'll feel empowered to make your web marketing fly faster, stronger, and better. Excited yet? Here's how to get started.

USING GOOGLE ANALYTICS

There are a number of analytics packages out there. Some are free (many hosting companies include web statistics in their package) and some have fees (like Webtrends and Omniture), but by far the most popular and easily accessible service is Google Analytics (www.google.com/analytics/). Google Analytics has become the industry standard. It has the benefit of being powerful and integrating effortlessly with AdWords (Google's pay-per-click ads), e-mail marketing, social media marketing, mobile marketing, and more. Oh, and it's *free*. Google Analytics is limited to five million page views a month; however, users with an active Google AdWords account are given unlimited page-view tracking.

No matter how large or small your website is, the smartest place to start tracking web marketing is with Google Analytics. The data tells you how people use your website and where your traffic comes from, which advertising (if any) works, how many visitors you have, how well the website design works, where visitors are located, and so much more. Many organizations think they need to buy expensive web statistics technology to have web marketing success. Although fee-based web analytics companies offer very robust add-ons and stellar advisory services (the art of analytics on top of the science), it is best to cut online marketing teeth on a free service like Google. You could spend years mastering and taking advantage of all the options available. Why learn web analytics on a pricey package when you can learn on a superior free version?

If you don't know what drives your web marketing, your web marketing may drive you. With good web analytics tools, you have high sensory vision to see what is making your site tick, leverage what is working, and optimize what isn't.

Still, there are many businesses that don't trust free software. They feel that you get what you pay for. Often the features of a free product are limited in function or expire after a set period. Most "freemium" software is served up free so that a small taste of it whets your appetite to buy the full package. Web analytics software seems to be the exception. Because most analytics software makers want the maximum number of people to use their products, they make the free version as fully featured as possible. Since the free packages like Google Analytics are so robust, most web marketers would do well to start there and then consider paying for more advanced analytics when their site gains very high levels of traffic.

What to Do Before You Start

Before you sign up for or log into a Google Analytics account, think strategically about what you want to accomplish with your analytics efforts. Or as web analytics guru Avinash Kaushik suggests, ask yourself "Who cares?" To help boost your marketing efforts, here are four important things to remember as you set up and eventually use web analytics:

- **Plan.** Know what questions you want to answer when you're reviewing your web analytics and make a checklist of your goals.
- **Measure.** Focus in on the metrics that matter to your business. Avoid analysis paralysis by establishing data priorities so you're not sidetracked by otherwise interesting but ultimately trivial data. No matter what your organization's mission is, know its key performance indicators (KPI). Look at the metrics that matter.
- **Analyze.** Ongoing review and analysis are key. You will also need to contextualize data against your current marketing activities. If you're a visual person, presentation can help you monitor trends (think color-coded spreadsheets and pie charts), and can help you view changes over time and know when you've hit targets that you've set.
- **Take action.** If your goal is to optimize your marketing efforts, you will need to be able to glean actionable insight from your data.

Whether you are looking at unique visitors, traffic sources, referring keywords, top content, web design feedback, conversions, or understanding your top content, be sure to ask yourself if and how these metrics are relevant (again, who cares?). The metrics that matter most will help you improve the customer experience as well as enable you to segment out characteristics of your most profitable users so you can drive more traffic and boost your sales.

SETTING UP WEB ANALYTICS

While this chapter will focus on Google products, the logic and methodology of web analytics are largely the same regardless of the software package used.

Start by signing up for a Google Analytics account (www.google.com/ analytics). This will take a few minutes, after which you will get a unique line of code that you or your organization's webmaster will place in the HTML of your website. Once this line of code is on the website, within a few days (or even hours, with a very high-traffic site), you will start to learn the following information:

- See which pages drive the most page views on the site.
- See which pages users abandon most frequently (your "bounce rate").
- See which landing pages (pages tailored to a specific marketing campaign) work best.
- See which traffic sources (search, pay per click, e-mail marketing, social media, etc.) are driving people and actions to your website.
- See how long people are spending on each page.
- See the location of your user base. You can see where people are coming from by country, state, and city.
- View conversion goals for your users. Different groups will have different desired actions they want visitors to take (buy, download, join, subscribe to free newsletter, donate, click on "About Us," ask for a consultation, etc.). All desired actions can be measured.
- Incorporate e-commerce metrics (if e-commerce happens on your website) and measure traffic sources, key phrases searched, and online advertising down to the sales amount and products purchased.
- See which organic search terms people used to find your website. (This will become very important when it comes time to discuss search engine optimizing in the next chapter).
- There are over 80 other reports you can get from your Google Analytics dashboard.

Setting Goals: Conversion Rate

A quick word about setting up goals with an analytics package. A goal is most often defined when a user clicks or takes action on something that generates a new page. For example, when a user completes a form and clicks on the "Buy Now" button and the "Thank You" confirmation of purchase page loads, a goal is seen as completed. Purchases are not the only web marketing action to measure, though. At its simplest, a goal is measured as completed any time a user clicks on something that loads a new page. By adding extra event tracking code to track behaviors such as e-mail sign-ups, downloads, clicking on outbound links, watching videos, completing a contact form, and more, the sales funnel can become increasingly clear. When someone completes a goal or desired action, web marketers call that a *conversion*. Many organizations evaluate several goals and use analytics to see the impact web marketing has on them.

Suppose you are selling an item and you want the user to click on the product page, view a demo video, add the item to his or her shopping cart, fill out the order form, and then click on the "Buy Now" button. You can analyze each of these steps in the sales funnel in the Funnel Visualization report. By tracking this process you can see where you lose people and take steps to correct whatever needs fixing.

Don't think that funnels are only for e-commerce. Most charities need to make 10 or more contacts with someone before that person donates. By creating a funnel (a series of actions), you can help your end users get to that conversion goal faster.

Different goals have different values for each website owner. For example, an expert may write for free for other websites but believe that the low traffic it brings has no value. If, however, the expert sets goals (like measuring the number of visitors from that site who sign up for an e-mail list), he or she may see that low traffic still converts to a huge percentage of e-mail sign-ups, thereby making the effort worthwhile. The more insight a marketer can have to look at the art of online marketing execution, the better. Think about what your organization's goals are and put a value (either dollar value or importance) on each goal.

Measuring a Goal's Return on Investment (ROI)

Putting a dollar figure next to a conversion event like a sale is easy, but don't forget to put an ROI value for the steps that lead up to the sale. For example, if your sales team converts 10 percent of leads generated by the website to an average purchase of $1,000, then the value of each lead the website generates is $100 (10 percent of $1,000).

When calculating a particular conversion goal's ROI, don't fixate on the immediate big sale. Keep in mind that web marketing is about having a relationship with the user. Some users may dip their toe in the water first by downloading free white papers, attending a webinar, then buying a small-ticket item before purchasing a big-ticket item. These small goals are part of a larger relationship funnel.

The true importance (or dollar value) of your conversion goals will emerge over time. As you make website optimizations, add new or different conversion goals, add web pages, and so on, conversion goals will change in value and importance. The key is to keep the online marketer's focus on creating value, however it is measured by the organization.

Making Sure You Get Good Data

After you insert your Google Analytics tracking code in your website's HTML, you'll need to wait a while (a few hours or a day) for the data to come in. Sometimes when people set up the analytics they don't configure it properly, so be sure to follow the verification steps outlined by your analytics provider. Here are a few tools and tricks to make sure you get the best data possible.

SiteScan

First, make sure you installed Google Analytics correctly. While the initial sign-up process will give you a nice, friendly verification mark (after you log in) to tell you that Google has found the code on your website, appearances can be deceiving. For a host of reasons too geeky to get into here, you may have the analytics installed on most, but not all, of your website.

To make sure you have a Google Analytics tracking code on every page, use EpikOne's Google Analytics SiteScan tool. According to Google:

> SiteScan picks up on some classic signs indicating that your site has improperly implemented tracking code like:
>
> 1. No data in your account. The tracking code was either never implemented or has the wrong account number.
> 2. You're seeing a high bounce rate even though your site isn't a blog and has more than one page. If you've only tagged your homepage, your Google Analytics account will be unable to identify any other page views from your site.
>
> SiteScan then reports each page in an easy-to-read file after you've installed the tool. This makes it easy for you to isolate the pages with tracking problems, fix them, and effectively manage your Google Analytics Tracking Code installation.

URL Builder

Google's URL Builder allows you to measure the success of specific online marketing initiatives by tagging your online ad URLs with specific information (like campaign, medium, and source), so that Google Analytics can track your marketing campaign and show you which activities (pay-per-click ads, Twitter links, blog mentions, etc.) are paying off. If you want to track specific marketing elements (like a text link versus a button in an e-mail marketing piece), you can create a unique link for each element you want to track in your marketing e-mails, social media campaigns, and pay-per-click (PPC) ads with the URL Builder tool (http://www.google.com/support/googleanalytics/bin/answer.py?hl=en&answer=55578).

Filter Yourself

Google Analytics has a filter option that further ensures the accuracy of monthly data, allowing you to remove your web use as well as that of your organization, your colleagues, and even your webmaster. Sometimes internal organization web use can really skew data. To create filters with Google Analytics, start by visiting www.myipaddress.com to get the code for your unique IP address, then put it into the Google Analytics filter, and your Analytics report will only collect visitors' data from people who are not filtered by the IP addresses. Filters give you a better picture of your actual monthly traffic patterns—specifically, the people you are trying to serve, support, and sell.

THE ART OF WEB ANALYTICS: AVOID ANALYSIS PARALYSIS AND FOCUS ON THE METRICS THAT MATTER

Web analytics can help you improve user experience by shedding light on how people find, use, and navigate your website, as well as segment out characteristics of your most profitable site visitors to drive more traffic and boost your sales.

When we think of web analytics, most people think of data. Lots and lots of data. So how do you avoid analysis paralysis and help ensure your analytics efforts are paying off?

While collecting data (the science) is definitely a large part of web analytics, the artful part is being able to analyze your data so that you can make optimizations and identify necessary actions.

After about a week or two (depending on the website's traffic volume), there's sufficient information to start gaining insights and make some decisions about how to optimize the website. Make it a daily, weekly, or monthly ritual to review data. Practice makes perfect, so the more often you drill down to see what the data holds, the more natural the art of analysis will become. The great news with analytics is that you can't mess it up. You can click all day long and if you get lost, you can always go back to the dashboard and start over. The sooner you work web marketing measurement into the overall marketing plan, the sooner you will wonder why you didn't start sooner!

Interpreting Web Analytics—Focus on Content

To get the best performance from your website, you need to constantly test both the medium and the message. The medium can be the marketing channel, your site layout, navigation, how different items are highlighted, the graphics, and more. The message is the actual content: the words, video, audio, Flash, photos, offer, headline, and so on. Ideally both need to work together, but often the content is hidden beneath layers of bad layout and navigation. Web analytics allows you to unearth these diamonds in the rough and cut them, polish them, and put them in a setting that will make them sparkle.

Let's look at the major analytics categories:

- **Top content.** What are the most visited pages on your website? What can you learn from this? Many sites are often surprised to learn that their top pages aren't their home or shop pages, but some obscure page deep inside their website. If that is the case, you might want to create more information around that topic on your home page to attract more users.
- **Top key phrase searches (paid and unpaid).** How does this change your key phrase optimization strategy? What terms are people searching to find your organization? You may find that searchers will change terms based on a variety of outside factors such as the season, or news events. If you see a spike in keyword searches around a topic, act quickly to capitalize on it. The next two chapters will discuss search engine optimization and paid search strategies in more detail.
- **Traffic sources.** Are you getting more traffic from search engines, traditional off-line marketing efforts such as radio spots, and social media links, or from links you've posted in comments in high-traffic blogs? Of all of the sources of traffic (both high and low volume), what sources convert the highest? If you see a pattern of traffic or goal spikes that relates to your marketing actions, can you do more of that? You may even find that other websites and blogs are referring you and you don't even know it.
- **Traffic volume.** Smart marketers want high-quality (the right kind of) traffic. Quality beats quantity. You could get a lot of traffic by posting search ads on broad phrases that may not be specific enough to your

products and services, but that high traffic probably won't convert to whatever the website's goals are. You need to evaluate traffic sources on more than traffic alone and focus on goal conversions and ROI.

- **Time patterns.** When do most of the website's visitors hit the site? Which days? During which hours? Are they surfing from work or from home after the kids are asleep? Do they spike after a coupon offer or a blog entry? Do they research on Monday but buy on Friday? You can fine-tune your offers and content to maximize impact. Many marketers realize their prime site traffic times and use this data to spend online advertising budgets targeted only to those times, saving thousands of dollars and laser-targeting their efforts thanks to web analytics feedback.
- **Geographic.** If the website has a specific geographic market, every search outside that market has limited value. Some organizations use the geographic feature to test market segments and make new store decisions by following visitors' geo-location patterns and performance.
- **Bounce rate.** If you have a high bounce rate, that means people are hitting your website and leaving almost immediately. A high bounce rate could mean that you need to change the entire website or how people are finding the site. Watch, learn, tweak, and test.

  A high bounce rate may simply mean that your web marketing efforts aren't connecting properly. Let's say you have an advertisement or link that promises specific content (40 percent off two items, a white paper about a specific topic, a special video, etc.). When the users clicking on that link land on your home page, they can't find that specific content and leave frustrated, probably never to return. If you create specific landing pages for those links, the users will find the content immediately, your bounce rate will fall, and your users will be more likely to explore the rest of your site.
- **Time on-site.** This one can be tricky to interpret. Generally speaking, the longer someone stays on the website, the better (especially if you are a content-rich website). However, long page-views aren't always a good thing if they don't convert to a desired action. If your users get lost trying to find something before they can complete a conversion goal, a long page-view may point to a need to simplify and highlight the steps to the conversion goal.
- **New vs. returning visitors.** There are few web marketing efforts that don't desire returning visitors. Some single-topic sites just want you to complete the conversion goal and never return. They haven't added any new content since 1998 and are selling fine, thank you very much. But

for most organizations, effective web marketing is about ongoing relationships. That means returning visitors. Not only do you want to know how many are returning, but how many of those returning visitors are converting to whatever your goals are. To increase the number of returning visitors, you need to create a content strategy that is "sticky," because it glues users to your website. Over time the more returning visitors you have, the more successful your web marketing efforts will be.

- **Success of marketing efforts.** Web analytics can help evaluate the effectiveness of both off-line and online marketing efforts. Create a print or radio ad that points people to a unique URL such as www.yourorganization.com/BigDeals. Analytics of that specific landing page will point up the success of those offline marketing efforts. Online links from PPC ads, specific links within your website, comments on other sites, social media, online coupons, and so forth can each have unique URLs and landing pages using Google URL Builder. Online marketing efforts that are not paid (like Facebook pages, Twitter, or YouTube videos) can be measured under referring sources. As long as conversion goals are set, the success of all channels can be scientifically evaluated.

THE ART OF ADVANCED ANALYTICS

Analytics numbers describe complex human behavior and you need to compare and contrast them with a variety of other data to get a true picture. Analytics do offer the easy exporting of data into PDFs and Excel files, but sometimes it is better to create a custom spreadsheet that specifically addresses your organization's online marketing data to review performance and compare data from one month to the next.

Start by creating a weekly or monthly report in the spreadsheet application of your choice. By creating a regular report you can see how your marketing efforts interact over time. You can measure other marketing media:

- E-mail
- Traditional media (print, radio, TV, direct mail)
- Blog (RSS feeds)
- Social media
- Online advertising (paid search, banner ads)

Looking at traffic, cost, conversions, influential patterns, and more can give an aerial view of what is working and how all the marketing is integrated together. For example, one online marketing medium may seem to have a very high cost per acquisition, but when compared to other channels, the volume of quality conversions from this traffic source is much higher compared to lower-cost channels that it justifies the larger expense. Artful interpretation reveals the dangers of myopically focusing on the wrong metric such as a cost per action instead of seeing a solid conversion generator.

Continual evaluation will uncover bugs and burnouts. Most web marketing efforts start slow and build. No matter how experienced you are, you should always be evaluating and optimizing. A reliable channel may lose its fire and need a copy change, or may have a broken link. By creating these reports, you can uncover the marketing efforts that work best together and make sure the efforts give maximum payoff.

Digging Deeper

Again, using Google Analytics as an example, the Content Overview menu is a great place to learn what works and what doesn't. You can see which pages bring in the most eyeballs, and study them. Understand what messaging makes the copy work (is it attracting search engines, does it communicate value well, does it have a helpful video and a clear call to action?), and employ this on other pages for maximum impact.

Click on the Navigation summary to see how people are moving within your site. This data can help you figure out the flow of your website and where people get stuck. To see which landing pages work best, look at the Entrance Sources and Entrance Keywords. Realize that people enter the site through many surprising doors. One travel writer who had written a review became a top listing when people Googled "Harvey's Bristol Cream Museum." The writer started getting calls from people all over the world who were interested in wine tourism and wanted to buy tickets to tour the museum! Moving the link from a buried section of the website onto a more obvious page increased traffic to the landing page, and reduced bounce and conversion rates for the writer.

A favorite Google Analytics functionality that helps online marketers is called Site Overlay. This feature allows you to review all pages of your website (as long as they have tracking code on them) to see an overlay of which items get clicked. You can also see which links achieve your conversion goals. The overlay shows data in boxes: the larger the box, the higher the activity. It is a nice visual way to see behavior over all of the pages at the same time. Sometimes a simple observation of a link low on a page getting tons of traction can prompt an easy optimization to move the link higher on the page to serve users better. The overlay allows you to see what users want so you can deliver more of it. When you modify the website, you can see almost instantly whether a change like a bigger button or a text link converts better.

Site search is an analytics feature that will show you what, when, and where people are searching within your site. This only applies if a website has a search feature. If you see internal search terms coming up again and again, that is a sign that you need to make information on that topic easier to find. People will often start to search for something internally once they are deep in your site and aren't finding what they were expecting.

This search feedback is also insight that can help you improve online marketing or search marketing efforts based on phrases your audience looks for. If you are a lending company, your search feedback may show more people looking for the term *borrow money*. This could lead to changes in the phrases used in the website copy, website navigation, overall marketing messaging, and so to serve your audience by speaking to them in their language.

Internal site search terms might point to the need to create new content and new goals that capture lost traffic. For example, if owners of a pet store in Clifford, Kentucky, keep seeing internal site searches for *Clifford the Big Red Dog* pet products, perhaps those store owners might consider selling some of that merchandise online. Although most of their customer base is local, people online are searching for product they want to buy. Why not sell it to them? Internal site search is your users' way of telling you directly how to improve your site.

Event tracking refers to events that don't create a new page, such as viewing an embedded video, downloading a file, playing a game, and more. These events can be crucial to track, especially if the video is a key part of your conversion goal's sales funnel. For example, if through event tracking you learn that 86 percent of people who played a given video converted to your goal, then you'd want to make sure as many people as possible saw the video. Without getting too geeky here, it may be better to track these events using event tracking rather than virtual page views because you can get more details. Check the Google Analytics help screen to get more details on this and what approach will work best for different cases.

Arguably, the most important sections in the analytics report relate to goals. As mentioned before, there may be lots of little steps users take before they convert to your biggest goals. A bridal shop owner could find that users who convert usually check out some wedding dress tutorials, upload their dress size and preferences, and look at 30 wedding dresses that fit their selection criteria before buying the one they like. Each step in that process is a goal that is part of the sales funnel. You can use the Funnel Visualization report to see how many people enter each step, how many fail to convert and where they go to next, how many people convert, plus the value of each conversion step.

When you are starting out, you'll want to measure all the goals (sales, leads, e-mail signups) to capture as much data about what users do on the site. Over time you'll discover which goals are important and which steps in your funnel need to be changed or optimized. Because you want as much data as possible, there is a temptation to make the user click on a variety of links to load a new page to capture each decision (A-line dress, size 12, with sleeves, etc.). While every dress variable is vital to the owner from an inventory point of view, exhausting the patience of a busy user doesn't convert to buying a dress. Instead of demanding the user click on a new page for each section, the owner might create check boxes or pull-down menus on a single page and then capture that data when the pages are created dynamically. Every click you demand of your user increases the chance the user will get frustrated and exit. The art of managing your sales funnel is to get to the big conversion with the user taking as few steps as possible.

If the website has an e-commerce element, Google Analytics will integrate with your online store to show you what is selling, how people find those products, and more. Go to your Google Analytics profile and click on the e-commerce tab under the left navigation to get details. If you are using Google AdWords for your PPC ads, you can get detailed data that dovetails easily with Google Analytics. Not only will you see which ads brought the most traffic but which ads converted to e-commerce purchases.

Where Google Analytics Falls Short

Most of Google Analytics is focused on anonymous users in the aggregate. The online marketer can narrow the segments to groups such as paid visitors (those who clicked on PPC ads) from Utah who spent over $100. This kind of advanced segmentation delivers very powerful data, but some sites need more.

Some sites (like Amazon) allow users to personalize the experience by signing in. Users can shop at online stores anonymously or can sign in to get benefits such as offers tailored to their viewing and buying history within the site. These users can see products specifically chosen for them and purchase them with a single click. In these instances, the website owner knows that this customer is a Mr. Wile E. Coyote, a very loyal Acme Products customer with an unlimited credit rating. This lucrative repeat customer is very important to Acme. An online marketer will want to track these signed-in customers with an even finer degree of data based on their history. This data detail is Google Analytics' blindspot. Currently there is no elegant way to track known individuals using Google Analytics. This is where pricier analytics packages have a powerful place in online marketing measurement.

Google offers a number of tools for searching (Google Product Search for a listing of competitors selling the same product and Google Commerce Search for presenting and searching for products within an organization's website), payment (Google Checkout), and more. But they offer nothing that dynamically creates custom pages by drawing on individual user history. Other vendors offer this kind of software and they have analytics built into it. By the time an organization gets into the business of dynamically creating pages for signed-in users and tracking their behavior, it is time to evaluate such software on a case-by-case basis. Organizations that rely heavily on the power of personas (having very distinct descriptions of users, their behaviors, etc.) can help model "ideal clients" with individual tracking technology, which helps them study in detail who their top clients are as well as their behaviors, preferences, and more. Online marketers can use this detailed information to design savvier websites, messaging, and more.

You can also send marketing e-mails to individuals and track their responses so that you can customize their experiences. These fall under the heading of customer relationship management (CRM). This software prompts Acme to e-mail Mr. Coyote to show him the latest bird-catching devices. CRM software allows an organization's sales force to track the success of their coordinated marketing efforts both online and off.

Salesforce.com (fee-based) and Zoho CRM (free for three users, fee-based for more) are both popular CRM software that works nicely with Google products.

OTHER ANALYTICS TRACKING TOOLS TO HELP OPTIMIZE MARKETING

Grader.com is a suite of online analytics tools provided by HubSpot.com. Their tools are free, although they do sell advanced technology that helps optimize web marketing performance. Website Grader is a free tool that measures the marketing effectiveness of a website, focused heavily on search engine optimization tips. Website Grader has graded over one million sites and won numerous awards. It's a free tool that allows you to enter in a website URL (along with those of a few competitors, if you wish), and then it rates the site based on an algorithm, taking into account different variables such as social media, search engine data, the structure of your website, site performance, how long the domain has been registered and when it expires, as well as approximate traffic to your site. Websites get a score of 1–100, and the free report spits out tips that can be put in optimization motion immediately. The grade can improve over time and can serve as a web analytics benchmark.

E-mail management companies have their own reports included in their dashboards that show open rates (how many people opened e-mails), click-through rates (the percentage of people who clicked on images or links within an e-mail), unsubscribe numbers, and conversion rates. Part of custom reporting often includes measuring e-mail success to look at integrated marketing efforts.

Companies like SiteTuners.com have an art-meets-science approach that is centered specifically around landing page optimization. Their fee-based service has a success-backed algorithm that measures performance, then their team of experts gives an analysis of how to make the site work better vis-à-vis image use, copy, site architecture, and more.

Anne Holland's Which Test Won? (http://whichtestwon.com/) has multivariate testing education for marketers. On this site, you can see sites similar to yours that tested different layouts, forms, e-mail subject lines, and more, and which tests proved the best. This is quick way to benefit from years of testing without the hassle.

Google Website Optimizer (www.google.com/websiteoptimizer) allows you to automatically test up to 50 website changes at once. You can test different headlines, art, text, offers, calls to action, graphic elements (button vs. text link), layouts, and more. The great thing about Google Website Optimizer is that it will not only tell you which headline and art worked best individually, but which combination of headline and art achieved optimal conversions.

Another hidden feature of Google Website Optimizer is that it kills creative conflict in its tracks. Frequently creative types want to fill a website with artistic flourishes. An easy testing solution like Google Website Optimizer allows you to try their designs and let the end user decide. If the changes convert, great! If not, go back to the previous optimal version of the website. In the end, the customer is always right.

HOW TO MAKE CHANGES BASED ON ANALYTICS

Web analytics can often prove that your organization's web marketing strategy isn't working to meet your conversion goals. If the numbers show this, you can:

1. **Panic.** When in trouble, when in doubt, run in circles, scream, and shout!
2. **Make changes.** Look at the data and think critically about what the numbers say and then make calculated opinions about why the data shows what it shows and work to make the site function better. Variables that impact success can include:
   - Bad advertising placement (not the right targeting, placement, or venue)
   - Messaging that doesn't speak to the end user
   - Design that doesn't appeal to the target customer
   - Poor website architecture (People don't know where to go or what to do.)
   - Low-visibility calls to action (People are not being funneled to where they need to go.)

Online marketing is a mix of creating ideas, executing them, monitoring them, then going back to the first step. Measurement is a critical success step and needs to be woven into the overall plan.

NEXT STEPS

There are literally thousands of ways to slice and dice analytics numbers. The key is not to get analysis paralysis. You need to translate these numbers into action. Don't worry about making mistakes. You will make them—hopefully lots of them. Mistakes are repeated until we learn from them.

The idea is to keep testing changes to see which produces the best results. You can make one change or you can make lots. The problem with testing lots of things at once is that you can't be sure which change made it better and which one made it worse. Also some changes work better in different combinations.

Remember what Thomas Edison is reputed to have said about his many attempts to build a storage battery: "I have not failed 700 times. I have not failed once. I have succeeded in proving that those 700 ways will not work."

Obviously you have a lot more web marketing mistakes to make, but web analytics will help quickly measure what works and what doesn't to easily expedite the success sauce. Web marketing is the most measurable medium if the time is taken to tap the power of web analytics. Get busy.

Chapter Quiz

1. One of the biggest distinctions of online marketing is _____.
2. True or false? Companies should use free web statistics, especially if they are new to web analytics.
3. Why would marketers want to filter out their web use and their web management team's web use?
4. What are some of the main metrics to review for analytics?
5. List ways to customize web analytics reports.
6. What is Google Analytics' biggest blindspot?
7. What is Grader.com?
8. Name some web variables that can impact success and be measured by analytics.

CHAPTER 8

SEARCH ENGINE OPTIMIZATION

Many marketers use the terms *search engine marketing* (SEM) and *search engine optimization* (SEO) interchangeably. For the purposes of Chapters 8 and 9, we define SEM as an umbrella term that means using search engines to market an organization. SEM can include trying to get higher organic (free) search rankings, buying paid listings, or using a combination of both. Search engine optimization is focused exclusively on attracting traffic to the natural or organic listings on search engine results pages. This chapter will focus on SEO, and how to attract as much free organic search as possible.

WHY SEARCH ENGINE MARKETING IS SO IMPORTANT

More than 90 percent of the online population uses a search engine to find products, services, and information, according to iProspect, a search engine marketing firm. Once a search engine visitor types a query into the search box and receives results, marketing studies show that:

- Natural search receives 250 percent more traffic than paid search.
- Natural search converts 30 percent higher than pay-per-click (PPC) paid search.

- The first page of the search engine results pages (SERPs) gets at least 80 percent of the clicks.
- The second page of SERPs gets about 10 percent of the clicks.

(2006 data from 1,000 sites using Urchin software, and presented at convertlinks.com)

According to iProspect, "research also clearly demonstrates that if your website isn't found within the top 10 to 30 search results (the first three pages), no one will find it. And if they don't find it, not only won't they become customers—they will find your competitors instead" (http://www.iprospect.com/search-engine-marketing-university/).

The definition of *search engine marketing* includes efforts that may incorporate improving organic search listings, running pay-per-click ads, and getting listed in vertical search placements. (In Figure 8.1, the local results are an example of a type of vertical search.)

Figure 8.1   In this example, paid and vertical search (the local search results) appear on the search engine results page.

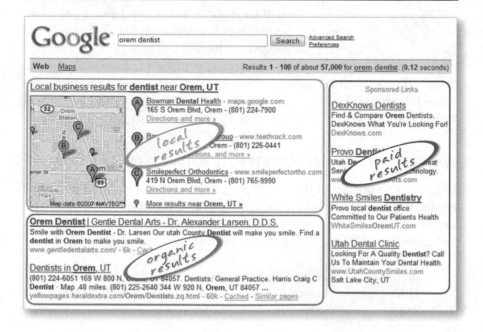

Organic, or natural, search results are a trusted source due to their lack of connection to paid sponsorship. Organic search findings are based exclusively on indexed results. Websites can maintain maximum visibility by employing search engine optimization best practices. Keeping a website optimized for natural search is an ongoing effort, as algorithmic patterns change all the time. The only constant with search results is change. Results are now often personalized to each searcher (based on prior individual behavior).

Pay per click allows companies to buy placement for search engine terms on sites like Google, Yahoo!, and Bing. Organizations can set up daily budgets to determine how much they will pay to have their ad place higher in (or alongside) the search engine results. Organizations compete for the top keywords in their categories by bidding higher cost-per-click prices on the keywords that are most likely to have a high click-through rate.

Vertical search is the most recent addition to search engine marketing. Vertical search is a streamlined solution that helps web surfers find what they need via a smaller search-topic universe. Websites can receive exposure on a free or paid basis, depending on the engine. Some examples of vertical search include local search engines like Yahoo! Local; Google Maps; industry-specific sites like WeConnectFashion.com (a search engine about fashion); and job search engines like HotJobs.com.

A way to remember the difference between paid and organic search (and a simple way to explain it to a superior or colleague) is that organic search is the way that your site *is* found. Paid search is the way you would *like* your site to be found.

SEM is a critical medium for brand awareness and customer acquisition. Organic search, PPC, and vertical search can *all* be engaged and optimized to remain competitive in the search marketplace. As with any promotional tool, getting in front of your target customer is desired, so companies need to be on top of search engine trends to stay competitive and visible.

SEARCH ENGINE OPTIMIZATION

Since organic listings are often more trusted and have a statistically higher likelihood of being clicked on, we will start the SEM education with SEO.

Getting a website optimized and indexed takes a lot longer than simply placing an ad on Google or Yahoo!, but once the organic efforts are indexed, the power of free visibility can't be beat. One of the reasons that getting found in the free listings is so attractive, aside from its zero cost, is that people frequently become ad blind, meaning that the sponsored listings do not catch their eye as quickly as the organic listings.

SEO is important because by optimizing a website around the key phrases that are important to a given audience, the online marketer can pull in prequalified traffic. The key is streamlining the process by understanding which phrases the audience searches and leveraging the website, blog, social media, videos, and more with these phrases so they can connect and accomplish their goals.

How to Uncover a Site's Magical Keywords and Phrases

The first step is determining the best keywords and/or phrases to focus on for visibility. These keywords should not only be relevant to the site, but also relevant to searchers.

The best way to start uncovering a site's magical keywords and phrases is by sitting down with a plain sheet of paper. Better yet, go back to the marketing questions you answered in Chapter 1 and expand on the descriptive words and phrases you identified there. Look at web analytics to see what your audience already searches to find the products, services, and information in your topic area and expand on those. If you are starting a website from scratch and don't have any analytics data, use one of the following keyword tools to get ideas. To get results from these free tools, you will have to insert some phrases to start, so think about what the web surfers will type in to find you. Think from their perspective.

- Google AdWords Keyword Tool: https://adwords.google.com/select/
  KeywordToolExternal
- Google AdWords Ad Preview Tool: https://adwords.google.com/select/
  AdTargetingPreviewTool

Check out the competition's websites to make a list of keywords and phrases that are given importance (in subject headings, sales copy, and so on).

If you have an existing site with web analytics installed, you can see the keywords and key phrases that people are using to find the organization's website. Some of the obvious keywords you may see are:

- Your organization name
- Your products
- Your slogan
- Your services

- Your location
- Keywords that are specific to your industry

Some of the not-so-obvious keywords may be:

- Your competitors
- Your senior staff or employees
- Misspellings
- Content related to an obscure page on your website (happens all the time)

Web analytics packages reveal not only which keywords and/or phrases brought in the most traffic but also which ones converted most. Conversions can be leads, sales, signups, or a combination of both. Being able so see which words and phrases yield actions is powerful data. It helps focus content creation and steer search optimization efforts around language that truly "clicks." Create a spreadsheet that lists the website's top converting keywords and phrases (people may search the same product under a variety of names). This list of key phrases will become your SEO compass as you begin optimizing your site.

How to Use Keywords

SEO works when people type in key phrases to come to a site in a prequalified way. There is more power in phrases than in single words, so once your list of phrases is defined, be sure to use those consistently in website copy, code, URLs, and more. If the site is selling a wrinkle cream called CraggyBeGone but "heavy wrinkle cream" is a more likely searched phrase, then be sure to spread "heavy wrinkle cream" liberally into site messaging.

If the website owner, for some reason, is adamantly opposed to the words *wrinkle cream* and insists that CraggyBeGone be called a *facial youthenizer*, for branding purposes, find a way to meet the art of branding with the science of pulling prospective customers in with content that they need. Show the owner the traffic data or free keyword reports, especially which keywords or key phrases led to increased goal conversions. When organizations debate strategy, the side armed with data instead of opinions usually wins.

By the way, there are ways of using "forbidden" keywords. There can be educational or online PR text saying "CraggyBeGone is so much more than a heavy wrinkle cream. . . ." Site copy could compare popular wrinkle creams to their product and "heavy wrinkle cream" could be used in invisible website code called meta tags (more on those in a bit). There could also be copy about "why facial youthenizers are more effective than heavy wrinkle creams" in articles on the site that use common jargon but still keep the branding messaging intact.

Share Your Optimized Key Phrases with Your Marketing Team

The important thing to realize about SEO is that while individual keywords are important, it is key phrases that will deliver the right audience. SEO is not about getting traffic; it is about targeting the right kind of traffic so your time is spent serving more qualified site visitors. Key phrases must be listed and shared with anyone at the organization working on any type of online marketing (people writing blog posts or online press releases or uploading website images; social media consultants) before any search optimizations are executed.

For a local search, use the following equation: Business or service + Location or region = Optimized key phrase. (For example: wardrobe consultant + Santa Barbara = wardrobe consultant Santa Barbara.) For other non-local businesses, the activating keywords could be descriptors of whatever the potential customer would search for, as in the following equation: Product or service + Distinction or description = Optimized key phrase. (For example: stock screening software + foreign exchange = foreign exchange stock screening software.)

The power of determining targeted phrases pays off when you begin optimizing page titles, meta tags, site content, internal links, and external links. Preplanning and researching and documenting the right phrases will help attract targeted search results and bring the right customers to your site.

SEO 101—THE NUTS AND BOLTS

The best SEO tactics aren't always the most obvious. In many cases SEO best practices are nearly invisible to humans but are seen clearly by the search engine "bots" that index a site. Having a grasp of the art and science of SEO will make the most impact, but getting down to the geek-speak is critical. The reason that there are thousands of companies across the world that do nothing but SEO is because the list of possibilities can fill entire bookshelves. Since we only have a chapter, we'll do a crash course on SEO 101 to identify the three main areas that determine how search engines index pages, then drill deeper with tactics.

Search engines look at three main factors when they are pulling results from the search engine results pages:

- Architecture
- Content
- Links

When someone types a query into a search engine, the search engines go into their database of billions of indexed web pages and, through mathematical equations (or algorithmic results), produce SERPs that have the most "relevant" content. Helpful hint: Do a search for the key phrase of your choice in Google, Yahoo!, or Bing. Pay attention to the bolded phrases in the first blue line, the text under the blue text, and even the URL. This is a sneak peek into how the search engines match up their mathematical algorithmic results. Note the importance of key phrases in the content and URLs and you will learn that what you see in the SERPs is also dictated by the code.

A search engine indexes pages thanks to millions of "spiders" (also called robots or bots) that scour the web. Search engine robots are not human, they are technological creatures, so the websites that are well architected get more priority. The better organized a site structure is and the better the site is built can make a big difference in SEO.

Content is king with SEO. Search engines look at the key phrases in content headlines, website copy, blog posts, online press releases, web articles, Facebook pages, tweets, LinkedIn profiles, and more. Using key phrases that your current and prospective customers search on throughout the website will help give the search engine spiders more "food." Help the search engines help you. If your company tagline is "Supermarket to Wealth," but in reality, your firm does small business consulting, make sure the phrase "small business consulting" is used in pages of your site. Frequency of content is also a critical player. The reason many blogs rank so well is because they are being populated frequently with content. Search engines want the freshest, most current content, so they note sites that get updated frequently (like blogs) and make sure their spiders are feeding there more frequently than an unchanging nondynamic site.

Link building helps show a search engine how popular a website is (it is easy for search engines to quantify the number of sites link to your site). It is not just external links (links from other sites to yours) that boost SEO, but internal links (links from pages of your site to other relevant pages within your site) that help search engines index a site better. The secret here is not just having links but having links with strong key phrases in them. "Click Here" used throughout a site is not going to help people find your "Online Fax Service." Using key phrases in links will make your site a super player in the SEO game.

Look at the website www.primevisibility.com. It is a website developed by a search engine marketing company that employs every best practice including architecture, content, and linking. For a fun example of the power of linking, search for "coolest guy on the Internet." Among the top listings, you will find Brad Fallon, an SEO guru who has lots of people linking to his site (and the links contain the key phrase "coolest guy on the Internet").

The Domain Name

Remember that you may register multiple domains for your products, trademarks, slogans, and more. For maximum SEO strategy, an organization may use several domains to boost search visibility. Each domain could go to a unique landing page that speaks to the desired key phrase and so will get a high SEO ranking. Buying a bunch of domains then pointing them all to the main website is not SEO. Frantic domain buying and redirecting is called being a domainiac. Search engines want to see unique URLs with unique content, so if key phrase–rich domains are purchased, they need to be used with a distinct purpose.

The Page URL

SEO architecture does begin with the URL, but the main domain is not the only location to strategically place keywords and phrases. Attracting search engines and getting your site into search engine results pages can be expedited by setting the suffix of URLs with search-rich phrases in subpage URLs, as well. For example, this subpage, which details public speaking (http://www.lorriethomas.com/the-marketing-therapist.php), uses the phrase "the marketing therapist" for search engine optimization.

Not all organizations need a key phrase–rich URL. Instead they might want a clear company-branded URL. However, if the domain name is only being used for search engine optimization, having priority key phrases in the URL can work well. Take a look at www.hybrid-rental-car.com. This particular site was built to do nothing but attract search engines and drive traffic to other sites through Google ads and affiliates like rental car companies, which pay the webmaster a percentage of referring sales.

The Page Title—Meta Title Tag

The introductory lines in blue viewed in most browsers on search engine results pages are title tags. They can dictate what SERPs show when a page is listed on the top title bar. When someone bookmarks a page, this is what the bookmark will say. There need to be unique meta titles for each page. Think of page titles as descriptions of each individual page. Many sites start each title with the company name, which is a waste of the 50- to 75-character space. Use key descriptions early on and make that effort count.

Descriptions and Keyword Meta Tags

Meta tags are invisible lines of code that tell search engines how to categorize the content on a given page. This is one of the most important steps for SEO, but many websites skip it entirely (or assume that it their webmaster's job, which is not usually the case). Every page of a website needs to include key phrase–rich meta tags that describe the content on each page. It's similar to how books are indexed in the library. No exceptions.

Meta Tag Management Best Practices

Managing meta tags for SEO is not especially hard, but to best organize the process of setting new or optimizing meta tags per page, it helps to create a spreadsheet to keep track of what needs to be done. This list makes it easier for a webmaster to manage the edits; allows you to make sure the webmaster did them correctly; or, if you are your own webmaster, helps ensure you keep tabs on your work. Here are the things to track in your spreadsheet:

- **Current name of the page or existing URL.** List each page so the webmaster knows to optimize the right page with the right meta tags. In the first column of your spreadsheet type the old URL. (Example: www .lorriethomas.com/training.php)
- **Proposed new URL name.** In the next column note what you want to change the name of the URL to here. Use memorable words and structures. (Example: www.lorriethomas.com/web-marketing-training.php)
- **Meta title tag.** Include the meta title tag in the next column. Each page should have a brief, unique, and descriptive title to let both users and the search engines know what the page is about. The character count is 50 to 75 characters, max. (Example: "Web Marketing Training = Increases in Business")

- **Meta description tags.** In the next column of your spreadsheet, list the meta description tags. These tags are up to 150 characters in length and are a summary of each individual page and what important information should stand out. Use this to educate and prequalify clicks. (Example: "Book Lorrie Thomas for expert in-house web marketing training. Topics include SEM and SEO training, social media marketing training, and more.")
- **Meta keyword or key phrase tags.** In the last column, list the meta keywords or key phrases for that page. These tags are individual keywords or phrases that are used to describe the page. List no more than 10 keywords or phrases. (Example: online advertising training, search engine marketing training, social media marketing training, blog strategy training, web marketing training)

Photos

Images are a big factor in the SERPs. Naming images properly can allow you to take three bites out of the SEO apple. Using underscores or hyphens in naming helps create natural spaces to attract more searches, as most people do not search for words all mashed together (like "onlinemarketingspeaker").

- **File names.** Save photos with file names that include key phrases that describe products/services. Instead of "image997.jpeg," the photo file name could be "Online_Marketing_Book.jpeg."
- **Alt tags.** Alt tags are text descriptions of graphics. For example, MSN.com uses alt tags (scroll your mouse over photos on their website to see) to credit photographers and describe images. Alt tags are used by the blind (as well as search engine bots) to understand visual elements of a website. Think of this tag as an opportunity to communicate to search engines what the image is, and use strong key phrase descriptions.
- **Captions.** Where layout allows it, put in keyword-rich captions that describe the photo.

Page Headline

In addition to the title tag, a headline refers to the headline that is on the top of each page. The headline is your first line of copy. Headline text usually has Heading 1 or Heading 2 style tags, which search engines rank highly.

Introductory text headlines on web pages can also have key phrases in them to also help boost search visibility. For example, a web page headline "About Our Firm" can be made much more "searchelicious" with a phrase like "About Our Atlanta Tax Attorney Firm."

Important Musts to Boost SEO

- Register site domains for five years or more. Search engines can see how long a URL is registered and they see the ones that are registered longer as more serious, which can help boost ranking. This also prevents cyber-squatters or the competition from snagging your domain.
- To stay on top of SEO and see what is being said about you and your company, add the name of the site, brand, organization, and owner/operator to Google Alerts (www.google.com/alerts). You will receive e-mail alerts about the pages, blogs, videos, and other items that Google indexes.

For an existing site, be sure to check for canonical URLs. Go the address bar of your browser and type in www.yourwebsite.com (insert your URL) and http://yourwebsite.com (minus the www). Does the URL appear the exact way typed with and without the ww or does it redirect to one or the other? Some websites have the same site but with two URLs, such as www.example.com and http://example.com. To avoid having a canonical URL (the same site landing on two different URLs) you need to declare one version of your home page the primary domain so the search engines know the main domain to index (and avoid tripping the search engines). If you don't do this, you could have 15 versions of your home page, and search engines may get confused as to what the main domain is.

OPTIMIZE OVER KEYWORD PRODUCT/ CONTENT CATEGORIES FIRST

Let's take the example of a hypothetical company in Duluth, Minnesota, called Minnie's Minnesota Minivans. The owner, Minnie, should optimize (based on the analytics data) around the key product searches, such as "Honda Odyssey minivans," with subject headings that call out each model name and year in her inventory. After the basic navigation headings are created, the copy on the Honda page (and perhaps the home page) could say "Duluth's #1 Honda Odyssey minivan dealer." Each paragraph of the Honda sales copy could include the full phrase "This 2011 Honda Odyssey Touring minivan has . . ."

Because the best SEO focuses not on traffic but on conversions, you want to optimize around phrases that attract quality "prequalified" traffic, not just large quantities. The main Honda site and sites like Consumer Reports are where people will do their primary minivan research. What Minnie wants to do is reach people who have already decided on a Honda Odyssey and are looking to buy in the Duluth market. So her meta tags and headlines, URLs, and so on should be more geo-specific, using key phrases like "Honda Odyssey minivans, Duluth, Minnesota."

LOCATION, LOCATION, LOCATION

If a business is mostly local, it will want to optimize around its location. In the above example, "Minnesota" is good to optimize around, but "Duluth" is far better. The web copy should say something like "Duluth's minivan headquarters, serving the minivan needs for Duluth and the surrounding communities of Superior, WI, Cloquet, Hibbing, North Branch, Brainerd, Forest Lake, East Bethel, Ham Lake, Hugo, Andover, Lino Lakes, Elk River, Stillwater, Ramsey, and Blaine." Below the fold of the home page, some sites even include all the zip codes they serve. That way when someone searches for "minivan 55802," they have a better chance of seeing Minnie's Minnesota Minivans.

This is where vertical search comes in. For Minnie to capture the most local buyers, she'll want to be sure that her auto dealer is correctly listed in free local directories like Google Places, Yahoo! Local, and Bing Local.

Since Google, Yahoo!, and MSN often include local businesses above other listings in their search results, local businesses can often leverage their geographic edge to get top listings. These local directories will display a company's location on a map, contact info, hours of operation, and company information including links to the main website, photos, videos, and comments.

Businesses that operate or have a mailbox in a geographic location can add their listing (usually at no charge) to Superpages, Yellow Pages, and other online phone book sites. Most businesses should see what traction they can get off Google, Yahoo!, and Bing first, then try the free online phone book listings. The majority of searches happen on Google, so start with the most heavily trafficked search engine first. Some local search engines require a call or will mail a postcard to verify your address, but with most all you need to do is add your business online. Once the listing is live, it cannot hurt to ask your clients or customers to post comments about your business on your local Internet listings to further boost credibility and awareness.

Build Links with External Websites

Increasing local links back to your website boosts search engine visibility. Local businesses can maximize links from other sites by taking advantage of their tremendous assets: contacts and community. Use your connections to initiate:

- Links in a local directory
- A link in the local Chamber of Commerce directory
- Links to your site in the blogroll of other local bloggers
- Partnerships with noncompeting local websites to exchange links

Whenever possible, request that the link have the key phrases you are targeting.

Place Contact Information and Place Names on Each Page of Your Site

The simple act of adding contact information to every page of your site can boost search visibility. If you serve multiple cities, provide your address as well as a descriptor such as "Serving the Tri-Counties, Small Business Bank for Ventura, Santa Barbara, and San Luis Obispo Counties."

GETTING INTO GOOGLE PRODUCT SEARCH

People will research products to purchase on the main Google website, but they will comparison shop vertical search engines like Google Product Search (found by clicking on the "Shopping" link at the top of the Google search page). Other search engines such as Yahoo! and Bing have similar product search offerings, so look over the website analytics for the top organic search sites to prioritize which product-searching sites are bringing the most traffic. If the website in question is retail, getting listed in *all* the top product search engines is mission critical.

Product searches are top priority for retail businesses because searchers using them are in a "transactional mind-set." They have researched the options and have decided on the specific product. They have already moved down the sales funnel. They are poised to purchase. The next few seconds of their sales experience are crucial.

Let's use Minnie's Minnesota Minivans as an example. Minnie sees that Google delivers 80 percent of her traffic, but when she tries to find herself in Google Product Search, she's invisible, while her crosstown rival, Criminally Cutthroat Cars, shows up. Minnie then lists her inventory as part of Google's Product Search (http://www.google.com/intl/en_us/products/submit.html), which allows searchers to sort by make, model, year, price, location, options, and more. This is free and all it takes is Minnie inputting the relevant information in Product Search. (She can create a weekly or daily feed to automatically make sure that Google Product Search has her most current inventory listed.)

For product searches, the lowest price usually wins. Price competition is a double-edged sword that can hurt as much as help. On price alone, Minnie's Minnesota Minivans is regularly beaten by her rivals over at Criminally Cutthroat Cars. But that doesn't mean that Minnie needs to slash her prices in a "race to the bottom" death spiral. If she is in roughly the same price ballpark, Minnie can tout her "#1 in customer satisfaction" rating, positive reviews, extended warranty, and Better Business Bureau status. Remember, credibility, good site usability, and visibility boost sellability! If she doesn't show up on the first page based on price, Minnie can pay for featured status at the top of product searches where her paid ad can tout her "#1 in customer satisfaction for 20 years running."

Minnie can also use Google Commerce Search (or similar competing services) within her website to allow users to search by make, model, year, price, options, and more. (This service costs merchants depending on the size and features they want.) An internal commerce search like Google's automatically architects the site in a way that makes it exceptionally search engine friendly. While each page is created dynamically out of current inventory, Minnie can still optimize the car descriptions and the site copy on the page to capture, for example, more of the people looking for "minivans under $5,000 in Duluth."

CREATING AN SEO CONTENT STRATEGY AROUND KEYWORDS

Some professionals are worried that if they stuff too many key phrases into the site text it will be awkward to read and turn off readers. This is a healthy concern. Remember that websites need to serve an end user first and a search engine second, so place key phrases strategically when you can, but do it in a way that never compromises user experience. Do remember that most web surfers scan versus read, so use keywords in headlines (which may seem like stuffing but is most often ignored by a human's perceptual filters).

Don't be shy about keyword stuffing your copy. The more descriptive terms that appear in the website, URLs, links, meta tags, image names, and more, the higher the page may rank. "Tell them, tell them what you told them, and tell them one more time" works for SEO too. As discussed in the "Content Marketing" chapter, this content should have value to the reader, not just be a piece crammed with buzzwords. These pages should answer the questions people have about the topic (which would be the same things people would search for). When in doubt about site copy, remember to serve, not sell. Try a Frequently Asked Questions (FAQs) page with key phrase–rich copy that answers questions, or a blog post that has helpful information but also has key phrase–rich links pointing to other pages of the site or older blog posts.

Search engines like what people like. External links show popularity, and search engines want to show relevant and popular results. Customers might want to link to Minnie's handy form that people could print and take with them when they kick the tires of different minivans. Maybe she has a list of things to check before a long car trip. Maybe she has quirky stuff like how to cook a chicken dinner with the heat from the minivan's engine block as busy parents pick up their kids after work. She could create a list of the top minivan models to use as commuting cookers. All of this content will find an audience and, if it is linked to, those pages will rise in the rankings.

SEO BEST PRACTICE: INTERNAL LINKS

Linking to internal material increases a site's ranking. Copy on the home page of a website may say "Get a Free ATV Insurance Quote" and the phrase that the organization wants to optimize (ATV Insurance Quote) links to the page to get a free quote, boosting user experience and creating optimized internal links to boost SEO. One of best places to set internal links is in a blog. Creating internal links within blog posts boosts SEO by giving new life to old blog posts so that they're not forgotten by search engines—or your readers. An example of blog text with an internal link to boost SEO is: *Last summer, I wrote a blog post on* Alternative Financing—New Ways to Secure Financing. *I wanted to readdress these points as it is very important for small businesses to know that there are places to go when the banks say no. . . .*

Integrating Related Posts into Your Blog

While it's a blogging best practice to offer additional value to your readers by linking to related articles within the copy of your posts (links that also have words in them that you want to get found in search engines on!), you can take this a step further by installing a simple plug-in that will automatically display a list of blogs related to the current post. This has great benefits for your site, both in terms of usability and search engine marketing.

There are a number of ways of doing this. For example, a WordPress blogger can use the Yet Another Related Posts Plugin to integrate the related links readers see below the posts. The plugin is customizable and allows users to set a threshold on the relevancy of the posts they want to show.

This is SEO that provides value to the reader. Showing related posts on your blog gives visitors an easy way to navigate through content that may interest them. This is a great way to keep readers engaged in your blog while boosting your page views!

THE NEW RULES OF SEO MARKETING

Social media ranks highly in search engines. In many cases, links to an organization's Facebook, Twitter, and LinkedIn pages will appear in the first page of SERPs for a company name. As you deploy your SEO strategy across your site, be sure to use those same principles in all your social media including blogs, Facebook, LinkedIn, Twitter, Flickr, YouTube, and other sites.

You can diversify your SEO portfolio by having lots of web collateral working for you to boost visibility. The more collateral on your site blog and in social media, the more likely your organization will be searched and found. Smart marketers even optimize their LinkedIn profile web links. When adding websites on the "Edit My Profile" page, instead of choosing "My Website" or "My Blog" in the Websites dropdown menu, they choose "Other:" so they can add a website title that includes key phrase–rich links like "Los Angeles Law Firm" or "Web Marketing Speaker."

SEO RESOURCES

SEO is not an online practice that you quickly spend money on and check off your strategic planning checklist. SEO requires investment. The investment is in learning, implementing, measuring, and contributing to SEO best practices. While there is a time and human resource commitment, know that there are great web tools available that you can use to boost your search optimization efforts.

- HubSpot's Website Grader: http://websitegrader.com/. This tool will share a bunch of SEO tips, such as seeing if your meta descriptions have the correct number of characters, if images have alt tags, or if you are maximizing your blog potential (for frequency of content).

- Google Analytics: http://www.google.com/analytics/. Google Analytics shows what phrases people actually use to find your site and allows you to benchmark success on SEO efforts.
- Google Webmaster Tools: http://www.google.com/webmasters/tools/. Google Webmaster Tools can help make sites more search-engine friendly. It actually tells you when you need to do SEO therapy on your site by showing if you have title tags that are too long, short, or repeated, as well as descriptions. You can also submit an XML site map (a search-friendly coded map of your site) to help Google's search engine read your site faster.

SEO BEST PRACTICES CHECKLIST

In addition to the topics mentioned already, here is a checklist of SEO best practices.

- Maximize your meta tags. Make them keyword-rich with unique meta tags for each page of the site:
  - Title tags
  - Description tags
  - Keyword tags (This section is a low priority; Google does not read this much, but make it a practice for other engines.)
- Remember, content is king. Make sure all your pages contain solid content. The home page is your most visible page and should also contain your most important key phrases.
- Keep the home page content fresh. Changing content on the home page gives the engines more to feed on.
- One hundred percent Flash can be trash to SEO. Have key content appear in text format so it is easy for spiders to detect. Flash is brilliant for selling on the web; just be aware that full Flash sites are tough for a search engine to read. Try using some HTML text in addition to Flash to give search engines some content they can read and index.
- Create internal links. Use strong key phrases in hyperlink text that point to various pages within the site. It's like setting cookie crumbs on every page so the hungry spiders will follow the crumbs.
- Create links in website copy with strong search-rich phrases (include the words you want used to search and find you). "Click Here" can be "Get a Free ATV Insurance Quote."
- Image isn't everything. Use the alt tag on all pictures to tag photos with key phrases. Name the image file with key phrases too. Key info can be

displayed even if image loading is off. The alt tag appears in code for search engines to read and to the human eye on photos when you scroll your mouse over an image.

- Go back to the basics. The H1 and H2 heading tags were used back when sites were hand-coded. Web designers do not need this anymore, but search engines can see the H code phrases in headlines, which boosts visibility.
- Play the name game. Incorporate your company and site description into the URL. Be mindful of keywords when you name all URLs and photos. (Example, http://www.shopirish.com/irish/Celtic-Rings-and-Wedding-Bands_13A.html)
- Content is king, but remember KISS (Keep It Simple, Silly). The best website copy is easy for a surfer to comprehend, and it's easy for engines to detect. Be clear with key phrases in copy whenever you can. Your "Meet the Team" page can say "Meet the San Diego Food Bank Team."
- Get keyword-rich external links. Link to relevant partner sites on your website and have them link back to you. Links from high-ranking sites can help boost your visibility. Ask the sites that link back to you to have the link contain optimal key phrases. (For example: A link that reads "www.nameofeventmarketingcompany.com" that links to your site could instead be a link that has your descriptive phrases, such as "Sales and Event Marketing Santa Barbara," which links to your site.)
- Standardize your URL. You know that "http://yoursite.com" and "www.yoursite.com" are the same, but search engines may not. If your URLs do not point to one main domain, a search engine may see this as two pages with the same content, which is SEO cheating. Make sure your webmaster picks a path and sets what is known as a 301 redirect.
- Map it out. Create an HTML site map with text links with strong key phrases to boost content and links. A site map is basically a table of contents for the engines to crawl. Also create and submit XML site maps with Google Webmaster Tools.
- Be "submissive." If your site or page is new and you want it to get found faster, you can let the engines know you exist by submitting your site to Google, Yahoo!, and MSN. Type in "Submit my site to _____ [Google, etc.]."
- Make sure your site is listed in the Open Directory Project (ODP) at DMOZ.org. This ensures a listing in Google and other key directories. It is free to submit your URL to the ODP editors, who will review your entry.

- Keep it real. Do not add hidden text or try to "trick" the engines. "Black hat" SEO tactics may work temporarily, but they will not sustain you for the long haul. Do not hire an SEO firm unless you know they are ethical. If an SEO company seems overly secretive about how they help sites get more traffic, you are better off not hiring them.
- More is better. Employing one natural search practice won't necessarily do the trick. Using all the best practices in unison will help you obtain the best visibility on a number of engines.
- Do your homework. Know your SEO options and terminology. You cannot achieve success or hire the right management firms until you know what search tools you have or can get to work with and what areas you want to optimize or implement. Check out sites like SEOmoz.org for tips.
- Time is on your side. Putting best practices into place so your pages will get indexed will gain traction as you build history with the engines. The age of a URL is a factor in search results.
- The only constant is change. Algorithms will always change, as will your listings. Have a well-architected site as well as content and links with strong key phrases, and you will ride the trends of SEO.
- Focus on what you want. Assess your current visibility, know the current key phrases people search to find your site, and use the Google AdWords Keyword Tool (https://adwords.google.com/select/KeywordToolExternal) to look up other key phrase ideas. Make a list, share it with the team, and get optimizing.
- Monitor your progress. Set benchmarks and track progress periodically. Web statistics are a must.
- Sign up for Google and Yahoo! accounts. You'll need them if you ever buy paid search or use Google Webmaster Tools to add an XML site map.
- Embrace Web 2.0. Blogs and social media sites are delicious to search engine spiders as there is new content every day. Video gets picked up in universal (or blended) search results, and social media sites like Wikipedia, Facebook, LinkedIn, and Twitter get really good search traction.
- Get your geek on. There is an art and science to SEO. Be prepared to resolve coding issues to get the most return on investment. This is an advanced SEO tactic, but worth noting.

NEXT STEPS

The more you apply search engine marketing, such as search engine optimization or local search, the more the pieces you learn will make sense. Some of you may decide that hiring help will be the best way to ensure good SEM. A good third-party SEO/SEM firm can become an extension of your marketing team. Many SEM firms have tools and advanced technology that will get the work done faster and smarter. The more you understand how they work, the better you can select the right firm for your organization. Know what you want before you pick up the phone. If you do up-front goal identification and prescreening work, you'll save yourself a lot of headache and cost in the long run. Be willing to collaborate with the third-party firm (you have to do some legwork on your end too), as your involvement will be key to your success.

You will dive more into the paid part of SEM in the next chapter. By now, you should see how all the pieces of online marketing start to work together to make a powerful impact.

Chapter Quiz

1. More than 90 percent of the online population uses a _____ to find products, services, and information.
2. Define *search engine marketing*.
3. Define *organic,* or *natural, search*
4. Define *pay per click* (PPC).
5. Define *vertical search*.
6. What is the first step required to start SEO?
7. What are the equations used to create strong key phrases that incorporate descriptions and/or geographic locations?
8. What are the three main factors search engines review when producing SERPs?

9

ONLINE ADVERTISING/ SEARCH ENGINE MARKETING

We have covered a boatload of options to boost awareness, communicate your message, connect, serve current and prospective customers, and make sales for little to no investment. But for most marketers, there comes a time when you need to spend money to make money.

Online advertising, when done correctly, can rocket your web marketing into the stratosphere, but if you don't have the right plan in place, you'll blast a giant crater in your budget. Online advertising isn't rocket science, but you need to know the basics to be savvy about where to invest your money.

John Nelson Wanamaker, the man who opened the first department store in Philadelphia in 1875, is reported to have said, "Half the money I spend on advertising is wasted; the trouble is I don't know which half." One of the largest distinctions of online advertising is its tracking capabilities, so there is no excuse for spending money on online advertising or search engine marketing without knowing what works and what doesn't.

Today you can sift through analytics data to get very granular information about the success of your advertising. Initial tests may not be immediately successful, but if you take calculated risks, execute them in an organized and methodical manner, and continually monitor results, you can optimize your expenses to remove any that do not support your overall marketing goals. Despite such a wealth of data available to online advertisers, many people who try online advertising (like banner ads and pay-per-click [PPC] ads) on for size end up losing their shirts.

Why? Because they did not plan to fail, they failed to plan. This chapter on online advertising and paid search engine marketing will help you understand what steps to take so your time and money work as hard as they can.

THERE'S MORE TO ONLINE ADVERTISING THAN SEARCH ENGINES

Search engine marketing (SEM) is the area of online advertising that secures the majority of overall online advertising dollars (a combination of all online advertising areas like paid search, display ads, affiliate advertising, video advertising, e-mail advertising, online classifieds, etc.). SEM wins so many marketers' online advertising dollars because it's easy to target campaigns around optimal key phrases that prequalify people who are in the most transactional mind-set. And, advertisers only pay when people click on their ads, making the spending more efficient. Search engine marketing is more likely to deliver people who are ready to buy, as the ads are focused around searches that are targeted to phrases that represent your product or service.

As powerful as SEM is, it isn't the only online advertising game in town. In order to get your brand out there, sometimes you need to build awareness via other online advertising vehicles. That means paying for exposure in other places your target audience visits.

Different Types of Online Advertising

Understanding how online advertising works is the foundation for spending money to make money. Online advertising goes far beyond the words *pay per click*. There are more tools to tap than just search engine PPC ads. Before we get too far into this, let's define a few online advertising terms.

Vertical Search
Vertical search is a streamlined search solution that helps web surfers find what they need. Vertical search engines focus on a smaller search-topic universe leading to more concentrated results. Online yellow pages, job searches,

local searches, and product searches are types of vertical searches. There are vertical search engines that are tied to a specific industry that organizations can advertise in. The beauty of vertical search is the specific targeting, so pick placements that make the most sense. For example, if you offer textiles to the fashion world you might want buy a listing on WeConnectFashion.com, a vertical search engine specific to the fashion industry. You might also test a buy for textile-centered key phrases on Google, Yahoo!, and Bing. No matter what the industry, there is a good chance there is a vertical search engine that specializes in reaching that audience. It can be a challenge to find and get listed in these engines, but if there are popular options in your industry, they may be worth tapping.

Display Advertising

Display advertising is an interactive way of promoting products and services online. Display ads are sometimes referred to as banner ads. They are, for the most part, image ads that you see on websites. Portals like Yahoo! sell display ads. Visit any of their sections like Yahoo! Shopping and you will see square ads. If you hit the refresh button on sites that have these display ads, you will often see other display ads in rotation. Display ads range in size and technical capability. See the Interactive Advertising Bureau's site (www.iab.net) for Ad Unit Guidelines (under the Guidelines navigation tab).

E-Mail Marketing

E-mail marketing involves reaching prospective customers in their e-mail inbox. Some companies sell ads in their targeted e-mail lists or sell their names directly to online advertisers. E-mail advertising could be in the form of a newsletter, an ad in another company's e-mail, e-mailing a list with a dedicated message, or communicating to current customers with your own e-mail list.

Viral Marketing

According to MarketingTerms.com, viral marketing (also referred to as word-of-mouth marketing) is a marketing phenomenon that facilitates and encourages people to pass along a marketing message. CareerBuilder.com invested in a successful viral marketing Monk-e-mail campaign in 2006 to spread the word about their website and services that still lives on the web (www.careerbuilder .com/monk-e-mail/) due to its success. In fact, CareerBuilder pays for Google ads for people searching for "monk-e-mail" because people are still talking about it via word-of-mouth, or viral, marketing.

News Sites

Google AdWords (among others) will allow you to place your ads on the news, opinion, entertainment, and other sites that your audience frequents. You can specify what general types of venues or specific blogs you want the ads to appear on. The publishers of these websites get ads placed around their content as part of Google's AdSense program (www.google.com/adsense). When a reader clicks on your ad, the publisher and Google both make money. (You should compare AdSense to competitors like Yahoo! Publisher Network [advertising.yahoo.com/publisher/index] if you want to do a revenue sharing plan and host ads on your website.)

Blog Marketing

Blogs can help build relationships, create strategic marketing partnerships, and drive new traffic to websites. Advertisers can buy ads directly on popular blogs (for example, an eco-friendly clothing company may buy ads directly on Tree-hugger.com), or advertisers can buy ads across a network of blog sites through companies like BlogHer (http://www.blogher.com/advertise), a women's blog network, or SocialSpark (http://socialspark.com), a blog marketing network that connects advertisers with bloggers through an online marketplace.

Behavioral Advertising

Behavioral advertising tracks users' actions online so ads that are relevant to their surfing behaviors (sites visited, products purchased) can be displayed. For example, if someone visits and leaves a banking website, an ad for a 401(k) assessment may appear on the next website the surfer visits. There are also retargeted ads, meaning that if someone visits a site and leaves, the advertiser can have their ads reappear on other websites that person visits to hopefully gain his or her attention with the "tell them, tell them what you told them, and tell them one more time" tactic.

Social Media Advertising

Social media marketing may involve creating social media advertisements to engage customers or buying advertising on social media sources. Blogs are a marketing tool that fall under the social media umbrella. Social media ads (ads on Facebook, Twitter, etc.) can be an option for some advertisers.

When you created your Facebook profile, you most likely included your age, city, interests, and more. Advertisers can target their ads specifically to people based on this. Visit http://www.facebook.com/advertising/ and create an ad (you can play with the feature without putting in a credit card) to see how targeted your ads can be. If you are a golf company, you can target men 45 and older who have labeled themselves as interested in golf. Ads can also be placed on Facebook group pages that cover a topic. The audience on those fan-based social media sites view the ads as desired content.

Social media ads can be lucrative for the right kind of product, but they do not work for everyone. Rupert Murdoch paid nearly $600 million for MySpace, expecting it to become an advertising cash cow. It never did. When the masses are using social media every day, your ads have to make an impression against a sea of noise. If you feel social media advertising will drive sales for your product, by all means take it for a test spin to discover your mileage.

Another place social media advertising can be tested is within work-related social media like LinkedIn. There are a number of human resources and employment-related advertisers who swear by LinkedIn. Advertisers can target by geography, job function, seniority, industry, company size, gender, and age (https://www.linkedin.com/directads/).

Contextual Advertising

Contextual advertising allows advertisers to target keywords and phrases within content on other people's websites. On free press-release sites, the online content often has links in it. If you put your mouse over these words, they sometimes link to advertisers.

Affiliate Marketing

Affiliate marketing is revenue sharing that occurs between online advertisers (also called merchants) and online salespeople (also called publishers). Compensation is based on performance measures, typically in the form of sales, clicks, registrations, or a hybrid model. The only time advertisers pay is if their publishers (website owners) take actions. This form of marketing has a reputation as the "black sheep" of online advertising. The "only pay for performance" compensation setup has caused some publishers to engage in unethical or "gray" marketing practices to enhance their percentage of revenue sharing. If your organization is in a heavily regulated industry, you should know that this medium is the most susceptible to regulatory flagging.

For most businesses, affiliate marketing can really pay off. Amazon has an incredibly successful affiliate marketing program called Amazon Associates, paying websites a percentage of sales for products sold (https://affiliate-program .amazon.com/gp/associates/join/landing/main.html). In fact, this program is the most successful affiliate program on the web. Often affiliate marketing can lead to larger partnerships. Sometimes affiliates will team up above and beyond revenue sharing.

With affiliate marketing, advertisers become affiliates by allowing other websites or adverting networks to promote an offer and get paid when they produce sales, leads, e-mail addresses, or whatever the desired "action" is. Affiliates must have a sound way of tracking the actions to make sure that they are:

- Paying their partners correctly
- Submitting accurate action counts for compensation
- Tracking the quality of the actions

Most affiliates use third-party affiliate management software companies like Commission Junction (www.cj.com), LinkShare (www.linkshare.com), Performics (www.performics.com), or ShareASale (www.shareasale.com) to track actions and pay and recruit affiliates.

ONLINE ADVERTISING STRATEGY

There are so many forms of web marketing, how does a marketer know how, where, or which options to select? Savvy online advertising execution occurs via sound web marketing strategy. Marketing strategy marries the art and science of web marketing so that all options are explored to best reach and serve the right audience. Web marketing strategy and execution often takes an integrated approach. Marketers may choose a combination of online advertising options that offer multiple means to generate awareness, traffic, and eventually, sales.

Web Marketing Pricing

The more targeted an advertisement is, the higher the cost. However, the targeting can also be very cost efficient, as it hits only the exact right audience. It is important to understand web marketing pricing language as it relates to online advertising. There are several types of online advertising pricing:

Cost per Thousand (CPM)

This pricing model is based on the cost per thousand impressions. *Impressions* are defined as how many times an ad is viewed. This pricing metric is similar to traditional advertising like radio and television. Online advertising purchased on a CPM basis is more likely to be guaranteed inventory (meaning that the ads will appear on the website). Think of impressions as views, or "eyeballs." CPM buys views. Anytime you hit the refresh button on a site with ads on it and new ads appear, that is considered an impression.

Cost per Click (CPC)

This model is based on the cost or cost-equivalent paid per click. A click is defined as a user who clicks an online advertisement as a way to get to the advertiser's destination. Note: If an advertiser's site is down or is having technical bugs, then clicks are most times still counted and billed for, even if the click does not go through due to a faulty site. Paid search ads (in search engine–sponsored links sections) are most commonly sold on a cost-per-click basis and are also referred to as pay per click (PPC). When ads are purchased on a per-click basis, there is no charge for impressions, only clicks.

Cost per Action or Cost per Acquisition (CPA)

Payment by advertisers is made *only* if qualified actions such as leads, sales, or registrations occur. Ads are also sold on a CPL (cost per lead) basis. Affiliate marketing is run on a CPA basis and has a distinct set of rules, norms, and management responsibilities. CPA deals are very likely to use co-registration deals as a method to initiate actions. (See the following.)

Co-Registration

Co-registration is an agreement in which a company hosts a registration form where multiple other companies can collect new subscribers from them. Sometimes web surfers opting into one program are unaware that they are opting into another program. This can yield lots of new leads for an advertiser, but some advertisers spend more time and money explaining to these "new customers" who they are and what they opted into, and crediting them for a deal they did not want or expect.

Sponsorship

Some websites, blogs, or portals sell their advertising on a sponsorship basis, meaning that advertisers pay to appear on a website. There are no guarantees for impressions, clicks, or actions. Sponsorship allows an advertiser to buy branded exposure and be visible to the audience that is on a particular website.

It is important to note that web marketing pricing options (the way ads are bought and sold) can dictate priority of placement, obligation to run ads for a length of time, control of brand/marketing message, and integrity of the advertisement.

For example, if a publisher (website owner) only gets paid per action, the publisher may want to alter the advertiser's marketing message to initiate action, or not be crystal clear about the offer, in order to create an action.

All pricing options need to be critically evaluated before a marketing campaign is launched. There are placement, branding, and quality pros and cons to all options. Knowing your options and testing return on investment is a must.

FIRST STOP: SEARCH ENGINE ADVERTISING

SEM and SEO are tied together in that the keywords you optimize around will also often be the words and phrases you create your PPC ads around. Minnie's Minnesota Minivans analytics package will tell her which keywords and phrases people use to find her website. If Minnie paid for ads around the optimized key phrase "Duluth minivans for sale" and others like it, based on her analytics data, she may get more eyeballs and website traffic. Or, if Minnie knows her business is a perfect fit for people searching the phrase "Duluth minivans for sale," and her site does not come up in the search engine results pages, she can buy this phrase through paid search advertising to get her website searched and found to attract quality visitors.

Google, AdWords, Yahoo! Search Marketing, and Microsoft adCenter (for Bing) make it easy to buy ads—anyone with a computer and a credit card can participate. AdWords also incorporates comprehensive tracking based on Google Analytics data, making AdWords performance easily measured via Google Analytics.

In this section, we'll focus on Google AdWords, but the following techniques will work with almost all ad packages.

HOW LOCAL BUSINESSES CAN PROFIT BY BUYING PAY-PER-CLICK ADVERTISING

Pay-per-click text ads, such as Google AdWords, are an advertising medium that a local marketer can afford to test once they understand the options available. When it comes to paying for advertising, you want to get people who are most ready to buy. That means you can restrict your ads from showing up in searches from computers outside your geographic area.

Target Paid Search by Local Phrase

Local business owners can laser-target their advertising budget to have text ads appear on search results for local phrases that will elicit a small quantity of searches. But small quantity aside, those people searching are likely to be quality prospective customers due to the specific phrases they searched for.

For example, a vacuum cleaner company in Austin, Texas, can buy phrases that are very specific, making them less competitive and, therefore, less expensive, such as "vacuum cleaner repair Austin" or "vacuum cleaners Austin."

Don't forget the place names of suburbs as you set up your campaign. The Austin vacuum company might want to include surrounding areas and towns like Rollingwood, Pflugerville, Georgetown, and Round Rock.

Phrases that have geographic locations built in may be less competitive than a broad phrase like "vacuum cleaner." They will cost less per click, and have fewer clicks, making advertising costs much lower than for a national or international company that can't target geographically.

Target Paid Search by Location

Local businesses can employ geo-targeting to their paid search message so that it appears only within a:

- City
- Metro region
- Zip code
- Three- or five-mile radius of the local business location

Now, with GPS-enabled phones, you can create location-aware advertising that says "you're just a short walk to . . ." This allows ads to attract prospective customers who may not type the city name in their search query. This is becoming more and more common as location aware search usage continues to rise.

For example, someone in Austin searching for "vacuum cleaner repair" may not include the city name "vacuum cleaner repair Austin," even if the search is local. Geo-targeting broad phrases to a city, region, or radius allows for greater exposure, yet attracts quality traffic.

Target Paid Search to Local Websites

Moving beyond the search results page, ads can be targeted by location on Google's "content network," websites that carry Google text ads on their content pages. This way, advertisers can have exposure on high-profile local websites, such as news sites, TV station websites, or popular city blogs, taking advantage of local geographic targeting. Campaigns can be targeted by category, topic, URL, or demographics. For example, Google AdWords campaigns can be targeted to the greater Los Angeles area *and* only appear on websites specific to sports.

Target Ads by Time of Day, Day of Week, and Frequency Capping

Ads can also be targeted to appear on certain days of the week, certain times of the day, or a maximum number of times to someone. Let's say your company is open Monday through Friday. Ads can be set to appear only on weekdays to avoid driving traffic to a site on days where there is nobody there to help interested customers. If there are certain times of the day that are better to drive traffic, this can be targeted as well. Lastly, if people see your ad several times and don't click, they probably never will, so ads can have a frequency cap set to minimize wasted impressions on uninterested viewers.

Organize, Plan, Test, Track, Optimize

Paid search advertising can work wonders for awareness, traffic, and sales, but you'll need to set up your accounts carefully and develop a plan to manage your various campaigns. Ad groups need to be organized into sections (by product, service, etc.) so performance can be monitored, quantified, and optimized.

For example, the Austin vacuum cleaner business might want to set up three separate campaigns for testing to see which works best.

- **Local place names.** Specific phrases with city names in them: "vacuum cleaner repair Austin"
- **Geo-targeting.** Broad phrases targeted to geographic location: "vacuum repair" (targeted to the greater Austin area or within a certain radius from the business location)
- **Geo-targeted content networks.** PPC ads on local websites or geo-targeted PPC ads on national websites.

Segmenting your campaigns by campaign group allows you to monitor traffic, conversions, spending, and click-through rates (CTR) so that you can make continual improvements to ensure that your ad expenditures go where they count.

Set a Budget

Local PPC advertising campaigns can be set up with daily or monthly caps to prevent you from overspending your budget. Start small and learn, optimize, and expand as you go. There is no need to spend a lot at once. Set a small test budget, then, as you learn what works, spend more money on phrases that more effectively drive traffic, leads, sales—whatever the desired action may be.

Targeting local regions can often result in very relevant ads, but with high click rates. Be prepared to invest and remember that when the going gets tough, local businesses that understand and utilize PPC marketing with best practices can leave their competition in the dust.

HOW TO TRACK PPC SUCCESS

Before you proceed, have a tracking system in place. Define what success means to you. Be prepared for the multiple variables in online advertising that can impact a campaign's success. Tracking points to evaluate may include some of the following:

Per keyword or phrase
Per engine (Google vs. Yahoo! vs. Bing)
Per offer ("Free Trial," "Save 20 Percent," "Offer Expires by _____")
Site-targeted ads (pay-per-click ads on sites)
Local ads
Per landing page (You may test several landing pages to see what converts best by
    setting up unique URLs using Google URL Builder or a similar tool.)
Time of day
Day of week
National
Regional
Geographic locations of traffic
Frequency of ads viewed
Interest groups
Industries

Web behaviors (sites visited, shopping habits, shopping trends)
Traffic
Conversions
Conversion rate (percentage of visitors that take a desired action)
Quality of conversions
Return on investment
Customer feedback
Interactivity
Google search network
Google content network

WHICH TYPES OF ADS WORK BEST? TESTED ONES

Online advertising success varies per product, service, goal, and industry. In order to find your optimal equation for success, you need to test everything. Ideas are created then implemented, but without commitment to managing, monitoring, and optimizing new efforts, success may never fully be achieved.

You can get amazing results by constantly testing, tweaking, and optimizing ads. Put two different ads up for a week and track conversions. If one wins handily, make that your "control," or the one to beat. Tweak your control. Change the words, the order of the words, landing pages, ad messaging, and more. Little differences can yield big results. Mark Twain said, "The difference between the almost right word and the right word is really a large matter—it's the difference between the lightning bug and the lightning." Once you have the text that works best, play with text size, text color, background color, and more. Each time you find a winner, crown that one the new king of the control, and keep trying to beat it.

If you are buying search ads, it is a best practice to tailor the advertising copy to fit with the searched keywords. Remember, web surfers scan. If they search for "Celtic gold jewelry" and the ad says "Celtic gold jewelry" in the messaging, the likelihood of attracting that web user's attention could be stronger than just having an ad with the company name and generic messaging in it. Think of it this way: the searched keywords are the question; the text of your ad should be the answer.

The goal of some ads is to spur the click. Some ad copy is more geared to really prequalify a user to help get closer to making a sale. The goal will be up to you to define. Once the goal is clear, the ad copy can support this. See the difference in ad copy that is price-based like "Honda Odyssey clearance sale—Prices under $5K" and teaser copy like "Secret Honda Odyssey deals—Offer closes Friday."

LANDING PAGES

A website has many entrances. Some sites create landing pages specifically to link to online ads or offerings. Instead of getting the home page when the user clicks on these links, some ads are set to go to a specific page that speaks to the particulars that the link promised.

If you have an online ad that says "Click here to get a 40 percent off coupon," send that user to the specific page that matches the promised content. Taking them to the home page and making them find that coupon on their own is bad service. Landing pages reinforce the message and the goal, and help guide people to where you want them to go.

Landing pages are also great for segmentation. If your 40 percent discount offer is addressed to parents, the text would be unique to that audience. If the pitch is to kids, the language would be different. From a design point of view, landing pages can't be an afterthought. You must look at online advertising from start to finish (ad placement, targeting, message, landing page) and include the site's look and feel into the campaign planning.

The most successful campaigns work when the ad brings users to a landing page specifically designed for that content. When landing pages and online advertising work hand-in-glove, goal conversions follow.

Optimize Your PPC Landing Pages to Increase
Paid Search Advertising Conversions

The landing page used in your PPC ads is an important factor in determining your Google Quality Score, and can help boost your paid search conversions. Search engines will find these landing pages. If they find keywords, they may rank the landing page higher than the home page for specific keywords and phrases, which can boost ranking in the paid search order. The quality of the landing page is part of Google's ranking order in addition to the bid price per click and the click-through rate.

Want to boost your pay-per-click advertising conversions and maximize your Google AdWords investment? Where you direct your users after they click on your ad is a critical element to consider. You should always link your ads to the most relevant page on your site. When users click on your ad, they want to be taken to a website page that matches your PPC ad message. Having a landing page that isn't relevant to your PPC campaign not only confuses users, it also confuses Google.

In addition to matching your landing page messaging to your PPC campaign, you should also optimize your landing page for relevant keywords that you are buying. This means that if you are buying multiple phrases, you may need to create several landing pages optimized for those keywords. This is a long-term investment, as Google rewards relevance by boosting Quality Score (which enhances ad positioning and helps you lower bids/costs).

Once you find a formula of keywords, PPC ads, and landing pages that seems to work with your audience, roll it out with more keywords, testing and tweaking your way to total world domination.

DEVELOPING AN ONLINE ADVERTISING STRATEGY

Before you start online advertising, you need to create a strategy. Follow these three steps and make sure they are part of your planning, management, and growth plan:

- **Assess.** What is your current situation? Do you rely on natural search referrals for traffic? What's worked? What hasn't? What terms do people currently search with to find you? Is your site employing best practices? What do you want to accomplish? Are there certain target markets you want to reach? What online advertising opportunities will help you get in front of the people that you want to serve? Do you have landing pages that effectively sell your products and services?
- **Plan/Optimize.** Traffic needs to be driven to a website or landing page that serves, supports, and sells. If the website needs improvement, do it before driving traffic there. If your assessment showed current online advertising spending areas that are not working well, fix those.
- **Test.** Once a plan is set and the areas that need optimization are managed, then test new online advertising channels. Diversify your web exposure. Ask for help, if necessary.

Asking for Help

A good third-party online advertising and/or SEM firm can become an extension of your marketing team. There may come a time for marketing managers when they realize that they may not be able to do it all themselves. There are thousands of companies who can assist you with search engine marketing and online advertising. Know what you want before you pick up the phone, and be prepared to research and interview firms to make sure their skill sets are the best fit for your company.

Be prepared to ask a lot of questions before you get into any contractual agreement. When evaluating third-party providers, ask them if they provide the following:

- Goal identification
- Current audit
- Keyword analysis/research
- Competitive analysis
- Content analysis/optimization
- Website landing page design and architecture analysis/optimization
- Paid ROI optimization
- Dedicated account management
- Collaboration with your internal staff: communication, education, reporting tools
- Online advertising management: setup, copywriting, reporting, conversion, tracking/optimization
- Reporting/reviews: search engine position tracking, link popularity trending, ROI, ranking by keyword or online ad, search traffic reviews, strategy recommendations, project updates
- Success stories/references

NEXT STEPS

Online marketing is *not only* online advertising. Advertising is simply one more tool in the wild, wild web marketing world that can be used to increase relationships. You can pay to maximize exchanges as long as you are ready to approach online advertising in a holistic way. Understand that the multiple variables online marketing presents need to all be considered, planned, tested, measured, managed, and optimized. Committing to building lasting, healthy relationships with your clients and customers is critical. Taking responsibility for buying online advertising and search engine marketing can be the missing link to building awareness and relationships.

Chapter Quiz

1. What are some of the big benefits behind search engine marketing as an advertising option?
2. Why is the quote from John Nelson Wanamaker ("Half the money I spend on advertising is wasted; the trouble is I don't know which half") inexcusable in online advertising today?
3. What are the main ways online advertising pricing is structured?
4. What are the main pay-per-click (PPC) search engines to advertise on?
5. What are the different types of online advertising opportunities that are available?
6. Name different ways pay-per-click ads can be measured.
7. Why are landing pages so important to consider in paid search?
8. What are the three steps to developing an online advertising strategy?

10

E-MAIL MARKETING

Traditional marketing methods like television and radio distribute messages in a way that is like shouting across a crowd. Today's "new school" web marketing is less of a shout and more of a private conversation.

E-mail marketing, one of web marketing's most powerful channels, taps both mass marketing and niche targeting power, depending on the application. E-mail marketing allows senders to broadcast a marketing message to appeal to the widest swath of audience, fine-tune it to a specific user based on their previous behaviors or purchases ("Since you bought X, why not try Z?"). It allows senders to track user behavior such as who opened an e-mail and who didn't, which links got clicked on and which did not. E-mail marketing is so effective because it connects you with potential clients in a place that they check constantly—their inbox. Used correctly, e-mail marketing can move prospects down the sales funnel automatically.

E-mail marketing can also offer tremendous value to recipients, bringing convenient, easy, value-added content and information that's customized to their exact needs. E-mail marketing can drive sales through special offers or coupons that are targeted to users' stated interests or past purchases. E-mail marketing not only makes it easy to follow a client through product, service, buying, and seasonal cycles, but through the cycles of life (as they get married, have babies, send their kids to school, and so on).

Because so many people suffer from media overload, e-mail marketing can be a challenge for marketers to implement successfully. Really, who needs more messages in their inbox? However, when done strategically, e-mail marketing can be extremely rewarding for both the sender and recipient. Despite the new social media age, e-mail marketing is still a quick and cost-effective way to reach out to target audiences. All too often talented professionals, with outstanding services to offer, are not approaching their e-mail campaigns with critical thought and execution. This chapter will present ways to think about how to apply e-mail marketing in a way that enhances overall online marketing strategy.

E-MAIL MARKETING WORKS

Online marketing with e-mail is a high-stakes, fast-paced survival game.

- According to Merkle Interactive Services, about 55 percent of the subscribers who receive promotional, permission-based e-mails delete them without even opening them (http//www.techradar.com/news/computing/spammers -get-1-response-to-12-500-000-emails-483381?src=rss&attr=all).
- One study by Salted Services indicated that more than 50 percent of e-mail recipients delete messages within two seconds of opening them (http//www.btobonline.com/apps/pbcs.dll/article?AID=/20100701/ FREE/100709996/1115/FREE#seenit).
- If an organization deploys best practices, then 77 percent of recipients will spend 10 seconds or more reading the e-mail.
- If the e-mail avoids being deleted, another study (by Experian) showed that 75 percent of opens and clicks yield 47 percent of transactions occurring the same day (especially when paired with a limited time offer; http//www.bizreport.com/2010/07/experian-first-24-hours-after-email -campaign-dispatch-busies.html#).

Your own success rate will depend on your commitment to continually refining your messages to motivate different audiences. As with all forms of online marketing, "quick and dirty is always quick, but also always dirty." Taking the extra time to employ e-mail marketing best practices can perfect the online marketing survival game and help an organization thrive.

- Despite the tough inbox competition for a reader's attention, e-mail marketing works. Here are the numbers from Email-Marketing-Reports.com:

E-Mail Marketing Statistics

- According to research conducted by the Direct Marketing Association, e-mail marketing generated an ROI of $43.62 for every dollar spent on it in 2009. The expected figure for 2010 is $42.08. As such, it outperforms all the other direct marketing channels examined, such as print catalogs .
- In Datran Media's 2010 Annual Marketing & Media Survey, 39.4 percent of industry executives said the advertising channel that performed strongest for them was e-mail.
- The Ad Effectiveness Survey commissioned by Forbes Media in February/March 2009 revealed that e-mail and e-newsletter marketing are considered the second most effective tool for generating conversions, just behind search engine marketing.
- A December 2008 survey of hundreds of marketers by MarketingSherpa saw pay-per-click search ads rank top for ROI, followed by e-mail marketing in second place.
- A February/March 2008 retailer survey by shop.org revealed that e-mail marketing has the second lowest cost per order (CPO) of any online marketing tactic. The CPO of $6.85 compares favorably with, for example, paid search's CPO of $19.33.
- A December 2009 survey of 300 e-mail marketers by Silverpop found that their companies were feeling the effects of recession, but "4 out of 10 marketers reported that their e-mail budgets in 2010 would increase, and nearly half (47 percent) said their budgets would stay the same."
- A Q2 2009 survey of over 5,000 senior U.S. executives revealed that e-mail marketing was the channel most likely to see an increase in marketing budget.
- In August 2009, Veronis Suhler Stevenson's annual Communications Industry Forecast suggested total spending for e-mail will grow from $11.9 billion in 2008 to $27.8 billion by 2013.
- In Datran Media's 2009 Annual Marketing & Media Survey, 58.5 percent of industry executives said they planned to increase investment in e-mail. Only 5.7 percent planned to decrease it.
- The Direct Marketing Association estimated spending on e-mail marketing (in the United States) will increase from $600 million in 2008 to $700 million in 2009.

(Source: http://www.e-mail-marketing-reports.com/basics/why.htm)

HOW TO SET UP AN E-MAIL MARKETING PROGRAM

Setting up an e-mail marketing campaign requires smart strategic planning. Online content strategies discussed in other chapters are still in play (the content has to be about helping the customer solve problems, educate, inform, or meet a need). In addition, while websites, blogs, and social media have few rules, e-mail is highly regulated. Making mistakes can be costly (up to $16,000 for each recipient who gets a piece of spam from you). Fearing e-mail marketing is unhealthy, the business case for e-mail marketing is very strong, but knowing how to do it the right way will spare marketing mistakes.

E-Mail Marketing Software

Even if an e-mail list has only a few hundred addresses on it, running it through your personal or organization's e-mail marketing program provider is not a best practice. Internet service providers (ISPs) watch for high-volume mailings—if there is any suspicion that something is marketing-related (such as a large number of recipients), even the smallest organization's list can be blocked. E-mail terminology calls this getting "blacklisted," and it will freeze an entire organization's (anyone sharing the @companyname.com hosting) e-mail system until the sender gets back on the ISP's good sender list (or "white list"). Setting an organization up with third-party e-mail management software allows marketers to work with larger, compliant, ISP-friendly companies, and enables productive list management for scalability. The more prevalent e-mail marketing becomes, the more lists can climb into the thousands and require segmentation and optimized management. Setting up an e-mail management system early in the planning phases helps set the stage for a smart and successful e-mail marketing strategy success.

If collecting opt-in e-mail addresses is part of the online marketing plan, then partnering with an e-mail service provider such as Lyris, Constant Contact, Silverpop, Infusionsoft, AWeber, My Emma, VerticalResponse, or Responsys is a must. Even if a hosting provider has a pretty good bulk e-mail program, most of them have limitations when it comes to creating e-mail campaigns that are dynamic and trackable. If you want to generate dynamic marketing e-mails that, for example, reference past purchases or user behavior, the hosting provider's off-the-shelf bulk e-mail program probably isn't up to the task. Be prepared to pay for a higher level of service, and reap the benefits.

If you want to track a particular e-mail recipient and move them through the sales funnel on an individual path (download this free white paper, attend this webinar, get this e-book, speak to a sales agent, and so on), you need customer relationship management (CRM) software. The level of sophistication and functionality (such as integration with an organization's e-commerce data) will vary depending on the needs of the organization.

How to Build Your List

If you are interested in growing your e-mail list, there are some pretty easy ways to do so.

Put your opt-in form everywhere, such as:

- Every page on your website (or at least on your most popular pages)
- The signature of your e-mail
- Coupons, printed ads, and marketing materials
- Landing pages from pay-per-click ads or marketing e-mails
- Confirmation of purchase e-mails or printed sales receipts
- Social media like Facebook

Here are some incentives to offer people in order to motivate a sign-up:

- Coupons/discounts
- White papers/e-books
- Webinars
- A multiple e-mail mini-course on your topic
- Contests
- Videos/podcasts

Note that, in today's world of mass communication and overflowing e-mail inboxes, the likelihood of someone feeling motivated to take action on a "Sign up for our e-mail newsletter" call to action is next to nothing. This type of call to action has zero value to the person contemplating whether or not they want to sign up. Instead, communicate the type of content (the value) of what you are trying to get people to opt into. Instead of "Sign up for our e-mail newsletter" (which reads as "please let us put more mess in your e-mail inbox"), try something specific like "Get our newsletter with free financial tips, tools, and helpful saving advice!" or "Get our e-book on the Six Simple Saving Steps that you can start today, and become a part of our financial tips e-newsletter list."

Beware that an e-mail collected from a person who has e-mailed your organization, purchased something from your website, or filled out a lead form is not implied permission to add them to an e-mail list. Use the e-mail best practice of getting people to opt in (meaning they specifically say "Yes, I want to receive your e-mail messages") so the list is high quality. Make opt-in for e-mail a separate check box on any online forms (such as leads, contest sign-ups, and contact forms) to boost e-mail list growth. Even when people have to register with your site to make a purchase, adding a user checkbox to opt in can boost a quality list build.

If you have the opt-in box automatically checked as a default on a form, or just take the e-mail and add it to a list without permission, when users get your e-mail, they may not remember that they have opted in and may label your e-mails as spam upon receipt. If enough people flag your e-mails as spam, you or your organization will generate a lot of bad will and possibly get your e-mails banned by most providers. Respect is reciprocal—ask for permission and you will get the recipients' respect back in return.

How *Not* to Build a List

A business card exchange is not permission to add someone to your e-mail list. A quality opt-in (confirmed request to send information) or double opt-in list is the best way to go. Think quality over quantity with e-mail marketing. Developing a list is not a sprint, it's a marathon.

While it may be tempting to grow the list and buy e-mail lists from other providers/partners, that method requires extensive research and may require professional advice to ensure the integrity of the list. Marketers who buy lists can never truly know how the names were acquired, the quality of the e-mail addresses, or how many times the names have been sold to other marketers. Most third-party e-mail management companies will only allow opt-in lists, and will cancel relationships with organizations that add names without permission attached to them.

Spam

E-mail marketing's prolific evil twin is known as spam. According to a 2009 McAfee Threats Report, spam accounts for 92 percent of all e-mails. That's about 183 million e-mails per day. Why, with all the spam filters and blacklists out there, does spam still exist? According to a spam study by the University of California, Berkeley, and the University of California, San Diego, spam generally gets one response per 12,500,000 e-mails, a response rate of just 0.00001 percent. A recent report has upped the number to 95 percent of e-mail as spam. Check out: www.net-security.org/secworld.php?id=8755.

The reason spam still exists as an unethical online marketing practice is because even a minuscule response rate can be hugely profitable. If unethical (otherwise known as "black hat") spammers can make a profit with such a microscopic success rate, imagine what an ethical, strategic, and scalable e-mail marketing program can do for your organization!

The main goal with e-mail marketing is to use it to serve, support, and sell as effectively as possible, without getting hit with a spam hammer by your users. Being branded as spam is more than an inconvenience. It could be a death blow to all of your web marketing. Once you're blacklisted, major web marketing efforts vanish with the flip of a switch. Most e-mail, hosting, and Internet providers have an anti-spam clause in their contract that states if a company is even accused of being a spammer, that is a violation of the terms of service and their account will be terminated immediately, stopping the ability to send marketing messages. Suspected spammers are found guilty before they even know what the charges are. It can take months or even years to restore a good e-mail marketing reputation.

The best way to avoid this fate is to use e-mail marketing best practices right from the start. People fear what they do not understand, and the biggest fear with spam is fear itself. It's easy to be compliant as long as you know the rules of the e-mail marketing game. The CAN-SPAM Act of 2003 is a law in the United States that was created to help clarify the multiple uses of e-mail communication and regulate the use of commercial e-mails to protect recipients. *CAN-SPAM* is an acronym: Controlling the Assault of Non-Solicited Pornography and Marketing. As online marketers, fun or not, you must learn, love, and live CAN-SPAM compliance.

CAN-SPAM had a clear purpose: to address the use of commercial messages, anything that was deemed promotional. Transactional e-mails (like a product recall announcement, a sales confirmation e-mail receipt, changes to an online privacy, etc.) are a separate type of e-mail and do not apply to the "spam" label. Dual-purpose messages that have both transactional and commercial content can be flagged for spam. To help marketers stay compliant, the Federal Trade Commission has set up a website that provides guidelines for how businesses must comply with CAN-SPAM. Here is the most important information right from the FTC:

The CAN-SPAM Act: A Compliance Guide for Business

The CAN-SPAM Act, a law that sets the rules for commercial e-mail, establishes requirements for commercial messages, gives recipients the right to have you stop e-mailing them, and spells out tough penalties for violations.

Despite its name, the CAN-SPAM Act doesn't apply just to bulk e-mail. It covers all commercial messages, which the law defines as "any electronic mail message the primary purpose of which is the commercial advertisement or promotion of a commercial product or service," including e-mail that promotes content on commercial websites. The law makes no exception for business-to-business e-mail. That means all e-mail—for example, a message to former customers announcing a new product line—must comply with the law.

Each separate e-mail in violation of the CAN-SPAM Act is subject to penalties of up to $16,000, so non-compliance can be costly. But following the law isn't complicated. Here's a rundown of CAN-SPAM's main requirements:

1. **Don't use false or misleading header information.** Your "From," "To," "Reply-To," and routing information—including the originating domain name and e-mail address—must be accurate and identify the person or business who initiated the message.
2. **Don't use deceptive subject lines.** The subject line must accurately reflect the content of the message.
3. **Identify the message as an ad.** The law gives you a lot of leeway in how to do this, but you must disclose clearly and conspicuously that your message is an advertisement.
4. **Tell recipients where you're located.** Your message must include your valid physical postal address. This can be your current street address, a post office box you've registered with the U.S. Postal Service, or a private mailbox you've registered with a commercial mail receiving agency established under Postal Service regulations.
5. **Tell recipients how to opt out of receiving future e-mail from you.** Your message must include a clear and conspicuous explanation of how the recipient can opt out of getting e-mail from you in the future. Craft the notice in a way that's easy for an ordinary person to recognize, read, and understand. Creative use of type size, color, and location can improve clarity. Give a return e-mail address or another easy Internet-based way to allow

people to communicate their choice to you. You may create a menu to allow a recipient to opt out of certain types of messages, but you must include the option to stop all commercial messages from you. Make sure your spam filter doesn't block these opt-out requests.

6. **Honor opt-out requests promptly.** Any opt-out mechanism you offer must be able to process opt-out requests for at least 30 days after you send your message. You must honor a recipient's opt-out request within 10 business days. You can't charge a fee, require the recipient to give you any personally identifying information beyond an e-mail address, or make the recipient take any step other than sending a reply e-mail or visiting a single page on an Internet website as a condition for honoring an opt-out request. Once people have told you they don't want to receive more messages from you, you can't sell or transfer their e-mail addresses, even in the form of a mailing list. The only exception is that you may transfer the addresses to a company you've hired to help you comply with the CAN-SPAM Act.

7. **Monitor what others are doing on your behalf.** The law makes clear that even if you hire another company to handle your e-mail marketing, you can't contract away your legal responsibility to comply with the law. Both the company whose product is promoted in the message and the company that actually sends the message may be held legally responsible.

(Source: http://www.ftc.gov/bcp/edu/pubs/business/ecommerce/bus61.shtm)

Countries like Germany have spam guidelines even stronger than the United States. No matter where home is, if your organization does business overseas, it may be bound by the spam guidelines of that country or region (such as the EU). Spam is one of the least fun parts of developing online marketing strategy, but knowing the rules will take the fear out of planning and give you a professional edge to ensure that the effort is done in a way that will work and continue to work.

Ensuring That You Have a Good List

The key to a successful e-mail marketing campaign is having a good list (or lists). In fact, having several segmented lists can be the healthiest approach to e-mail marketing success.

Double the E-Mail List Quality with a Double Opt-In
The first step to having a good list is making sure right from the start that you have good addresses from people who actually want your content. The best way to do that is what's called a double opt-in. The steps are simple:

1. Someone enters their e-mail address in a form saying they want your content e-mailed to them.
2. Within minutes, an automatic confirmation e-mail is sent to that e-mail address asking them to click on a link to confirm that they want the content.
3. The person should then get their first e-mail immediately. Ideally it should be a welcoming e-mail, or at least the latest relevant e-mail (regardless of when they subscribe in your edit cycle). This gives users immediate gratification and also establishes in their mind what your content looks like.

It might seem like having a double opt-in will create another step, and make it more likely to lose potential names in the e-mail list. In fact, the opposite is true. Having a double opt-in has two immediate benefits:

- It confirms the e-mail address, saving sending e-mails to bad addresses.
- It gives clients another opportunity to confirm that they want your e-mails. This means that they are far less likely to label your e-mails as spam or unsubscribe, and are far more likely to open them and act on them.

Customer Questionnaire Best Practices
The initial sign-in (or sign-up) screen is a good opportunity to ask clarifying questions and get detailed information on each customer. You can ask questions about their e-mailing preferences (daily, weekly, monthly), shopping habits, location, psychographics, and more. Only ask questions that will help you deliver more relevant e-mail messages. Potential customers usually only answer additional questions if they see the value in giving that information: a pregnant mother may be interested in getting offers/advice timed to her delivery date; the car repair buff may self-select to get information about certain types of cars and not others. Only ask for state information if it is very relevant, such as for special offers and shipping issues that are location-specific. For example, it is possible to ship scarves to all 50 states but not wine. In some cases, such as loan applications, asking lots of detailed questions is okay. But

it's not the norm for a basic e-mail marketing opt-in, so make your clarifying questions count. Every question asked will reduce the likelihood of someone completing the sign-in form. Most forms ask only for a first name and e-mail address. That's it. Pick your marketing questions wisely.

Questions can also be asked after sign-up, as you get to know your customers better. Additional questions will help further refine and segment the lists. Every purchase (or action such as downloading a white paper) can be added to a customer's profile with solid database management. Even non-purchase browsing can be tracked if your website has a sign-in that relies on cookies (for example, you can browse Amazon anonymously or signed-in).

An easy way to get clarity on how to deliver e-mails that users want is being up front and e-mailing new subscribers to ask them a few questions to help serve them better.

The opt-in page can also be a place where customers determine the format of their e-mails (text versus HTML), frequency (daily, weekly, monthly), and types of communications they want (newsletter, coupons, tutorials, etc.).

Most third-party e-mail management companies have representatives or account managers who can support marketers on best practices or have e-books or FAQs with tips on their websites.

Avoiding E-Mail List Churn

The best way to avoid e-mail list churn (those people who unsubscribe from a list) is to send quality, relevant messages. Deliver what was promised and what the user wants. Communicate when you or your organization have something important to say. Most websites see an annual churn rate of 25 to 30 percent. The more relevant the content to the users, the lower the churn rate will be.

A strategic online marketing tip that can sometimes help slow a churn rate is to offer e-mail preference changes at the bottom of every e-mail. If the e-mails aren't striking the right chord, the user can go in and modify their settings. This reduces the unsubscribing rate, as it offers the option to optimize message preferences to what the recipient wants.

E-mail list hygiene is a real term in the e-mail marketing world. Keeping a list current, scrubbed, and polished can amplify the power of the delivery. Many marketers are afraid to let e-mail addresses go, but people who do not open e-mails after three to six deliveries, consistently take no action, or bounce (meaning the e-mail address is no longer active or the inbox is overflowing) should be removed from a list to optimize results. Before names are scrubbed, it can be a good idea to do a "clean up" to try to re-engage potential customers (segment them with new lists that are specific to the behavior being targeted) who haven't opened or acted on recent e-mails. Special offers often reignite interest.

E-MAIL CONTENT BEST PRACTICES

There is no secret sauce to online marketing. It is how the art and science of web marketing are paired strategically that makes the maximum impact. It is the practice of coming up with a plan, refining the plan, executing the plan, monitoring the plan, optimizing the plan, and then going back to the first step. The bottom line with e-mail marketing, like all online marketing, is that the best practices are what work to support an organization's goals. Now let's get to the e-mail itself.

Types of E-Mails You Can Send

Successful e-mail marketing means sending the compelling, relevant content that the client wants to receive. There are dozens of kinds of e-mails clients might want to receive. Here are a few ideas:

Welcome series ("You're new to X, here's what you need to know.")
Surveys of potential new products
E-mail mini-courses (made up of 5 to 10 e-mails) on your topic
Step-by-step product tutorials
Post-purchase care/maintenance
How to get the most out of X
A new way to use X
New features
Upgrades
Recalls
Accessories
Relevant third-party or partnership offers
Answers to questions
New deals
Trends to watch
Resourceful newsletter with helpful links, resources, and advice

Formatting

Remember the "web surfers scan, they don't read" tip from Chapter 2? The same applies to e-mails. The easiest thing for e-mail recipients to do is hit the delete button before they even open the e-mail. Stop them with these best practices.

Create a Compelling Subject Line

The subject line is the first thing a recipient sees. Make the message work. The primary goal of the e-mail's subject line is to motivate the recipient simply to *open the e-mail*, not accept the offer—yet. There are just 50 characters to entice them; on mobile browsers, half that. You only have a split second to grab your audience's attention.

Make sure the subject line is concise and to the point. Don't waste space with excess punctuation (Example: Read This!!!!!!). Sometimes words that marketers think will work are hackneyed, overused buzzwords like *free* (Example: FREE Download!!!). Instead, entice the audience into opening the e-mail with something they can relate to (Example: Learn How to Blog at Our Free Workshop).

Use a Descriptive "From" Address

People are more likely to open e-mails from entities that they recognize, know, like, and trust. In order to save valuable space in the subject line, try to make the "from" address as descriptive as possible. For example, instead of ABC Company, it might be ABC Wedding Planners or a value proposition name like ABC Electronic Deals. Having a descriptive "from" address puts the message and value proposition in context. Some marketers have found that it helps to have a real person's name in the "from" line to create affinity. This "from" address section is an easy area to test and compare approaches for maximum return on investment (ROI).

Set Up HTML E-Mails with Text-Only Mode Backup

Although HTML e-mails (e-mails with graphics) look more appealing, many people receive e-mail in text-only mode. Be sure to include alt text on the graphics that repeats the deal offered, and set up a text version that can be shown in lieu of the image-based version. Since most readers will only be able to see the first few words in the preview pane, put your best and most engaging offer at the very top of your e-mail.

Test in Different E-Mail Clients

It's a good idea to check out prospective e-mails both with and without graphics in the most popular e-mail clients. Also, look at how the e-mails are rendered in the top web-based e-mail providers such as Gmail, AOL, Yahoo!, and Hotmail. Don't forget that more and more people are reading their e-mail on the small screens of their iPhones, BlackBerries, Androids, and other smartphones. If it makes sense for your niche, consider sending text messages with links instead of full e-mails to phones.

Use a Spam Evaluator

Some e-mail service providers have a spam content evaluator that goes through your e-mails before they are sent to determine the likelihood that they will be labeled as spam by filters or users. If this service is not built into your e-mail provider, here are some guidelines to keep your e-mails from getting smashed with a spam hammer:

- Don't use excessive exclamation points (Learn More!!!!!).
- Don't use a lot of capital letters (BUY PRODUCT NOW).
- Be aware of the F-word (as in *free*), as it can be a big spam-filter flag. If you do use it in your subject line, try not to use it with capital letters or an exclamation point.
- Don't use too many pictures. Overuse of images can also be a flag for spam.
- Avoid using certain words that are affiliated with high-volume spam use, such as *loans*, *insurance*, and *prescription drugs.*

Do Internal Testing Before the Real Send

Send an e-mail to a "seed list" (a select group of internal people) and have the group open the e-mail on different browsers to make sure that all the links and buttons are working properly and the copy is spelled correctly. Nothing is worse than sending an e-mail with spelling errors, or having a client click on your call-to-action link that sends them to a nonexistent web page. E-mail management technologies often offer a preview and test e-mail functionality, making internal testing very easy and manageable.

How to Avoid Critical E-Mail Marketing Mistakes

Web marketing tools alone will not help your business. How you use the tools is what makes the difference.

Me-Mail Marketing

Sending e-mail newsletters and messages that are all about you or your organization (rather than serving your audience) is not e-mail marketing. This egotistical use of e-mail is called me-mail marketing, and it doesn't work.

Me-mail marketing is selfish and alienates subscribers. They will get annoyed, see no value, unsubscribe, and have a negative reaction to the brand. If an e-mail is more about you than it is about your customers, it is not helpful to anyone.

It is okay to talk about your mission or organization, as long as it is helpful, relevant, and educational, and serves and supports the readers. Just be mindful of the intention. Being less egotistical with an e-mail makes a big difference in the results.

Lack of Strategy

Think critically about your use of e-mail as a marketing medium. Define whom you are targeting. What information can be included in the message that would be of value? Where is the call to action? The goal here is to create an e-mail marketing campaign that will:

- Serve the customers
- Support the sales and marketing messages
- Sell from a place of education and value

Neglecting the Core Foundation of Your E-Mail Marketing

Loren McDonald, Vice President of Industry Relations at Silverpop, has boiled down the core foundation of a successful e-mail program to three Ps:

- **Proposition.** What value do customers/subscribers get from the e-mail program?
- **Positioning.** How does your offer differ from the competitors?
- **Personality.** What tone and image do your e-mails convey?

Be Authentic and Relate to Your Audience

Whether you're a famous defense attorney, a respected marketing expert, or a shop owner, you have something valuable to offer your audience. Show that you can relate to your audience's problems by understanding their perspective. Empathy + Personality = Great e-mail!

Think Beyond the Box

Don't stick to any prescribed box of marketing. Have fun with e-mails—make them interesting and engaging. The result could be more subscribers forwarding them to their contacts.

Make Sharing Easy

Insert social media, forward, and share widgets so that recipients can easily share your e-mails with friends. Online marketing multitasks when e-mail has connections to social media, giving your audience choices about how they can interact with your organization. See if your e-mail newsletter service can insert sharing widgets for social media like Twitter, Facebook, MySpace, Digg, and LinkedIn directly into your templates. Have a call to action that is clear and easy. Having one social sharing link increases click-through rate (CTR) 30 percent, while having three or more sharing links increases CTR 55 percent, according to a study by GetResponse.

List Segmentation

Segmentation will save your lists. Too many organizations e-mail to the same list over and over rather than segmenting it into specific groups to serve relevant content. Why work to build an e-mail list if it is abused with irrelevant message overuse, causing the recipients to opt out? When a single list is slammed with nontargeted messages, unsubscribe rates increase. Do your e-mail marketing a favor and customize messages to different groups. Lists can be segmented by location, demographics, psychographics, buying behavior, sales funnel buckets, and more. Online marketing success comes from listening to and understanding the audience. The more you can define lists based on interest, behavior, and patterns, the more relevant your message will be.

When it comes to e-mail lists, quality is more important than quantity. Target the people most interested in the service or product, and track their behavior. Find out not just who opened the e-mail, but how many clicked through to the website, how many converted, and which products or services they looked at.

Ways to Segment Your List

You can segment with information provided when users opt in or, if you have a robust CRM software package, using the information they provide when they interact with your site. Here are a few basics:

- Preferences stated at opt-in (See the earlier section about customer questioning.)
- Information self-selected (date of upcoming birth, cars liked, etc.)
- Actions taken in e-mail
- User behavior on the website
- Previous buying history
- Geographic location
- Personal demographics (gender, age, income, etc.)
- Collecting information from online surveys

Segment with Landing Pages

The best way to track user behavior is to link the e-mail to a specific landing page that mirrors the language and the offer in the e-mail. Landing pages are defined as pages that communicate a specific product or service or funnel a particular purpose. Landing pages can be part of a website, or can be specifically designed to support a campaign. Landing pages can be used for:

- Keeping track of results from a specific online ad or special offer code for off-line ads
- Building search visibility using a key phrase–rich URL and great content for search engine optimization
- Supporting a new product/service as a communication tool that sales reps send (It lives on a website, and has ads directed to it.)

The landing page can be as simple or as complex as you desire. Those who click on a link to a landing page are already telling you something about themselves. Because the landing page has a narrower focus than the rest of your site, users may self-select to give you more information to narrow their search even more. For example, suppose your client sells men's sportswear. In your e-mail marketing you have a link for a big-and-tall sale. Clicking on that link tells you that the user is or shops for someone who is big and/or tall. The landing page for that sale then displays content choices for different sizes and different kinds of sportswear (jogging versus basketball). Based on that user's behavior you can then target him or her with more information about tall basketball sportswear.

If you are doing any split testing, where you are trying out different copy, offers, layouts, and so forth in your e-mails, then each variable should have separate landing pages (they may look identical visually to the casual user, but are coded with web analytics to track the results of each variable tested).

This sounds like a lot of work, but the process gets easier and pays off once you decide which variables and goals you want to test.

TESTING

Once you've got the basic art and science steps of e-mail marketing down, it's time for the most powerful word in e-mail marketing: *testing*. Testing (called split testing, A/B testing, or multivariate testing) is all about discovering the most effective way to meet your organization's e-mail marketing goals.

Testing is vital for both e-mail marketing and PPC ads. Before sending out the final message, it's important to know which elements will be the most effective. It's kind of like when you were first building your website and couldn't decide on the color scheme. Success depends on having the goals clearly defined (traffic, leads, branding, sales) and a comparison set (Message A or B, Image A or B, Offer A or B).

Common variables to test include:

Subject line
Offer
Call to action
Time/day of week sent
Creative copy/layouts (button vs. text, wording, position, size, color, repetition)
Landing pages
"From" address

Results to measure include:

Open rate
Click-through rate
Conversions rate
Value of conversion (items purchased)

While testing sounds like a lot of needless work, it is the very essence of what makes web marketing so effective. Testing allows you the opportunity to use e-mail to achieve your personal best on whatever goals you are tracking.

The simplest way to test is to send one message to half of your list and another message to the other half. But to get more bang for your buck, take the two versions of your e-mail and send them to a smaller subset of your e-mail list, perhaps 10 to 20 percent. Then take the winner from that contest and send it to the remainder of your list.

CUSTOMIZATION

Customization is the platinum standard for e-mail marketing. With great CRM, ideally every piece of information in the database about that user will be reflected in unique messages sent to him or her. Customization turns e-mail marketing into a very personal conversation. Its targeted messages are specific to a prospective customer's wants and needs.

Even good list segmentation is a "throw the spaghetti against the wall and see what sticks" approach. Today's consumers are empowered, busy, and want information that is specific to them. In order to customize, you need to create customer profiles that go beyond segmentation.

A simple segmented customer profile shows that people who purchased X also purchased Z. So after they purchase X, send them e-mails about Z. Customization gets much more granular and personal. Take a woman getting married in a year. A wedding planning site can give her a countdown calendar that includes information that she has entered. ("Did you get measurements for your bridesmaid's dresses yet?") But it can also present customized choices. Say the bride-to-be has chosen a color scheme of blue and gold—all the potential bridesmaid dresses and other items presented in the e-mail will have blue and gold in them.

While customization may seem like very expensive back-end information architecture, the payoff can be huge. How would you respond to these two hypothetical love letters: a beautifully handwritten note that was passionate about making your specific innermost hopes and dreams come true, or a badly photocopied form letter that was addressed to "Occupant"? Which love letter would you answer?

NEXT STEPS

E-mail marketing is one of online marketing's most elegant and effective channels, yet it has earned a rough reputation due to its evil twin—spam. As social media marketing continues to gain strength, sometimes professionals forget about the tremendous power e-mail has. People use e-mail for work and play. If marketers can capture attention in a place most people spend daily time, then e-mail can become a very sustainable part of overall web marketing.

   The next steps for e-mail marketing are to understand who your audience includes and brainstorm content that will be of interest to them. Incorporate ways to build the e-mail list, manage the list, segment it, test it, and track it. Don't forget that an e-mail signature can be an easy way to boost traffic to your site, build awareness, and promote new offers. Set up an e-mail signature with a purpose. Use that valuable real estate to connect with the people you already converse with.

   E-mail is a great information distribution medium for facts, reports, statistics, quick notes, and news. E-mail is a way to pass information, share information, and receive information. Productive professionals who use multiple communication mediums will always win at the web marketing game. E-mail is not going away any time soon. Be sure to think about ways to create, optimize, and try new communications via e-mail.

Chapter Quiz

1. Distinguish the difference in communication styles between traditional marketing and online marketing methods like e-mail marketing.
2. How much can it cost an organization for a spam violation?
3. What are Loren McDonald's "Three Ps" that form a core foundation of any e-mail program?
4. List some best practices to help keep your e-mails from being hit hard with spam hammer.
5. What is CAN-SPAM?
6. List e-mail marketing formatting best practices.
7. What is me-mail marketing?
8. E-mail testing can optimize performance, keeping communications fresh. What are areas of an e-mail that can be tested?

11

ONLINE PUBLIC RELATIONS

Traditional public relations, where organizations paid fast-talking flacks to telegraph press releases to fedora-wearing hacks, seems very old-school today. Those days of pricey PR are long gone. Today, any organization, large or small, can tap the power of online public relations. Online PR is organization-generated content distributed to various web marketing channels to generate buzz, which multitasks to boost credibility, visibility, and sellability. These days you can instantly connect with hundreds of thousands of journalists, bloggers, news wires, and customers all over the world. Better yet, you can do this work in your pajamas. As long as you have something interesting to share and a computer with an Internet connection, "PJ PR" can be a brilliant part of an online marketing strategy.

When organizations produce their own educational, informative, valuable online news content, it increases search engine rankings, traffic, and business. News releases are not written exclusively for the media anymore. The "just the facts" format has evolved to complement the web world's time-crunched nation to deliver information, educate customers, and connect directly with buyers.

Many newspapers do not have a massive staff of reporters on-site anymore, relying more on freelance writers, so the old approach of faxing press releases will often go unnoticed. Freelance writers are always in search of stories and win work based on delivering great content. Where do these writers and the mainstream media go when they need stories? They are more likely to search the web: Google, Yahoo!, news feeds, Twitter, video, and social media.

When organizations incorporate online public relations into their overall online marketing strategy, they begin developing more content that serves, supports, sells, and gets media attention. The sooner you and/or your organization are positioned as experts, the higher the likelihood you will secure a piece of the media pie. On the web, information is intended for mass consumption. Retrain your brain to think of news releases as people-to-people pieces to educate and connect with your customers directly. A well-crafted news release works in three ways:

- It addresses the needs of journalists (who are always looking for a story).
- It addresses the information-seeking needs of your current and prospective customers.
- It helps maximize search visibility (when content is crafted to include key phrases that your audience is searching for).

Journalists go online for their information and they go to the web to get quotes and expert sources. They are usually on a tight deadline and they need expert spin at their fingertips. Are you providing it to them, or are your competitors? Most of what you read in the media is spoon-fed to journalists by PR firms. Add press releases to your website for credibility and repurpose the content to several online channels for long-term visibility. Even if the media does not cover all your news, your time and effort count with your customers.

The power of online PR can accomplish the following:

- Get your news in the news.
- Add valuable content for your website.
- Boost your natural search visibility.
- Enhance credibility and increase awareness.
- Drive traffic to your website.
- Amplify content you already have to get more eyeballs and media professionals' attention.
- Attract more online conversation and partnerships (bloggers, fans, social media followers, etc.).

Get it? Got it? Good. Let's get started.

HOW TO GET STARTED: BRAINSTORMING

It is a common misconception to think that your organization doesn't have much to say that is "PR worthy," but this mind-set is wrong. All organizations, whether their business is small, large, start-up, established, B2B, or B2C, can generate buzz and possess PR power. A company that makes high-quality, high-priced blenders—Blendtec—showed the world how a small company could turn online PR into a true art form. They did it by using videos and demonstrating in a comical way how powerful their blenders were by blending media-buzzed items like the iPhone. Blendtec didn't create press releases that said "Blendtec Blenders Are the Most Powerful Blender" (truthful but boring). Instead, they showed via a video the superpower of their blender. If it can blend an iPhone, it has to be strong! Whether you use video or text-based "story-selling," as long as you have an interesting angle to share, your organization can reap multitasking marketing benefits.

As discussed in Chapter 4, "Content Marketing," you can create lots of content that you'd want to spotlight. Everything from your latest article or blog post to a video tutorial can be the subject of an online press release. Think of the online press release not as an echo of the original content, but as a megaphone that draws much more attention to it. Start by brainstorming things that could become online PR. This could be sponsoring a charity event to show your organization's values, sharing a new product release, or making a media statement that educates the market on things they need to know.

Start with Basics

As an organization goes through its business cycle, it is generating events that can be press-release fodder. The trick is spotting these opportunities and capitalizing on them. If the iPhone launches and your company's super blender is powerful enough to blend it, then that could be a release. If your CEO receives an honorary mention for her work in her local Rotary (and your audience is in that market), then a release about that can show the personality and values behind your organization and its community connection.

The key is to realize that your organization is interesting and getting over the "well, that isn't exciting enough" impulse. When you go back to Online Marketing 101 and remember your marketing questionnaire questions, you will remember the power of marketing comes by making relationships. We make relationships by sharing our stories. What is your professional story to share? A few release ideas include:

- **Launch press release.** Create buzz around the release of a new product or service or even the launch of a new blog or website. If it was launched to help people or fill a market need, then this is content-worthy. Share pertinent information to draw readers to your new product/service/blog/site. Online PR can make a simple business evolution into an interesting piece of content to educate, inspire, and connect with readers. An exciting "launch" release can be a piece of content that lives on the press or news page of a website, gets e-mailed to your audience, gets published on a blog, and gets sent to online PR distribution sites.
- **General news.** General news could be anything from "We're expanding our business" to "Our nonprofit has helped 7,000 Santa Barbara families get out of homelessness" to "We've gone green with our towels" to "95 percent of our customers say they've had lasting weight loss results." Write down the important information that you hear within your organization and repurpose this into a press release, blog post, and/or video. Online PR addresses the who, what, when, where, why, how, and "who cares?". Educational releases that inform are incredibly valuable, and your customer service departments may even use them too.
- **Event press release.** Any time your organization is supporting an event, this is news. Many times, local online newspapers allow events to be published to their event calendars for free. Create additional buzz around an event you will attend or host to get publicity and more attendees. Be sure to share the critical details: who, what, where, when, and why (and why the reader should care) to guide your release writing.
- **Expert positioning press release.** Position yourself as the industry information go-to leader to provide potential customers with useful information and possibly attract media attention. Write down what expert information you can share with people so that they trust you and turn to you for that kind of information in the future (whether it's tax problems, pain removal, or dating advice). Use press releases to share your expertise and boost credibility, visibility, and sellability.
- **Reaction to industry or world news.** When news breaks, your organization needs to be there to shed light on the issue and sometimes simply be a thought leader to your customer base. If major media buzz hits your industry or area, or makes mass media news, share your perspective on the issue. Your customers and the media will thank you for it. Increase your company's relevance by piggybacking on current events and positioning yourself or your organization as the experts you are. Make it

news people can use. This is good customer service and we serve and support to sell.

Pushing press releases and content that shares why your company is great is not as compelling as connecting with the hearts and minds of the people you want to serve. In Chapter 5, "Blogging," we learned the power of marrying fact and opinion (thank you, Arianna Huffington, for that tip). The same concept applies to online PR. The power of perspective is what takes the ordinary organization to extraordinary PR heights. Own your opinion—publish it online!

PR Brainstorming Example

Let's take a company like XShot (http://xshotpix.com/), which sells a brilliant camera extender (with this digital camera extension's long arm, you are never left out of your own photos), and see how many press release ideas we can generate.

- Launch press release: "XShot Launches iPhone Case with Built-in Tripod Adapter Unleashing New Possibilities for iPhone Camera Users."
- General news (repurposing media mentions to share with customers): "CNN Recommends XShot Camera Extender for Travelers to Photograph Themselves Anywhere on Vacation."
- Event press release (in line with current events): "One-of-a-Kind Graduation Gift with the XShot Camera Accessory" and "XShot Camera Extender: Affordable Mother's Day Gift That Lets Mom Be in the Pictures She Takes."
- Reaction to industry or world news (addressing XShot's connection to the social media phenomenon): "XShot Revolution Brings a New Focus to MySpace, Facebook, and YouTube Users."
- Expert positioning press release: "IZEAFest 2009 Highlights Latest Trends in Blogging and Social Media Including the XShot Camera Extender."

How to Write the Press Release

The Headline
The headline is the most important part of an online press release. You have mere seconds to earn reader interest. Capture your audience with a catchy and informative title that is interesting to *them*. Write down what value you

will provide to your readers (Are you launching a new service/product that will help them? Did you just sponsor a charity event that is in line with reader values?).

Headlines have to do a lot of work. Headlines should communicate who, what, where, when, and why, and be keyword-rich to help attract search engines. For example, XShot's event press release headline includes descriptive phrases like "camera extender" and "Mother's Day," which might be specific words they are targeting. Your headline must be compelling and "newsy," but always remember that this online marketing medium, like other online marketing media, is a relationship-building tool. The power of story-selling is where selling power gets rolling.

The Subhead

The subhead is one or two short sentences under the headline. This is an italicized summary of what the press release will say and why readers should care. Think of it as the "Cliffs Notes" for the release. Ideally in the subhead, but no later than the second paragraph, after introducing the main point of your press release, tell them why they should care. What value are you offering them? What is the point of the release? How will this affect or help them? Here are a sample headline and subhead for a company called US Capital Partners:

About US Capital Partners, Inc.

Since 1998, US Capital Partners has been providing prompt, innovative, and reliable financing solutions, including lending, corporate financing, and debt restructuring, to businesses across the United States and abroad. US Capital is a private investment bank, direct lender, co-lender, and lead financial arranger that specializes in asset-based debt for small- to middle-market private and public companies. The company's innovative approach allows it to provide the best financing available, not only for companies in excellent financial condition, but also for companies who may have been refused credit by traditional lenders.

The Dateline

Your release should start with your city and state (plus the date, if it's not in the header). This will help localize your story. Sometimes the month and year of the release is sufficient. Pick the locale that will have the greatest impact on your organization. If your organization is opening a new sales territory you can create two press releases, one in the headquarters location and one for the new territory.

The Lead Paragraph

The lead paragraph should briefly address who, what, when, where, and why. The "who cares?" needs to be addressed, as well.

Quotes

Quotes add character and credibility to the release. They also give deadline-driven journalists easy "copy and paste" content into their article. The easier you make their jobs, the more likely you are to get media coverage.

Quotes are not a science; they are an art. Make the quotes meaningful and story-rich. Don't say, "We are pleased to announce . . ." and then just recap the press release details with quotes around it. The best quotes put the press release in context, and put a human face on the news. Quotes can tell a story: "We can expect the number of IRS audits to continue to rise for small-business owners in 2010," says Michael Rozbruch, CEO of Tax Resolution Services. "About 25 to 30 percent of our tax-relief clients are small businesses with tax problems, so I know how important it is to avoid or quickly resolve IRS problems that could be detrimental to your business." Quotes can also illustrate the real benefit of your solution. Perspective in quotes equals PR power.

Product/Service Mentions

If you are promoting a product or service, the first mention of your product should be followed by a brief description, something simple you can imagine journalists running in a short blurb. It is good practice to include keywords here.

The Closer

Close press releases with compelling content. End on a positive note that reiterates how you are solving problems for consumers. Also, since this is a web release, include a call to action that invites people to visit a website, learn more, and so on. Include any details that would be necessary for consumers or media to engage with your organization.

The Boilerplate

A "boilerplate" is a consistent one-paragraph marketing message added to the end of each press release that describes your business, its value, what it does, and who it serves. It establishes your credibility. This content should remain consistent from one press release to another. Writing a boilerplate for online PR also gives your organization a succinct marketing message that can be used on other web marketing channels like e-mails, website copy, and more. From an SEO perspective, the boilerplate could be the most important part of the press release. Here is an example:

About US Capital Partners, Inc.

Since 1998, US Capital Partners has been providing prompt, innovative, and reliable financing solutions, including lending, corporate financing, and debt restructuring, to businesses across the United States and abroad. US Capital is a private investment bank, direct lender, co-lender, and lead financial arranger that specializes in asset-based debt for small- to middle-market private and public companies. The company's innovative approach allows it to provide the best financing available, not only for companies in excellent financial condition, but also for companies who may have been refused credit by traditional lenders.

If you would like to know more about how your business can secure the funding it needs, visit www.uscapitalpartners.net or call (415) 882-7160.

SEO and Anchor Tags

Select the key phrases that are search-friendly and, when you can, make them text links. Anchor text links are so important because they are search-friendly. Linked text must be relevant to the landing page. Since the objective of search engines is to provide highly relevant search results, you can use anchor text to help search engines. The code looks like this: <a href=http://www.xshotpix. com/>XShot Camera Extender</a>. The content looks like this: "This year, the XShot Camera Extender makes it easier than ever for Mom to be in the picture too."

Link other descriptive keywords like "special discount for Mother's Day" to relevant landing pages to boost search. Select key phrases for branding, such as:

- Camera extender
- XShot
- Digital camera accessory

Select more targeted key phrases ("long tail" keywords), such as:

- Unique Mother's Day gifts
- Flip camera accessories

Interactive Press Releases

As online press releases get more and more advanced, think about creating an interactive news release that includes video, audio, photos, PDF documents, or any other supplemental materials that might enhance your release. These additions are highly searchable and add value to the reader, customer, or media. Interactive press releases also have huge SEO benefits. Your video encoded into the press release can get extra pickup by the search engine results pages. Press release distribution companies like PR Newswire and PRWeb have interactive press release distribution options.

Look and Feel

When you are sending a press release, be sure that the PDF versions are on a professional-looking template containing your logo, website, and contact information. Press releases look the most professional when published on a well-designed template that conforms to the look and feel of your business identity or logo. Use your letterhead for press releases every time.

Readability

When writing online press releases, use active verbs. No passive voice allowed. This is the wild, wild web! Do not write in flowery language. Fluffy marketing-speak does not sell. Use easy-to-understand sentences so that readers who skim do not have to reread your release. Do not include overtly commercial language or overhype your product with unnecessary adjectives. Use catchy keywords and phrases that captivate your audience. Avoid business jargon and write for a more mainstream reading level.

If you are stuffing keywords into your copy, 2 percent is a good maximum keyword density percentage to achieve in a press release. Anything too high could sound an alarm to the search engines that your release is more spam than content. If possible, put technical terms in a detail block in the last third of the press release. Always proofread for spelling errors, as the smallest error can compromise the professionalism of your brand (not to mention the SEO).

SEO Press Release Checklist

Online PR shares your stories, connects with customers and the media, and supports your SEO efforts. One of the biggest factors in SEO is frequent content creation, and online PR was primed to support that. Here is your personal checklist to make your online press releases multitask for search engine optimization.

Headline (What's Your Story?)

- Does it communicate who, what, where, when, why, how, and who cares?
- Use priority key phrases early in the headline and often in the press release.

Who

- As a direct-to-consumer piece, does your message resonate and target your ideal audience (photography buffs, families, travel enthusiasts, etc.)?
- Are key phrases that they search for in the content?
- Is your release interesting enough with a smart story angle to attract customers and media professionals?

What

- Does the headline make sense to a reader?
- Do you communicate your key message *exactly*?
- Do you weave in key phrases (for SEO) to illustrate your point?

Where

- Is your news location-specific, national, or international? If it's local, write out full city and state descriptions.

When

- Does your release communicate a sense of urgency?
- Does your press release link to prompt action?

Why

- Is your headline compelling and "newsy"?
- Does it relate it to your target audience?
- What solution are you proposing?

Subhead

- Did you include a short subheading—a one- or two-sentence summary of your news?

Dateline

- Does your release start with your city and state (plus the date if it's not in the header)?

Lead paragraph

- Does your lead briefly address who, what, when, where, and why?
- Do you clearly and succinctly address why people should care?
- Is the first mention of your product followed by a brief description?

- Did you include a quote from someone involved that supports your story?
- Did you include any details that would be necessary for consumers or media to engage with your news?
- Does the lead paragraph have priority keywords and phrases in it?

Boilerplate
- Did you include the boilerplate?

SEO Final Check
- Have you selected appropriate keywords (including longer, more descriptive phrases) to include?
- Does your release have at least two to three anchor text links?

Sample Press Release

Company Name
For Immediate Release
Date
Media Contact

CNN Recommends XShot Camera Extender for Travelers to Photograph Themselves Anywhere on Vacation

Revolutionize Your Summer Vacation: CNN technology expert Chris Pirillo recommends the XShot as an essential digital camera accessory that allows travelers to take better vacation photos and be part of the memories they capture.

SANTA BARBARA, CA – The affordability and convenience of digital cameras has made it easier than ever to take top-quality vacation photos. However, travelers still face the age-old problem of trying to take a photo or shoot a video while including themselves in the shot.

For travelers wondering <u>how to take better vacation photos</u> this summer, CNN's Tech Enthusiast Chris Pirillo recommends the XShot as an essential travel accessory.

The XShot is a telescopic <u>camera extender</u> that attaches to any compact digital camera or hand-held video camera so that the photographer or videographer behind the lens can be part of the memories he or she captures.

(continued)

The cleverly designed digital camera accessory makes it possible for travelers to photograph themselves anywhere.

"This is something you're going to want to take with you on your travels because inevitably you're going to need it," Pirillo said.

With the lightweight digital camera accessory, travelers no longer have to ask strangers to take their pictures or struggle with their arms awkwardly extended to capture themselves in a photograph. And unlike a bulky tripod that can be cumbersome when traveling, the XShot collapses to 9 inches to pack easily into your bag or suitcase.

According to Pirillo, the XShot simply mounts to your camera, where you can adjust its angle and hold it at the perfect position to ensure a good shot. Additionally, the XShot effortlessly extends to more than 3 feet of reach, which is enough extension to include as many as five people in the shot.

"People have photographed themselves around the world with the XShot and submitted some amazing pictures to our website," said Michael Daoud, co-founder of XShot, LLC. "Whether you are traveling to the ends of the earth this summer or enjoying a much-needed stay-cation, the photos you take will end up being your best travel souvenirs."

About the XShot

The XShot 2.0 is a telescopic camera extender that attaches to any compact digital camera or hand-held video camera (including the Flip) so that the photographer can be part of the picture too. Everyday photographers no longer have to try and stretch their arms as far as possible to get a picture, let alone capture the background. The XShot 2.0 extends over 3 feet so you can be in the picture and closes to 9 inches to fit easily in a pocket or purse. The digital camera accessory has become popular with travelers, social media users, honeymooners, outdoor lovers, families, and digital scrapbook fans.

The XShot is affordable at $29.95 and is available online at http://www.xshotpix.com.

LOCALLY FOCUSED PRESS RELEASES

Far too many local businesses think they can't have a news section because they aren't big enough or don't have any news articles written about their business. Local organizations, be they profit or nonprofit, actually have additional online PR power as long as they know their options and how to put online PR to work.

All local businesses need to do is get into the habit of writing their own news to generate buzz. For example, if your organization adds a new product feature or service, write an interesting press release about it, add it to your website to share with current clients and potential clients, and boost search engine exposure with keyword-rich content. Write a short description of the event to clearly communicate what it was for, who attended, and why. The informative press release can increase your website's local search visibility.

Use a title with strong local key phrases to boost local search engine visibility. For example, if someone is speaking at a conference for female entrepreneurs, the local key phrases would look like this: female entrepreneurs + business owners + Ventura, CA. The final title becomes: "Female Entrepreneurs and Business Owners Get a Healthy Dose of Web Marketing Advice at Women's Expo in Ventura, CA, [Date]."

Send Press Releases to Local Online News Sites and Event Calendars

If content is king with web marketing, then outreach is queen. Local businesses need to submit press releases to local newspapers and media stations to receive free visibility. Remember, these local news sites need content. They want to hear from you. If you send a press release to a local newspaper, chances are you'll get exposure. In fact, when you send well-written press releases, often the local online papers will copy and paste the release in its exact form. Newspapers and local media are happy for the content. You will be happy for the free exposure.

Local online event calendars are another rich resource for local businesses, and submitting is usually free. Look for calendars on local newspaper websites, local radio websites, TV websites, chambers of commerce, and community college websites. Local sites need to fill their event pages, so when you have events, get them on these sites and help local websites help you.

Communicating your own news, events, awards, and content online will win you free exposure and wider visibility.

DISTRIBUTION: DISTRIBUTE YOUR NEW RELEASES AND ARTICLES FOR MAXIMUM VISIBILITY

Creating well-crafted content is only the first step. If nobody sees your content, then your time is wasted. Use what you've got to get the marketing results you want. The expertise in your brain needs to be on the web.

Your brain is for thinking, not storing. Use the web to store what you think and what is going on at your organization, in your industry, and more so you can use it for marketing.

Publish news on your blog, share free e-books, forward press releases about events you are doing, or send prospects articles you have published that live on the web. It takes time to write and distribute content, but the time you save by publishing it in multiple online venues, plus the visibility and credibility you reap, is well worth the up-front investment.

When you have great press releases or articles, you can publish the content on and off your website to get more readers and help attract people to your organization. Below is a list of places you could distribute your press releases or articles for more traction.

DISTRIBUTION CHECKLIST

Add a News Section to Your Website

Every business needs a news section on its website. News pages are a web-savvy way to manage content about events, sponsorships, new products or services, media mentions, and online press releases. When news content is written with keyword-rich titles that link to web pages with more great content, it boosts credibility, communication, and search engine rankings.

If you build RSS feeds in your website (very easy to do), have one for the main page and another for your news section. This way interested parties can subscribe and have every website update automatically delivered to their inbox or feed reader. Make sure your news page on the website is set for scalability. Many press pages have only the most recent press releases showing. Visitors interested in more can click to view a full page of all online press releases. This spares scrolling and allows content to be managed effectively.

Use Your Blog for News

A blog is a brilliant place to add news. Press releases are one way to share news, information, and stories. Do not forget that your blog and its conversational, fun, engaging style is a perfect place to share news. Content on a blog is more conversation than structured press releases, but that is no excuse not to put the power of blogging to work to share information and create relationships with your customers and the media.

VPI Pet Insurance releases their "Wackiest Pet Names" from the entries in their database. This was not launched in a formal press release, but instead posted on their blog. The content is interesting, speaks to pet lovers, is humorous, and became viral marketing by the mass of people sending this around. For a simple story, this company generated awareness, buzz, and more name recognition for their services.

Article Distribution

Online PR can also happen through positioning you or your organization as experts and crafting and posting articles on the many free article sites out there. Get your expertise in the news and build credibility, visibility, and sellability. Your analytics will show you which article marketing sites drive the most traffic, leads, sales, and so forth to your site. A few distribution options are below. All you need to do is create an account and get posting. (Note: These sites do have article guidelines, so be sure to follow them. Many times they do not want authors doing a hard-core sales push.)

> EzineArticles
> GoArticles
> Article Dashboard
> ArticlesBase
> ArticleSnatch
> IdeaMarketers
> Amazines
> Isnare
> ArticleCity
> ArticleCube
> Scribd
> Squidoo

How-To Sites

How-to sites are growing, not only as a social media phenomenon, but also as an online PR opportunity. Use your expertise to share what you know, whether it is "How to hire the best trademark attorney in Atlanta" or "How to train your greyhound in five easy steps." The more you can educate, the more your content can serve customers and position you or your company as experts. Here are some ways to post how-to–type content.

> eHow
> YouTube

BlogTalkRadio
PodcastDirectory
iTunes (You'll need to download the iTunes software.)

Your E-Mail List

Your e-mail list is a great place to share news and information. Some organizations send out the releases in true online PR format and some repurpose the content in a more conversational tone to share with readers.

Press Release Distribution Sites

Posting a press release on your website is great, but getting it out to online marketing sites is also important. By posting on PR-specific sites, you increase search visibility and the likelihood of attracting media attention. Here are some online PR distribution options.

- PressReleasePoint: www.pressreleasepoint.com. Submit press releases to more than 50 free PR websites in one easy place (rather than sending them one-by-one). This service charges a small fee to distribute releases.
- PitchEngine: www.pitchengine.com. This social media press release site allows you to creatively share stories with editors, bloggers, consumers, investors, and others. This release tool is distinct in that it is a social media online PR tool. It includes the option to write a Twitter message, you can share images, and these releases have social media widgets making it very easy for other people to share your news. There is a free service and a paid service. The latter ensures that releases live on the web longer.
- PR Newswire: www.prnewswire.com. Distribute your news through the largest PR tool and get exposure to 11,000 outlets total—5,500 newsrooms, including wires like AP, and 5,500 websites—plus thousands of relevant trade lists.
- ProfNet: https://profnet.prnewswire.com. Spoon-feed story angles to journalists to get yourself or your organization media coverage. ProfNet's journalist-only advisories go out to more than 4,000 news organizations via PR Newswire's national newsline. They are also posted on appropriate beat pages on PR Newswire's media site and distributed via e-mail to more than 7,500 subscribing reporters. You can distribute succinct expert alerts and also get access to media queries so you can reply to PR inquiries that fit your expertise. This is a paid service.

- PRWeb: www.prweb.com. PRWeb gets your news straight to the search engines that everyone uses, like Google, Yahoo!, and Bing. When people search for you or your industry, they'll find you more easily. This is a paid service.

Social Media

Don't forget to announce your news to your social media networks (Facebook, Twitter, Flickr, etc.) and your e-mail list, and post it on your website and blog. Here are some additional ideas:

- **Connect with journalists.** Respond to journalists' queries for story sources at HARO (Help A Reporter Out) at http://www.helpareporter.com. Connect with media people and outlets using social media platforms like Twitter, and remove the barriers that once prevented the average person from connecting with media professionals. Build your relationships and position yourself as a resource.
- **Engage in additional social networks.** Make your content available on communities like Digg and StumbleUpon.
- **Engage your happy customers and fans.** Reach out to your loyal customers, your social media contacts (on Facebook, Twitter, etc.), and your best customers to help spread the word.
- **Reach out to bloggers.** Bloggers are becoming a powerful force in the media. Send them your press releases and story angles. Don't discount blogs; they can help you get noticed by mainstream media.
- **Tap Twitter.** Check out http://twitteringjournalists.pbworks.com. This site is dedicated to journalists on Twitter and is organized by geographic location. Also visit @ProfNet on Twitter: http://www.twitter.com/profnet to see what journalists are wanting story-wise. ProfNet is a service powered by PR Newswire that helps connect journalists with expert sources for stories. (The only way to receive a full query feed is to have a paid PR Newswire account.)

NEXT STEPS

In the sales/marketing world there is a saying, "The more you require someone to do, the less likely you are to get the outcome you want." Online PR does not entitle you to getting customer attention and media news, but if you make it easy for your customers to understand your value, or the media to capture your story, the more likely you are to get the sale.

PR used to stand for "public relations." In the new world of online marketing and the new power of online PR, the "people-to-people" approach has given the *PR* acronym more meaning. Today, *P* stands for:

- **Positioning.** This applies to your or your organization's perspective and how you want to be perceived in the marketplace.
- **Perspective.** The media and your customers want to know your point of view.
- **Personality.** The more social media grows, the more companies can use online PR and pack it full of personality to create connections and get the word out.

The *R* stands for:

- **Relationships.** Use content to connect to build trust and relationships.
- **Responsibility.** You have a responsibility to communicate your value, values, and voice to the media and your customers. If they don't know what's going on, that is your fault, not theirs.
- **Rewards.** There are great rewards when you use online PR to communicate and collaborate. It will accelerate your business.

A coordinated effort of online PR combined with outreach, reviews, and SEO work will best position you for success. Online PR content builds SEO and works like compounding interest. Other efforts like paid search are great (and necessary), but when you turn them off, the traffic dies. Online PR multitasks and has online longevity!

Chapter Quiz

1. Define *online public relations*.
2. List the three main things an online press release can do.
3. What is the new way to define the acronym *PR*.
4. List five ideas for creating online PR content.
5. What are the checklist items you need to consider when writing an online press release?
6. List several ways to share online PR content.
7. What are online PR distribution options to spread releases on the web?
8. How does online PR multitask?

12

MANAGING MULTITASKING WEB MARKETING

Online marketing has tremendous multitasking marketing power. Web marketing is like a spider's web. Its interwoven parts support, attract other creatures, and can grow larger and larger, and all of its sections are critical. No single piece does the lion's share of the work. The best results come from the harmonious interplay of the parts. To attract the right people to your web, you need to make sure you weave your online marketing plan artistically and technically, with a strategic plan. This chapter explains how all the pieces of the puzzle (or spider's web) will make your marketing click (or stick!).

MANAGING MULTITASKING MARKETING

Multitasking marketing means that one online marketing effort can multitask for you in multiple ways. It can work in more than one way, often boosting more than one of the marketing goals:

- Awareness
- Communication (information distribution and education)
- Connection

- Customer service
- Sales
- Credibility
- Usability
- Visibility
- Scalability
- Sellability

By the time you've gotten to this chapter, you will have realized there's so much to do and you may not know where to start. The hard part is prioritizing. You need to separate the wheat from the chaff, the necessary from the nice.

Prioritize those elements that are essential for your multitasking marketing to work and the procedures you should follow to get the biggest multitasking ROI. We'll assume you've got the theory down but need the practice.

We're going to break this down in bite-size steps, showing an example 14-day period.

DAY 1: MIND GAMES

Before you assemble your tools, ask yourself: Is your head in the game? Know that the game you are playing is a long one. You have to be prepared for a lot of work with minimal payoff...at first. You will start small and then snowball. Don't be discouraged when the world doesn't race to your door the second you upload your latest piece of online marketing brilliance. The right people will come in time, but first you have to lay the right foundation.

Think about marketing not as spending but investing, and make the investments count. Online marketing collateral is a brilliant place to invest (it's low- or no-cost), and lives forever (unlike print ads, online ads, direct mail, or TV/radio ads that die when you stop paying for them). Invest in marketing that supports attracting, developing, and retaining relationships, and it will be an investment that carries an organization for years.

Day 1 is all about "strategy first, execution second." Clearly defined goals become the guide to online marketing execution. Answer the following questions:

- How will your product or service change or help your customer? Remember that the most effective benefits to tout are the emotional rewards, not the features. Is there a personal story of change you can attach to your product or service?

- Is what you have to say different? If you are saying the same thing and in the same way as the competition, you're in trouble. You must differentiate yourself.
- Do you know how to tell your story?
- Can you say your message boldly? If you've got something to say, say it loudly and clearly.
- Who is your target audience? Decide whom to target and what motivates them, then design your website, videos, and advertising campaigns to trigger every hot-button, motivating message you can. It must have purpose, be focused and concise, and deliver a clear impression of identity. This means that you can't be all things to all people. By focusing on a clear audience with a precise message, you have a better chance of capturing nontargeted audiences as well.
- Are you prepared to deliver the message in the most memorable manner possible? Are you ready to give up on nonproductive audiences and concentrate on those motivated to say yes? Are you able to ignore the odd complaint or nasty e-mail objecting to a cutting-edge approach? Are you ready for the web-video revolution?
- Where do you want to go? What is it that you want to accomplish? Think big.
- Have you crafted a unique selling proposition (USP) or value statement of the product or service that highlights the benefits? A good USP should be short, sweet, and to the point.
- Do you have a list of the competition's messaging and their media? Can you use a different message in the same media? Are there opportunities to tap blue oceans they have not yet discovered? (If they are on Twitter, Facebook, and a service for your target market, you should be there too.)
- Can you visualize the ideal customer (his or her age, income, etc.)? It will help you craft effective marketing messages. What would cause someone to want or need to buy what you sell in the first place? These are called *trigger points*.
- What is your goal—direct sales or lead generation?
- What do you want people to do when they visit your website or web pages?

DAY 2: DO YOU HAVE THE TOOLS YOU NEED?

Now let's make sure you have everything you need to get started. Here's your preflight checklist.

- Are you happy with your current website? If your current website isn't converting to your goals, then no marketing push in the world will change that. Make sure your calls to action and other conversion goals are working the best they can.
- Critically evaluate who you are, what you do, and whom you serve, then look at the website and ask if the people you are trying to reach and serve are truly being served well.
- If your main website isn't working for all your important audiences, discuss whether it is wise to create multiple sites and online marketing strategies for different audiences, or make the home page a North Star that guides all types of folks who come for various products and services. Remember, it's the wild, wild web. There are no rules.
- If you are going to create landing pages (or multipage mini-sites) for special offers and audiences, you need to budget the time and resources now, to make sure that the landing pages' URLs are selected and branding, design, SEO, and calls to action have all been optimized.
- If you are going to start an online advertising campaign like "Brand X makes everything better," consider registering a domain with those words in it or create a separate landing page on your site to support this campaign. Create laser-specific messaging to show and tell value and capture leads or sales.
- Assuming you have a website, do you have at least a few weeks of analytics data yet? Do you have the keyword list of organic searches? Do you have words or phrases that convert best?
- Does your organization have social media accounts at Twitter, LinkedIn, Facebook, Yelp, Squidoo, YouTube, Flickr, and other networks? If there is social media that is specifically relevant to your organization's mission or audience, now is the time to open the account.
- Does your website have an effective news section? Does it have a blog? Are there RSS feeds for both?
- Does your website (and blog) have social media buttons and widgets that make it easy for users to link to your news?
- If you have a blog, do you allow and monitor comments?
- Do you have a list of blogs and news sites that cover your topic area?

- Have you compiled a list of marketing assets and collateral? Is it all in digital form? If someone videotaped a relevant speech or presentation, can you have it digitized? YouTube has a 15-minute limit, so if you have a long presentation, you'll have to edit it into chapters. If you have brochures, do you want to upload them as simple PDFs or active forms where users can type in relevant data?
- As you assess your assets, look where the content can multitask as educational content. List what assets you've got:
  - Website
  - E-mail list(s)
  - Team members (writers, web people, a strong leader with valuable expertise that can be shared)
  - Blog
  - Press coverage
  - Photos
  - Business alliances
  - Content (old articles, previously written content, helpful information)
  - Data from past web history or marketing campaigns to guide future decisions
  - Success stories
  - Videos

DAY 3: BRAINSTORMING

Take a look at key phrases. Choose relevant product/service descriptions that can be worked into content to create actual news (like a product launch, public event, or new hire). Start brainstorming content ideas around those keywords and phrases.

Ask yourself what news around these topics does your audience need or want to know.

Gather content ideas from your frequently asked questions (FAQs), your product manuals, and so on. Every question can be the topic of an article, blog post, tutorial, or video, showing people how to apply knowledge about the topic.

Use a free web tool like the Google AdWords Keyword Tool (or use your favorite keyword research tool) to find relevant keywords and phrases in your topic area.

Create a repeatable process around the website's most popular key phrases and think about ways to help educate and empower prospects. To get the biggest bang for your content buck, figure out how much of your existing material can be reused and focused around those key phrases. You will be creating new SEO-enhanced frame around that old material.

To make the process repeatable, start a monthly editorial calendar, using the magazine model for your topic area. Figure out:

- What are seasonal topics that you can write about (holidays, events, etc.)?
- What are the features?
- What are the advice columns?
- What do beginner, intermediate, and advanced folks need to know?

DAY 4: WHICH CONTENT GOES IN WHAT FORM?

Whether you're repurposing old material or creating new content, you have to be systematic to make sure nothing is forgotten. Make a spreadsheet with the content item on the left and all the categories (from the list below) that it might be converted to along the top row.

Any given idea can take the following forms:

- Blogs
- Online press releases
- Articles
- Product/service descriptions
- Technical support
- User guides/technical manuals
- White papers
- Case studies
- E-books
- FAQs
- Tutorials
- Videos
- Podcasts
- Reference materials (from a simple glossary to a full encyclopedia on your topic)
- Printable items (procedure checklists, guides, recipes, flash cards, posters, etc.)

- Diagnostic questionnaire (designed to help the user solve a problem)
- Help desk or knowledge base
- Q&A advice
- Demonstrations on how your product/service works with a third-party product/service
- Company news
- Deals/coupons
- Online store
- Calendar
- Online utilities (online mortgage or retirement calculators, calorie counters, etc.)
- Software downloads
- Games
- Music
- Your commercials (Believe it or not, this can be a huge draw.)
- Twitter feeds and other social media updates
- Activism tools (tools that will allow users to promote your message)
- Industry news aggregating (an automatic feed of the latest headlines in the topic area)
- Lists of outside blogs, industries, or resources that users might find useful

Even if you're doing a cut-and-paste job, creating and SEO-ing all this content will take time. Not every item will work for all 32 categories, but every item will work for at least four, probably more. Prioritize.

DAY 5: CHOOSE THE BEST EXTERNAL SITES TO SHOWCASE YOUR CONTENT

External venues to consider as part of your coordinated content marketing strategy include:

- Online press release sites
- Video sites
- White-paper sites
- Guest posts on industry blogs
- Guest blogs on a popular site for your audience
- Radio show or podcast
- Social media sites including, but not limited to, Facebook, Twitter, LinkedIn, Squidoo, online communities, eHow.com

- Online newspaper guest columns
- Online trade magazines
- Consumer magazines in a topic area
- Third-party websites that don't compete but reach the same audience
- Affiliate marketing
- How-to sites
- Article marketing sites

DAY 6: WRITE THE ARTICLE

Write the article for that idea, showing your value, values, and voice. To get you started, here are some top article marketing directories to consider submitting to:

www.ideamarketers.com
http://ezinearticles.com
www.goarticles.com
www.oneminuteu.com
www.articlesbase.com
www.amazines.com
www.addme.com/article-submission.htm
http://digg.com/submit
http://www.selfgrowth.com/expertform.html
www.authorsden.com
www.scribd.com/upload-document#files
http://bx.businessweek.com

DAY 7: WRITE THE PRESS RELEASE

As discussed in Chapter 6, "Content Marketing," you can create lots of content that you'd want to spotlight. Everything from your latest article or blog post to a video tutorial can be the subject of an online press release. Think of the online press release not as an echo of the original content but as a megaphone that draws much more attention to it. Just be sure your press release has the following elements:

- The headline. Catchy, short, and loaded with priority key phrases
- The subhead. Tell them why they should care.
- The dateline. Localize.

- The lead paragraph. The lead paragraph should briefly address who, what, when, where, and why. The "who cares?" needs to be addressed, as well.
- Quotes. Quotes add character and credibility to the release.
- Product/service mentions. If you are promoting a product or service, the first mention of your product should be followed by a brief description, something simple you can imagine journalists running in a short blurb. It is good practice to include keywords here.
- The closer. Close press releases with compelling content. End on a positive note that reiterates how you are solving problems for consumers. Also, since this is a web release, include a call to action that invites people to visit a website, learn more, and so on. Include any details that would be necessary for consumers or media to engage with your organization.
- Don't forget the boilerplate. From an SEO perspective, the boilerplate could be the most important part of the press release.
- SEO and anchor tags. Select the key phrases that are search-friendly and, when you can, make them text links. Use unique URLs for tracking.
- Interactive press releases. As online press releases get more and more advanced, think about creating an interactive news release that includes video, audio, photos, PDF documents, or any other supplemental materials that might enhance your release.
- Look and feel. Use your letterhead for press releases every time.
- Readability. When writing online press releases, use active verbs. No passive voice allowed.

On launch/announcement day send your press release to your distribution list, which could include:

- The news section of your website
- Local online news sites and event calendars
- Your blog
- Your e-mail list
- Press release distribution sites:
  - PressReleasePoint: www.pressreleasepoint.com
  - PitchEngine: www.pitchengine.com
  - PR Newswire: www.prnewswire.com
  - ProfNet: https://profnet.prnewswire.com
  - PRWeb: www.prweb.com

DAY 8: WRITE THE BLOGS THAT WILL KEEP
THE STORY ALIVE FOR TWO WEEKS

Blogging is the mega multitasking tool of online marketing. A blog entry can highlight an article, a press release, a new video, and more. A blog entry can include all that content itself. Blogs can do a lot, not just during the announcement phase, but keeping the story alive in the days and weeks before and after the announcement. To keep yourself sane, write as many of these blog entries as you can before the announcement. Let's take an announcement like a product launch and see how a blog can keep this single story alive for two solid weeks of blog entries.

- Blogging Gives the Organization a Human Face: After the announcement, write about the team working on the project and their struggles, role in the product launch, etc.
- Blogging Demonstrates Customer Service in Full View: Blog about your customer base's reaction to the announcement, their questions, etc.
- Blogs Can Develop Niche Markets: If there is a niche market that you can spotlight, the blog is the place to do it.
- Blogs Help You Make "Long Tail" Sales: Highlight the other accessories/ services that will help make this new product more useful.
- Blogging Helps Reputation Management: Talk about the industry blog/ press buzz about your announcement. Link to positive blogs and refute the negative ones. Keep the story alive. All press is good press.
- User Experiences: Users of the new product or service can tell how it has improved their lives.
- Support: Blog about how to use this product more effectively.
- Blogs Build Communities: Talk about the new community building around the product or service. If you use social media links or message boards, talk about the buzz. Ask users to share the news with friends who they think could use this product or service.
- Blogs Can Build Existing Partnerships and Cultivate New Ones: Reach out to blogs and third parties that could use the product and service.
- Blogging Allows the Organization to Quickly Respond to Industry News: Write a "think piece" about your announcement and how it reflects or is a step ahead of industry trends.
- Link to Internal Resources That Related to the Announcement. You may know about X, but have you seen our tutorial on Y?

You could come up with many more topics, but you get the idea.

Important: On every entry, don't forget to include "categories" and "tags." A category may be applied to more than one post, whereas tags are keywords or short phrases used to describe a single post. This helps usability and search visibility.

Offer to write about any of these topics as a guest blogger on relevant sites.

DAY 9: A WEEK BEFORE LAUNCH

Tease your announcement on Twitter and on user message boards. If the audience can reasonably know what's coming ("We're working on a new version of the software," etc.), mention on Twitter and message boards that you're working on the project and that a major announcement is coming soon. Do this a week or so before launch. Be sure to send teasers to your press list to put it on their radar.

If you are going to make it a public event, get it on press calendars a month beforehand.

DAY 10: DOES THIS MARKETING PUSH HAVE SPECIFIC BACK-END REQUIREMENTS?

- Be sure to create trackable URLs for each of your distribution channels so that you can track which specific links located in various content pieces brought the most traffic. (If you create two trackable links in a press release and realize that most people click on the top one, you will learn to make sure that each item has a link up top.)
- If you make changes to the website, be sure to update the site map and, if the changes are substantial, resubmit it early to search engines for indexing.
- Does this marketing push prompt a new segment for e-mail sign-ups ("Want to learn about product announcements?" "Want to donate to our campaign?" etc.)?
- Will this new announcement mean any changes to the mobile website?
- Will it mean any changes to your privacy policy?
- If you expect/hope something on your website will go viral, don't crash your server. (You'd be lucky to have such problems.) Contact your hosting provider now to discuss how to deal with an uptick in traffic.

- If there is an e-commerce element (like a product launch), double-check fulfillment times so you can post on the relevant web pages how long it will take customers to get the product. Few things anger consumers more than the perception of "late" product delivery or, worse, vaporware.

DAY 11: PUTTING THE PIECES TOGETHER

Do you have any testimonials connected to the announcement? If it is a product launch, do you have early tester comments? Maybe you can get the product in the hands of industry figures to get a quote. If someone will be affected by the announcement, get a quote from him or her. Any time you leave the confines of your organization, everything takes more time, so start early. Remember that when it comes to testimonials, the best structure is to make a claim and then have a testimonial (sometimes in a box) that speaks to that claim.

Before you post this announcement to a new page that lives under your news section of your website, double-check the code, including:

- Meta title tag.
- Meta description tags (150 characters max).
- Meta keyword tags (no more than 10 keywords or phrases).
- Photo file names have key phrases in them.
- Photos have alt tag with key phrases.
- Photo captions are keyword-rich.
- Page headline (H1 or H2 tags) has keywords.

DAY 12: ON ANNOUNCEMENT EVE, TEST YOUR E-MAILS

At midnight before announcement day, test two e-mails by sending them to a small percentage of your list (no more than 20 percent). The e-mail that converts the best can then be sent a few days later to the rest of the list. Keep testing your e-mails to find the most effective ones.

Common variables to test include:

Subject line
Offer
Call to action
Time/day of week sent
Creative copy/layouts (button vs. text, wording, position, size, color, repetition)
Landing pages
"From" address

Results to measure include:

Open rate
Click-through rate
Conversion rate
Value of conversion (items purchased)

Segmentation: Send the announcement e-mail only to people who ask to receive such e-mails. If people only want to receive deals and coupons, design an e-mail that announces the news "To celebrate X, we're giving a 20 percent off coupon on Y."

- Create a concise subject line.
- Use a descriptive "from" address.
- Set up HTML e-mails with text-only mode backup.
- Test in different e-mail clients.
- Use a spam evaluator.
- Do internal testing before the real send.
- Does the e-mail need specific landing pages?

DAY 13: ANNOUNCEMENT DAY: GET YOUR SOCIAL MEDIA STREET TEAM TO SPREAD THE NEWS

When you officially make your announcement, the day your press releases go live, engage your social networks. Link each blog post to the following social media (if applicable):

- Facebook
- Flickr
- LinkedIn
- YouTube
- All the other social media that is relevant to your topic area

Add social media tools like a Retweet button or share buttons using AddThis or AddToAny to each blog post, so blog readers can share the blog posts, articles, and press releases and widen your audience.

Be sure to consider an active social media bookmark at the following sites:

- Twitter
- Digg.com
- Reddit.com
- Mixx.com
- Technorati.com
- StumbleUpon.com
- Yahoo! Buzz: http://buzz.yahoo.com
- Google Buzz: http://www.google.com/buzz
- TweetMeme.com
- Delicious.com
- Kaboodle.com
- BlinkList.com
- coRank.com
- Slashdot.org
- Propeller.com
- Folkd.com
- Netvouz.com
- Mister-Wong.com

Ask users what they think about the announcement and ask for feedback on the following:

- Message boards
- Product reviews
- New uses for your product or service (sometimes called "hacks") such as using clear nail polish to treat insect bites and stings, using a dishwasher to cook a whole salmon, etc.
- Testimonials or case studies (how users solved problems)
- Social media pages
- Twitter feeds
- Video contest submissions
- Q&A interviews with users
- Online groups or communities like LinkedIn, Ning, etc.

DAY 14: TIME TO ADVERTISE?

Obviously your stellar marketing multitasking efforts will bring millions of customers without spending a single ad dollar. But just in case it doesn't, it is time to map out an advertising strategy. After a few days of traffic coming in from organic sources, you can start to build up a profile of keywords and sites that are converting the most. If you tested your e-mail, you have an idea which words had the highest open rate. Now you can start to design ads for different online venues such as:

- PPC search engine advertising
- Display advertising
- E-mail marketing
- Viral marketing
- News sites
- Blog marketing
- Behavioral advertising
- Social media advertising
- Contextual advertising
- Affiliate marketing

Landing pages: For each campaign you'll have to create unique URLs and landing pages, so budget that time and expense into your planning.

And on Day 14, you'll repeat the process with a new announcement.

DOES MULTITASKING MARKETING EFFORT REALLY PAY OFF?

Here are a few examples. For reasons of confidentiality, the organizations will be anonymous, but the results are real. Their situations may not apply to all companies, but this is what worked for them and shows the steps they took, demonstrating how web marketing works in unique ways for each company.

Example: Organization A

In business for eight years, in the service industry.

Goal

To generate more leads. The percentage rate from lead to sale was already calculated, quality lead volume was the goal.

Assets

Media coverage, website, success record, testimonials, content from printed newsletter, years of web analytics to review, paid search results to apply to

SEO, CEO who is an expert in the field and full of educational tips, videos, photos.

Optimizations

- The website needed brand synergy with off-line materials like logo, letterhead, or client giveaways (mugs, etc.). Needed to clean up the major brand inconsistency.
- Needed to make media coverage visible on the website to boost credibility.
- Testimonials needed to be peppered throughout the website so they were read for better usability.
- Site was lacking SEO best practices for natural search visibility.
- Paid search campaigns needed to be organized better by categories to get conversion rate in a better state.
- Printed newsletter content could get repurposed into blog posts, online articles, online press releases, etc.
- Needed a press page to house online press releases.
- Needed a blog to share all their educational tips.
- No social media marketing—needed to get on Facebook, Twitter, LinkedIn, and YouTube.
- Selling message (the value of the services) was not fully communicated on the website; needed to make a USP, have more sales messaging that communicates value.
- Call to action (the form to fill out to get leads) was too low on the page; needed to move this up for more visibility and action.

New Channels

Post-optimization of the website (to make it a web solution), ongoing web marketing management included:

- Monthly website updates to keep testimonials current
- Monthly search engine optimization management
- Daily paid search management
- Weekly blogging
- Training of in-house staff about SEO and paid search and hiring of several outside consultants to help and work with the traditional publicist
- Weekly web analysis reviews to understand patterns and make improvements

- Article marketing to get more content out for credibility and visibility
- Monthly repurposing of the printed newsletter into content for the blog
- Display ads purchased on advertising networks
- Facebook page created and managed with updates
- Twitter accounts created
- LinkedIn profiles optimized with full bios, website links (external links for SEO)
- Flickr account created to store all photos
- YouTube account created to share video clips
- Blog was fed into the Facebook page, Twitter, and LinkedIn
- Online press releases created and sent weekly to online PR distribution sites
- Used Google Alerts to stay on top of company web mentions and watch the competition
- Networked with social media contacts
- Added e-mail sign-up to the site and started sending monthly newsletters

Multitasking Marketing Results
- Blog earned a "best of" content award for its educational quality content.
- Blog secured company's credibility and search visibility, steadily grew traffic 10 percent month after month.
- Blog gained PR interest and secured guest-writing opportunities with high-ranking sites (visibility/credibility).
- Twitter posts also gained media attention, securing two large media wins and media mentions.
- Paid search conversion rate due to ongoing optimization dropped the cost to acquire a lead by 35 to 45 percent, depending on the month.
- Natural search grew as a traffic driver to the website, decreased the need to spend as much on paid search, dropped paid search spend by 43 percent.
- Conversion rate on the articles distributed online converted three times better than paid search and two times better than natural search.
- Overall lead volume increased 50 percent and quality of leads (that become sales) increased monthly with increased optimization.
- Company doubled revenue year after year for three years in a row.

Using Multitasking Techniques

- An online press release goes on the press page, it gets sent to PR wires, gets repurposed for the blog, gets posted to the Facebook page, LinkedIn, and Twitter to multitask marketing power.
- Data from paid search shows what key phrases convert best so those words that yield most get put on the SEO phrase plan and get optimized.
- Top phrases get used in website copy, blog posts, online press releases, tweets, and YouTube labels.
- YouTube videos live on a private channel and get republished in press releases that allow video as well as on the blog and website.
- Social media builds prospective client connections, boosts credibility, and secures trust from the media that the expert-backed company is an authority.
- Top blog posts get repurposed into articles to be posted on article marketing sites.
- Website optimizations boost usability, search visibility, credibility, and sellability.

All the pieces are woven together to make web work click.

Example: Organization B

In business for one year, in the consulting industry.

Goal

To attract more awareness, show value (especially against the competition, who are bigger with a bigger marketing budget), grow business, and branch into the product business (instead of just services).

Assets

Credentials, background, expertise in industry, website, some paid search data to review.

Optimizations

- Needed web analytics to measure overall website traffic and leads and to fully understand ROI of paid search (company was going off click-through rate, not sales; the form to fill out to get leads was too low on the page).

- Website design looked very amateurish and was not showing the professionalism to build trust or sell the high-value and high-cost consulting packages.
- Needed SEO best practices.
- Needed to add blog, Facebook, Twitter, improve LinkedIn profile, start a podcast, share all the expertise to position consultant as an authority.
- Needed to measure traffic, leads, optimize to spend money where it makes the most money.
- Needed to automate blog to feed into Facebook, Twitter, and LinkedIn.
- Needed to build network with other bloggers in industry to get awareness by the target market, post comments on their blogs, make mentions of complementary blogs in social media to win friends and influence people.

New Channels
- New website with blog and social media widgets (LinkedIn, Facebook, Twitter, YouTube, BlogTalkRadio) was added in.
- Published articles on article marketing sites.
- Added a press page and created/distributed press releases.
- Productized expertise by doing an e-book, webinars to maximize time and revenue opportunities. Added e-commerce to capture direct sales.
- Added e-mail sign-up to the site and designed an e-mail template and sent monthly e-mails.

Multitasking Marketing Results
- Blog put this company on the map, became number one marketing tool—cost-free!
- Content creation and social media presence showed consultant's talents building credibility and increasing search visibility and sellability (blog is often mentioned as "I hired you vs. the competition because I read your blog [follow you on Twitter, etc.] and see how much you know and share, and I saw you are the best fit for me").
- Content on multiple channels increased search visibility by 75 percent.
- Hired a consultant to manage paid search who helped clean up the campaign, find top phrases for SEO, and decrease overall spend by spending money on phrases that count.
- E-mail drives traffic to the blog, Facebook, and Twitter.

- Website sells the value and has minimized unqualified lead calls by 50 percent and increased sales by 150 percent.
- Content is visible when searched by journalists, builds credibility and prompts contact, secured several huge media inquiries including a television appearance.
- Content can be sent to clients, saving time and boosting customer service.
- Blog, Facebook, and Twitter are used by clients to self-serve, communicate, and collaborate, decreasing one-on-one time, adding value to consulting work (via the community and immediate news, tips, advice), and has cut consultant's work hours by 37 percent.
- Product sales have become a large piece of the revenue model, allowing the service part of the business to require fewer hours. Consulting fees have increased, and the business owner works less, makes more, and attracts more quality clients.

Using Multitasking Techniques
- A press plug gets posted to Facebook, Twitter, press page, sent to PR wires, and repurposed for the blog.
- E-mail newsletters link to full articles on the blog.
- Blog articles become online articles published on article sites.
- Website boosts credibility, visibility, and sellability.
- Consultant becomes a "weblebrity" or "webceleb" when Google-searched, boosting credibility and sellability. Name is searched and website, blog, Twitter, Facebook, other bloggers blogging about this consultant, videos, press releases, and more come up.

YOU HAVE TO GIVE TO GAIN

Giving away expertise, tips, tools, downloads, white papers, free trials, blog content, podcasts, and videos all build trust, connections, educational empowerment, and more. Find your value and give some away. Some marketers call this the "pink spoon" or "sample taste," analogous to ice cream stores giving away a sample of the ice cream. You take that free taste and end up wanting more. Test the ROI of people trying something and see if it pays off. This could be a short e-book, helpful blog posts, valuable tweets, and so on. Give it away, learn, optimize, and build evangelists. Sharing is caring—people want to feel cared for and empowered, and be able to trust you. That is what the social web is all about. Generosity pays.

You don't need to go out and buy new tools. You can use what you have (analytics, databases, in-house resources, expertise, old content, etc.). Assess your situation, optimize what is not working, get the foundation healthy, then move on to new channels. Many times everything you need already exists; it just needs to be put to work.

Take inventory of your intellectual capital. People, technologies, products, expertise, data, and content are all things you can use to get more out of online marketing. Assess your situation, optimize things that need immediate attention to have a healthy online marketing foundation, then scale with new channels.

ASK QUESTIONS, TAKE ACTIONS

Marketing means making meaningful relationships. Relationships, not web tools, are what make sales and create new sales. When organizations invest in web marketing as a relationship-building tool to brand, build, and boost business, they win big. Online marketing works when there is a clear strategy and mindful execution. We do not always know the best web marketing path to pick at first, but when strategy is set before execution, you save time, money, and backwards-work. Remember that the real meaning of *marketing* is maximizing exchanges (leads, inquiries, connections, etc.). Online marketing includes websites, content creation, blogging, reviewing web analytics, social media, online PR, search engine marketing, and more. How these tools work in unison for multitasking marketing is what will *make your marketing click*. Bridging the art and science of online marketing with strategy is the question you will ask yourself. Taking action to make sure these ideas happen and are monitored, optimized, and continually managed makes it all matter.

Always think marketing investing, not spending (see, even we are "telling you one more time" to make sure this sticks!). Congratulations on investing the time to understand online marketing. It is never about what we know; it is what we are open to learning. Your commitment to learning online marketing has paved an educational foundation that will support you no matter what online marketing trends come and go.

It has been a pleasure facilitating your educational journey. This book is complete, but our ability to stay in touch is not, thanks to the power of the web.

- www.lorriethomas.com
- www.webmarketingtherapy.com

- www.themarketingtherapist.com
- www.facebook.com/lorrie.thomas
- www.twitter.com/webtherapist
- www.linkedin.com/in/lorriethomas
- http://www.youtube.com/user/webmarketingspeaker
- http://www.blogtalkradio.com/marketing-therapist

Chapter Quiz

1. Define *multitasking marketing*.
2. How is web marketing like a spider's web?
3. Name types of social media you could link a blog post to.
4. When it comes to online marketing planning, the rule is always _____ first, _____ second.
5. What are different ways to collect and show customer feedback online?
6. What are SEO points to address when adding a new page of content to a website?
7. What are the different online article sites you can submit your article to?
8. Explain the concept of "give to gain" in online marketing.

ANSWER KEY

CHAPTER 1

1. P2P—people-to-people marketing
2. Awareness, communication/information distribution, connection, service, and sales
3. Change
4. Remember that marketing means maximizing relationships. Tap free online marketing tools. Be an educator. Be authentic to differentiate your company. Repurpose marketing assets and collateral online. Stop selling and start serving.
5. Local search directories; Google Analytics; social media (blogs, LinkedIn, Facebook, Yelp, Squidoo)
6. Serving
7. Strategy first, execution second.
8. Sales and clearly defined goal(s). Clearly defined goal(s) become the guide to online marketing execution.

CHAPTER 2

1. Credibility, usability, sellability, scalability, and visibility
2. Selecting a domain name
3. Length of the domain name; memorable domain name; possible domain name confusion; problems caused by misspelling; domain

names that relate to the organization's name or core values; selecting the best domain suffix (*.com, .net, .org, .de, .fr.,* etc.) Is the domain used for search engine optimization? If so, the key phrases may be built into the domain name.

4. Home page that clearly communicates who you are; "About" page; professional design; easy-to-find contact information; clear calls to action

5. Use a maximum of five lines per paragraph. Use a combination of upper- and lowercase letters in URLs if you are mentioning website links in website text. Keep lines of text to 21 words maximum to boost readability.

6. Introduction, project details, goals/objectives, audience, competitive landscape, value/value proposition, critical communication points, communication media, design preferences, budget outline, references, approval process/considerations and contact information.

7. There are sources for free, safe stock photos that are "I didn't steal them"–proof, including Stock.xchang, FreeFoto, OpenPhoto, Photocase, Stockvault, and Flickr.

8. If the organization ever wants to change hosting providers or manage the site itself, the design may have to be re-created all over again.

CHAPTER 3

1. A website map is a list of pages that will be accessible to website visitors. It is also a visual hierarchy that will help a designer incorporate all the critical pages and website musts that will be part of the website.

2. A wireframe shows the basic architecture, or "bones," of a site, minus the skin.

3. Create a menu or a list of navigation items from your website map (navigation can be horizontal or vertical). Show calls to action. Include an e-mail list opt-in. Make a decision about social media widgets. If there is an e-commerce component to this website, have this designed into the wireframe.

4. Remember KISS: Keep It Simple, Silly—no welcome letters or music. Be conventional, because conventions work. Cut the clutter. Design the website to move vertically, not horizontally. Create a

visual hierarchy. Design your site so that every page is self-evident. Make navigation easy. Make clickable items obviously clickable. Try breadcrumbs (a usability design/development technique that leaves "crumbs" at the top of the page that allow visitors to easily find their way back). Use color. Check out a great book on usability called *Don't Make Me Think* by Steve Krug.

5. False. It is the job of marketers to become their own media department, creating properly formatted press releases that live on their websites.

6. Privacy policies address the use of personally identifiable information (e-mail addresses, contact information, website activity, and credit card information). The second a website asks for a prospect's e-mail; the law requires a privacy policy.

7. Testimonials, value propositions, clear calls to action, self-generated news releases, sharing your story or credentials and having an accurate privacy policy.

8. Assets can include anything from previous media coverage, descriptive sales copy, taglines, e-mail sign-up, and demonstration videos.

CHAPTER 4

1. *Content marketing* is simply defined as publishing content on the web that educates and empowers readers.

2. Editorial-based (or long-form) content; marketing-backed; behavior-driven; multi-platform (print, digital, audio, video, events); targeted toward a specific audience

3. False. Content marketing lives both on the originator's website and on the websites of others. This can include YouTube, article marketing sites, and more.

4. Message boards; product reviews; new uses for your product or service (sometimes called "hacks"); testimonials or case studies (how users solved problems); social media pages; Twitter feeds; video contest submissions; Q&A interviews with users; online groups or communities like LinkedIn, Ning, etc.

5. Creativity, a web camera (some are built into mobile devices or laptops), off-the-shelf video software (some is free or low cost), and a willingness to roll up your sleeves to publish the content online

6. Educational/customer service, media/branding, republishing speeches, entertainment, user-generated community video contests
7. Offer web transcripts of podcasts to help boost search engine optimization.
8. www.ideamarketers.com; http://.ezinearticles.com; www.goarticles .com; www.oneminuteu.com; www.articlesbase.com; www .amazines.com; www.addme.com/article-submission.htm; http:// digg.com/submit; www.authorsden.com; www.scribd.com.

CHAPTER 5

1. A web log of entries (or posts) about a particular subject or subjects where a writer or writers can post opinions, news, and more, and where readers can have new content fed to them via RSS and post comments back to the writers
2. Really Simple Syndication
3. No. True blogs allow readers to comment. Blog owners can moderate the comments, but that functionality must exist.
4. The four main factors to consider are whether or not it is important to have the blog live on the main domain of the website (www .website.com/blog versus,www.blogname.blogspot.com); if you want the blog content to live on your website or if a third party plat- form like Blogger is okay; if you want to own the blog or are okay with it being controlled by a third party that could shut it off; and how flexible you want the design to be (customization).
5. [Open-ended essay] When complete, go back to the chapter and see how your answers compare to the text.
6. List social media directories to submit to for more visibility and note appropriate social bookmarking sites to add your blog in order to increase traffic.
7. False. Bloggers must disclose payments for endorsements. It's the law!
8. Comparison blog posts; entries addressing how to solve problems; posts showing better ways to do things; entries sharing alternative/ new uses; posts featuring product or service news (new features, new prices, short-term sales); entries highlighting user stories

CHAPTER 6

1. Communication, collaboration, and entertainment
2. True. With social media, conversations will happen about organizations whether or not they participate. Being aware of what conversations are happening is very important.
3. Value, values, and voice
4. Social media has distinct power allowing companies to C.O.U.P.L.E.: **C**ommitment, **O**utreach, **U**nderstanding, **P**assion, **L**ove, and **E**ffort.
5. Facebook builds awareness. Facebook brilliantly distributes information. Facebook creates community. Facebook can offer additional low-cost customer service. Facebook can boost sales.
6. False. An organization can create its own page or group. Some organizations have people create pages on their own, or actively participate in content sharing.
7. LinkedIn is a professional's social marketing network to exchange information, ideas, and opportunities. A public LinkedIn profile acts as an individual's résumé, creating the opportunity to share expertise and credentials.
8. Social media like LinkedIn profiles, YouTube videos, Wikipedia entries, blogs, and Facebook pages dominate search engine results. Organizations can achieve "TWD" (total web domination) for visibility when social media is put to work.

CHAPTER 7

1. Its immediate tracking capability
2. True. Although fee-based web analytics companies offer very robust add-ons and stellar advisory services, it is best to start with a free service like Google Analytics.
3. Filters give you a better picture of your actual monthly traffic patterns—specifically, the people you are trying to serve, support, and sell.
4. Top content, top key phrase searches (paid and unpaid), traffic sources, traffic volume, time patterns, geographic, bounce rate, time on-site, new vs. returning visitors, success of marketing efforts
5. Start by creating a monthly report in the spreadsheet application of your choice. By creating a monthly report you can see how

your marketing efforts interact over time. You can measure other marketing media: e-mail, traditional media (print, radio, TV, direct mail), blog (RSS feeds), social media, and online advertising (paid search, banner ads).

6. Google Analytics does not provide insight into individual behavior, which does not allow marketers to follow top customers and use this data for persona creation.

7. Grader.com is a suite of online analytics tools provided by HubSpot.com. Their tools are free, although they do sell advanced technology that helps optimize web marketing performance.

8. Bad advertising placement (not the right targeting, placement, or venue); messaging that doesn't speak to the end user; design that doesn't appeal to the target customer; poor website architecture (people don't know where to go or what to do); low-visibility calls to action (people are not being funneled to where they need to go)

CHAPTER 8

1. Search engine

2. Search engine marketing means using search engines to market an organization. It includes efforts that may incorporate improving organic search listings, running pay-per-click ads, and getting listed in vertical search placements.

3. Organic search (also called natural search) results are a trusted source due to their lack of connection to paid sponsorship. Organic search findings are based exclusively on indexed results.

4. Pay per click (PPC) allows companies to buy placement for search engine terms on sites like Google, Yahoo!, and Bing.

5. Vertical search is a streamlined solution that helps web surfers find what they need via a smaller search-topic universe for more concentrated results. Websites can receive exposure on a free or paid basis, depending on the engine. Some examples of vertical search include local search engines like Yahoo! Local, Google Maps, industry-specific sites like WeConnectFashion.com (a search engine about fashion), and job search engines like HotJobs.com.

6. The first step in SEO is determining the best keywords and/or phrases to focus on for visibility. These keywords should not only be relevant to the site, but also relevant to searchers.

7. Business or service + Location or region = Optimized key phrase; Product or service + Distinction or description = Optimized key phrase
8. Architecture, content, and links

CHAPTER 9

1. Big benefits to SEM as an advertising option are that you can target campaigns around optimal key phrases that prequalify people who are in the most transactional mind-set. Advertisers only pay when people click on their ads, making the spending more efficient. Search engine marketing ads are targeted to phrases that represent your product or service, making spend more "laser targeted."
2. One of the largest distinctions of online advertising is its tracking capabilities, so there is no excuse for spending money on online advertising or search engine marketing without knowing what works and what doesn't.
3. Cost per thousand (CPM), cost per click (CPC), cost per action or cost per acquisition (CPA), co-registration, sponsorship
4. Google AdWords, Yahoo! Search Marketing, and Microsoft adCenter (for Bing)
5. Vertical search, display advertising, e-mail marketing, viral marketing news sites, blog marketing, behavioral advertising, social media advertising, contextual advertising, affiliate marketing
6. Per keyword or phrase, per engine (Google vs. Yahoo! vs. Bing), per offer ("Free Trial," "Save 20 Percent," "Offer Expires by _____"), site-targeted ads (pay-per-click ads on sites), local ads, per landing page (you may test several landing pages to see what converts best by setting up unique URLs using Google URL Builder or a similar tool), time of day, day of week, national, regional, geographic locations of traffic, frequency of ads viewed, interest groups, industries, web behaviors (sites visited, shopping habits, shopping trends), traffic, conversions, conversion rate (percentage of visitors that take a desired action), quality of conversions, return on investment, customer feedback, interactivity, Google search network, Google content network

7. It is a best practice to send users to a dedicated landing page that matches the promised content in the link. Taking them to the home page of your website and making them find that coupon on their own is bad service. Landing pages reinforce the message and the goal and help guide people into going where you want them to go.

8. Assess, plan/optimize, test new channels

CHAPTER 10

1. Traditional marketing methods like television and radio distribute messages in a way that is like shouting across a crowd. Today's "new school" web marketing is less of a shout and more of a private conversation.

2. Making mistakes can cost an organization up to $16,000 for each recipient who gets a piece of spam from them.

3. —Proposition: What value do customers/subscribers get from the e-mail program?
   —Positioning: How does your offer differ from the competitors?
   —Personality: What tone and image do your e-mails convey?
   Read more in his article "E-mail Mistake No. 10: Lack of Personality, Positioning and Proposition."

4. • Don't use excessive exclamation points (Learn More!!!!!).
   • Don't use a lot of capital letters (BUY PRODUCT NOW).
   • The "f" word ("free) can be a spam filter flag. If you use it in your subject line, try not to use it with capital letters or an exclamation point.
   • Overuse of images can also be a flag for spam.
   • Certain words that are affiliated with high-volume spam use (such as "loans," "insurance," "prescription drugs," etc.) have high flag rates. Using these words less in the body of the e-mail can help get an e-mail through the filters.

5. The CAN-SPAM Act of 2003 is a law in the United States that was created to help clarify the multiple uses of e-mail communication and regulate the use of commercial e-mails to protect recipients. *CAN-SPAM* is an acronym: Controlling the Assault of Non-Solicited Pornography and Marketing. As online marketers, fun or not, you must learn, love, and live CAN-SPAM compliance.

6. Create a concise subject line. Use a descriptive "from" address. Set up HTML e-mails with text-only mode backup. Test in different

e-mail clients. Use a spam evaluator. Do internal testing before the real send.

7. Sending e-mail newsletters and messages that are all about you or your organization (rather than serving your audience) is not e-mail marketing. This egotistical use of e-mail is called me-mail marketing, and it doesn't work.

8. **Common variables to test:** Subject line, offer, call to action, time/day of week sent, creative copy/layouts (button vs. text, wording, position, size, color, repetition), landing pages, "from" address; **Results to measure:** Open rate, click-through rate, conversions rate, value of conversion (items purchased)

CHAPTER 11

1. Online PR is organization-generated content distributed to various web marketing channels to generate buzz, which boosts credibility, visibility, and sellability.

2. It addresses the needs of journalists (who are always looking for a story). It addresses the information-seeking needs of your current and prospective customers. It helps maximize search visibility (when content is crafted to include key phrases that your audience is searching for).

3. The "P" stands for
   —Positioning: you or your organization's perspective.
   —Point of view: the media and your customers want to know your perspective.
   —Personality: the more social media grows, the more companies can use online PR and pack it full of personality to create connections and get the word out.
   The "R" stands for
   —Relationship: using content to connect to build trust and relationships.
   —Responsibility: you have a responsibility to communicate your value, values, and voice to the media and your customers. If they don't know what's going on, that is your fault, not theirs.
   —Rewards: there are great rewards when you use online PR to communicate and collaborate. It will accelerate your business.

4. Launch press release, general news, event press release, expert positioning press release, reaction to industry or world news

5. The headline, the subhead, the dateline, the lead paragraph, quotes, product/service mentions, the closer, the boilerplate, SEO and anchor tags, interactive press releases, look and feel, readability

6. Add a news section to your website; use your blog for news; article distribution; how-to sites; your e-mail list; press release distribution sites; social media

7. PressReleasePoint: www.pressreleasepoint.com. PitchEngine: www.pitchengine.com. PR Newswire: www.prnewswire.com. ProfNet: https://profnet.prnewswire.com. PRWeb: www.prweb.com.

8. Online PR multitasks by creating content for your site, can boost search engine optimization, connect with readers, be published on local news sites, shared, and more!

CHAPTER 12

1. Multitasking marketing means that one online marketing effort can multitask for you in multiple ways. It can work in more than one way, often boosting more than one of the marketing goals: awareness, communication (information distribution and education), connection, customer service, sales, credibility, usability, visibility, scalability, and sellability.

2. Its interwoven parts support, attract other creatures, and can grow larger and larger, and all of its sections are critical. No single piece does the lion's share of the work. The best results come from the harmonious interplay of the parts.

3. Facebook, Flickr.,LinkedIn, YouTube, and all the other social media that is relevant to your topic area

4. Strategy first, execution second

5. Message boards; product reviews; new uses for your product or service (sometimes called "hacks"); testimonials or case studies (how users solved problems); social media pages; Twitter feeds; video contest submissions; Q&A interviews with users; online groups or communities like LinkedIn, Ning, etc.

6. Meta title tag. Meta description tags (150 characters max). Meta keyword tags (no more than 10 keywords or phrases). Photo file names have key phrases in them. Photos have alt tag with key

phrases. Photo captions are keyword-rich. Page headline (H1 or
H2 tags) has keywords.

7. www.ideamarketers.com; http://ezinearticles.com; www.go
articles.com; www.oneminuteu.com; www.articlesbase.com; www
.amazines.com; www.addme.com/article-submission.htm; http://
digg.com/submit; www.authorsden.com; www.scribd.com/upload
-document#files; http://bx.businessweek.com

8. Giving away expertise, tips, tools, downloads, white papers, free
trials, blog content, podcasts, and videos all build trust, connections, educational empowerment, and more. Find your value and
give some away. Some marketers call this the "pink spoon" or
"sample taste," analogous to ice cream stores giving away a sample
of the ice cream.

INDEX

INSTRUCTIONS FOR ACCESSING ONLINE FINAL EXAM

I f you have completed your study of *The McGraw-Hill 36-Hour Course: Online Marketing*, you should be prepared to take the online final examination. It is a comprehensive test, consisting of 100 multiple-choice questions. You may treat this test as an "open book" exam by consulting this book and any other resources. Answers to both the online exam and the chapter-ending quizzes can be found on The McGraw-Hill 36-Hour Course Information Center landing site for each book (please see the instructions below for accessing the site).

Instructions for Accessing Online Final Exam
1. Go to www.36hourbooks.com.
2. Once you arrive on the home page, scroll down until you find The McGraw-Hill 36-Hour Course: Online Marketing and click the link "Test your skills here." At this point you will be redirected to The McGraw-Hill 36-Hour Course Information Center landing site for the book.
3. Click the "Click Here to Begin" button in the center of the landing site. You will be brought to a page containing detailed instruc-

tions for taking the final exam and obtaining your Certificate of Achievement.

4. Click on "Self-Assessment Quiz" in the left-hand navigation bar to begin the exam.

ABOUT THE AUTHOR

Lorrie Thomas is a speaker, trainer, marketing expert, and CEO of Web Marketing Therapy, a boutique web-marketing agency and training company that diagnoses, prescribes, and guides healthy marketing solutions. Her success-backed approach to web marketing empowers professionals to create scalable web solutions that brand, build, and boost business. In addition to running her agency, she is hired by organizations to lead marketing workshops and also teaches workshops through UC Berkeley Extension. She speaks nationally on a number of marketing-related topics and writes for several online publications. She has a breadth and depth of web-marketing industry expertise that encompasses developing web-marketing strategy, optimizing websites, search-engine marketing, search-engine optimization, affiliate marketing, social-media marketing, selling and buying online advertising, and educating students and businesses on a variety of web marketing–related topics. Ms. Thomas was on the founding team at ValueClick Media. Her thought leadership as a web-marketing expert has appeared in the media including *Inc.*, *Forbes*, the Associated Press, *eCommerce Times*, *Entrepreneur*, *DM News*, and *Tech News World*. Thomas's companies support http://www.1% for the planet.org/en, a growing global movement of companies that donate 1% of their sales to a network of environmental organizations worldwide. You can learn more about the author by Googling her or visiting www.webmarketingtherapy.com, www.themarketingtherapist .com, and www.lorriethomas.com.